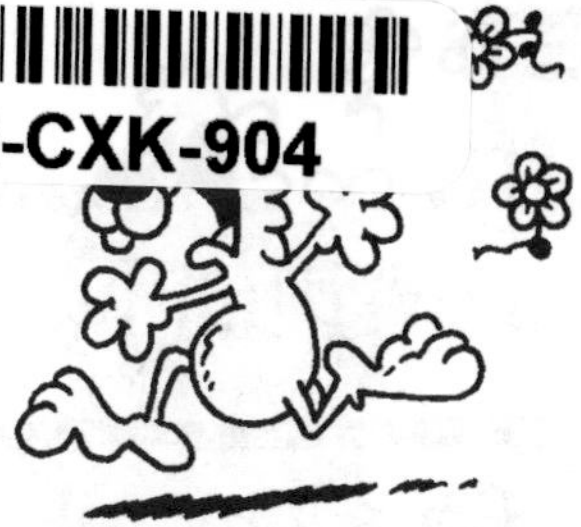

TUNDRA

NATURE'S FINEST COMIC STRIP - PACKED IN ITS OWN JUICES!

Written & Illustrated by Chad Carpenter
Co-written by
Darin Carpenter &
Mark Dickerson

TO BARBARA & DAVID!
I'LL BET BUSTER WINS
FOR "CHEAPEST WEDDING
GIFT."

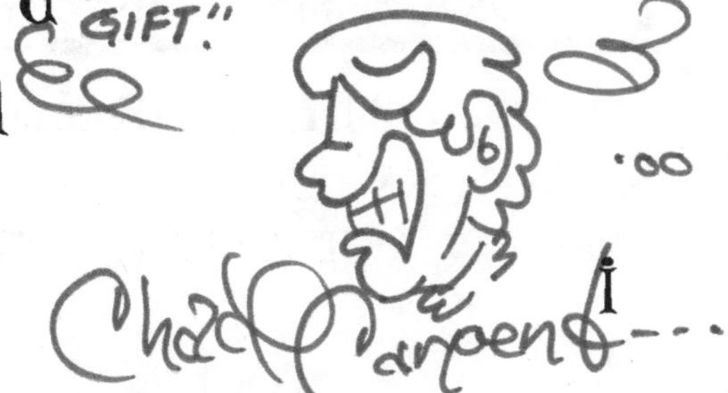

Chad Carpenter...

Published by...
Off-The-Wall, Inc.
PO Box 112743
Anchorage, AK 99511

TUNDRA... NATURE'S FINEST COMIC STRIP - PACKED IN ITS OWN JUICES!

Written & Illustrated by Chad Carpenter
Co-written by Darin Carpenter & Mark Dickerson

For additional volumes of this or other TUNDRA books, please mail $13 (includes postage & handling) to...

TUNDRA & Associates
PO BOX 770732
Eagle River, Alaska 99577 USA
www.tundracomics.com
tundra@arctic.net

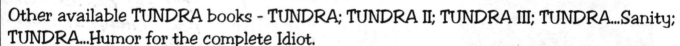

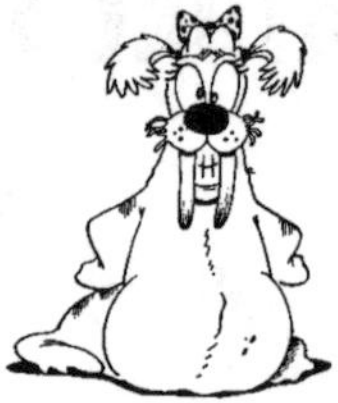

Other available TUNDRA books - TUNDRA; TUNDRA II; TUNDRA III; TUNDRA...Sanity; TUNDRA...Humor for the complete Idiot.

Library of Congress Catalog Card Number: 00-103507
First Printing: May 2000
ISBN 0-9665033-1-7
Printed in the U.S.A

Photo by Darin Carpenter

I would like to dedicate
this book to my dog, "Flea-Bag".
Not only does he whisper cartoon
ideas to me while I'm sleeping,
but he's also willing to share
anything & everything with me.
(except fire hydrants)

- Chad Carpenter

iii

CARTOONIST, CHAD CARPENTER'S BIO:

Chad Carpenter was originally a trained Shakespearean actor. However, while debuting on Broadway as the lead in "Phantom of the Laxative Factory," he was unceremoniously heckled off the stage by an angry mob – his fellow actors. Having suffered this traumatic setback, Chad decided to move to Botswana and begin a new career utilizing his hard-earned 12-year Bachelor degree. He became a street mime. Unfortunately, not many people in Botswana understood English, so Chad's pantomime act fell on deaf & confused ears. This latest crushing blow sent Chad tail-spinning into years of self-imposed exile within the walls of an abandoned asbestos plant. It was there that Chad discovered his true calling – taste testing lead paint chips. But, since there was very little chance of advancement in this career field, Chad decided to just draw pictures with goofy captions instead.

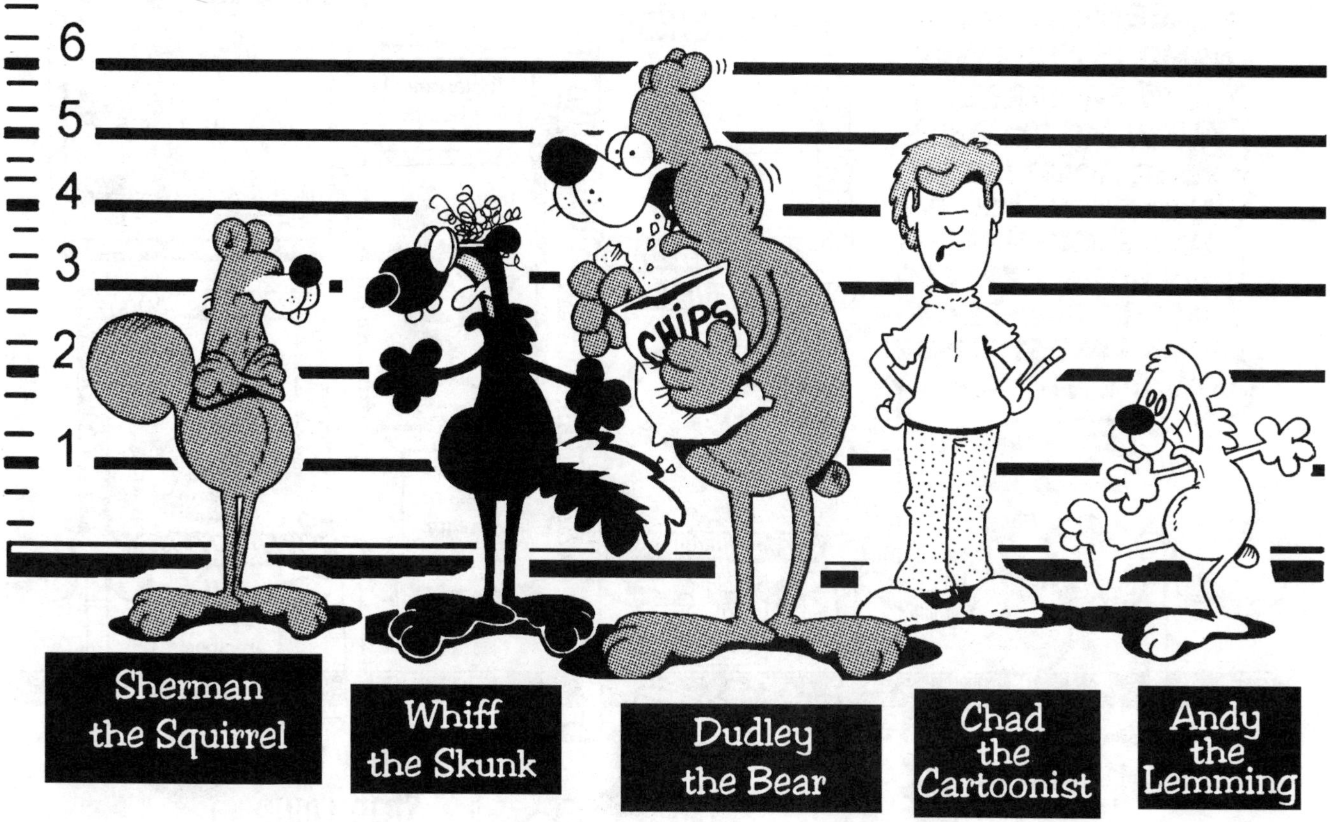
6
5
4
3
2
1
CHIPS
Sherman the Squirrel
Whiff the Skunk
Dudley the Bear
Chad the Cartoonist
Andy the Lemming

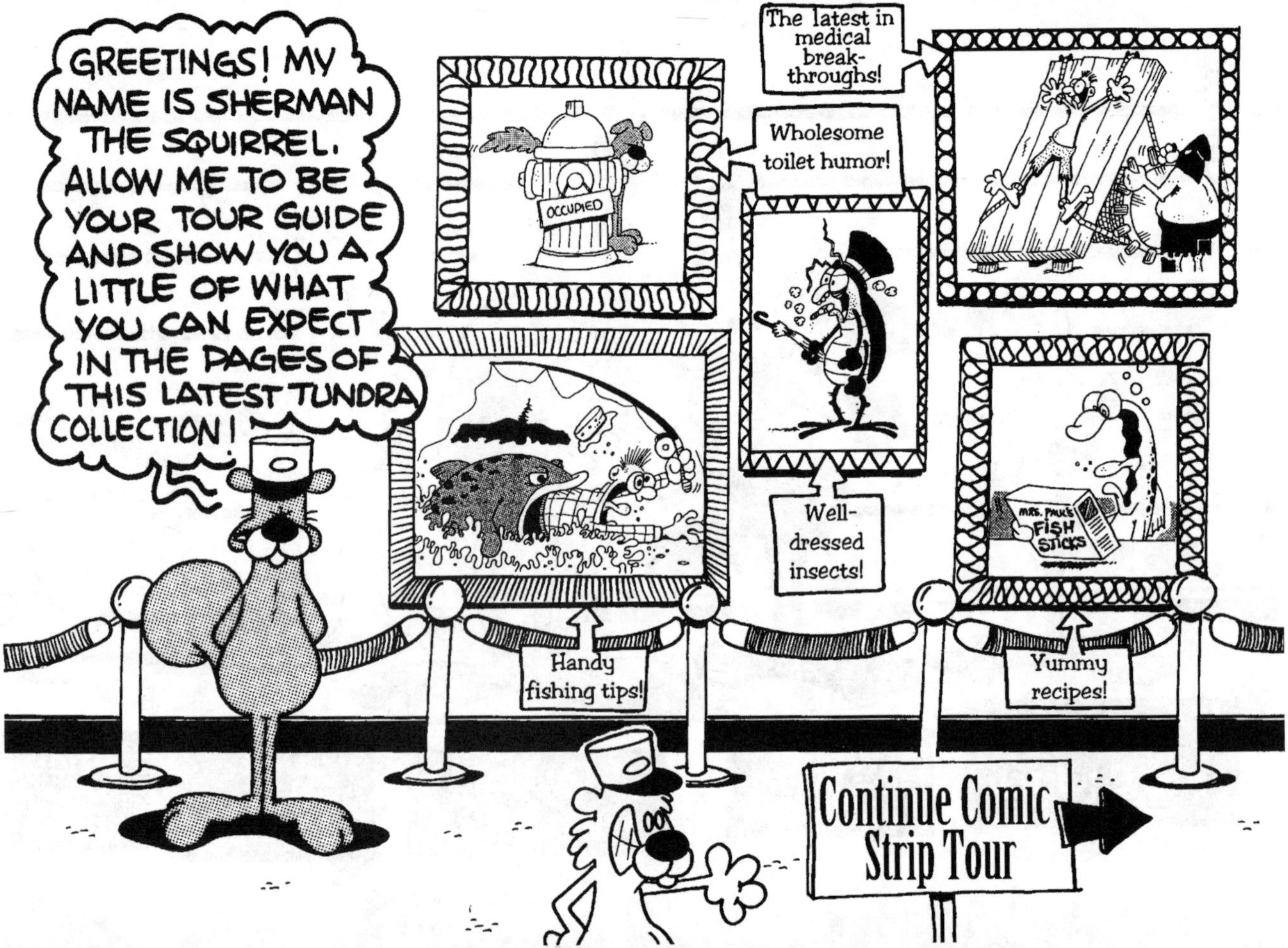
GREETINGS! MY NAME IS SHERMAN THE SQUIRREL. ALLOW ME TO BE YOUR TOUR GUIDE AND SHOW YOU A LITTLE OF WHAT YOU CAN EXPECT IN THE PAGES OF THIS LATEST TUNDRA COLLECTION!
OCCUPIED
Wholesome toilet humor!
The latest in medical break-throughs!
Handy fishing tips!
Well-dressed insects!
MRS. PAUL'S FISH STICKS
Yummy recipes!
Continue Comic Strip Tour

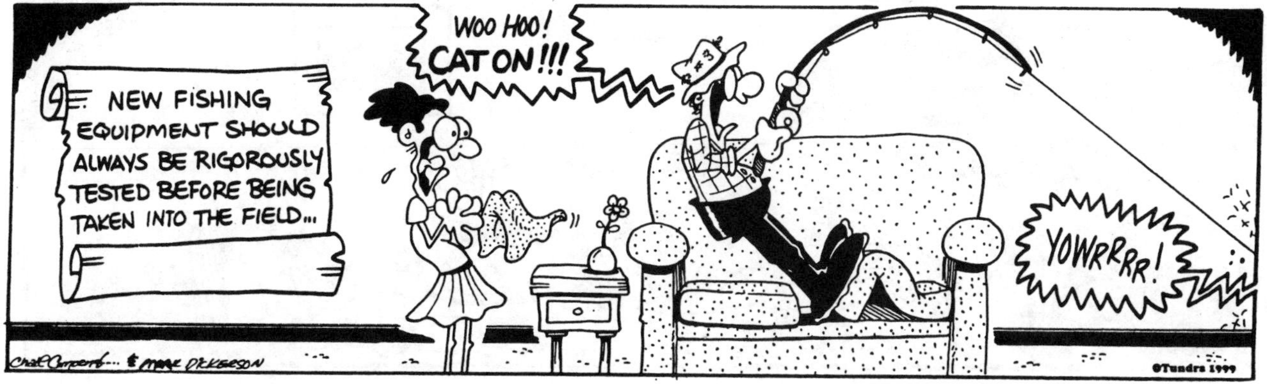
NEW FISHING EQUIPMENT SHOULD ALWAYS BE RIGOROUSLY TESTED BEFORE BEING TAKEN INTO THE FIELD...
WOO HOO!
CAT ON!!!
YOWRRRR!
Chad Carpenter ... & MARK DICKERSON
©Tundra 1999

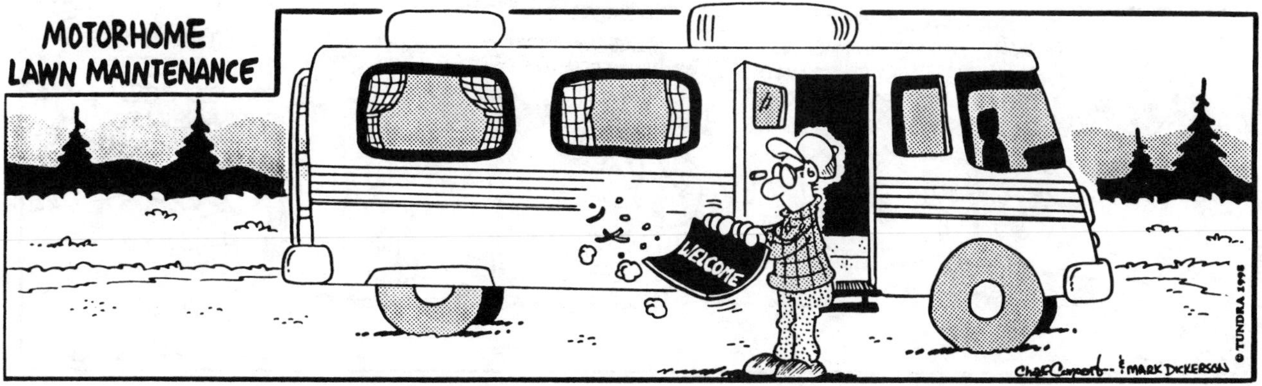
MOTORHOME
LAWN MAINTENANCE
WELCOME
Chad Carpenter ... & MARK DICKERSON
© TUNDRA 1998

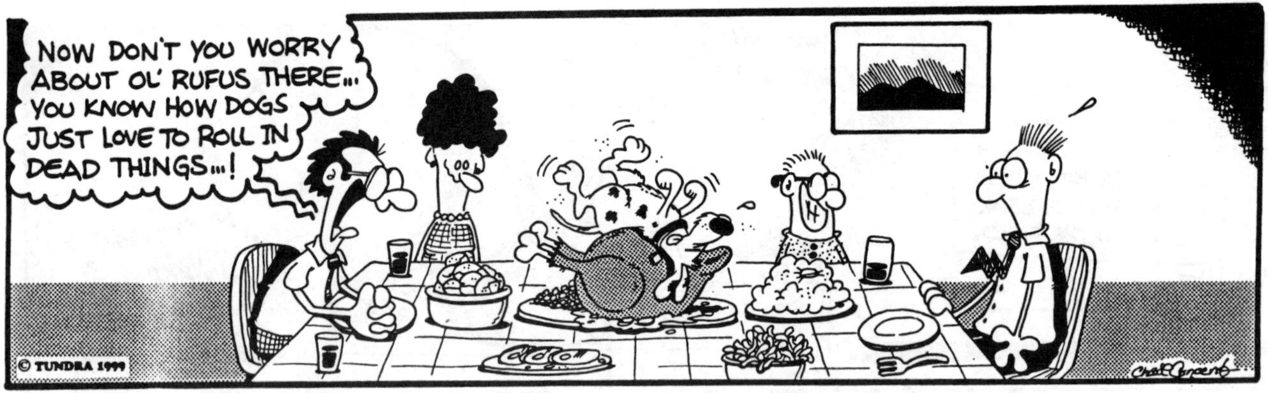
NOW DON'T YOU WORRY ABOUT OL' RUFUS THERE... YOU KNOW HOW DOGS JUST LOVE TO ROLL IN DEAD THINGS...!
© TUNDRA 1999

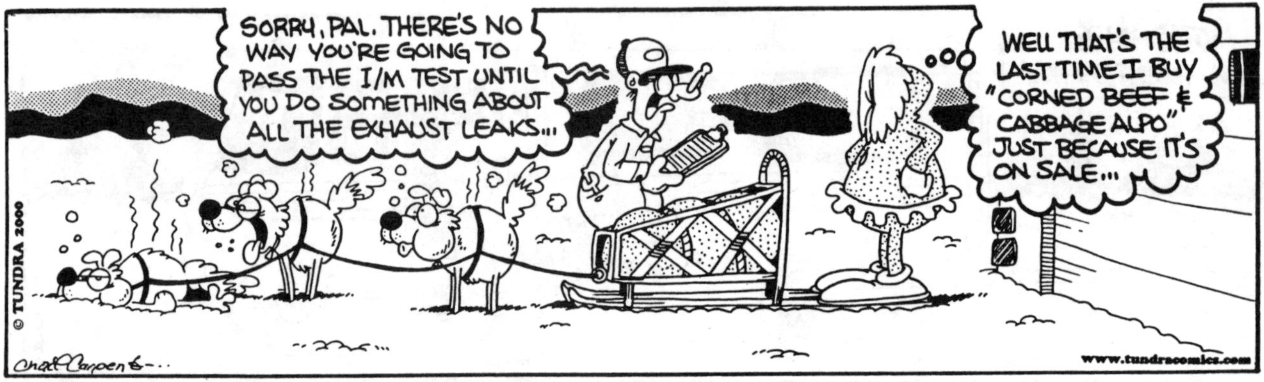
SORRY, PAL. THERE'S NO WAY YOU'RE GOING TO PASS THE I/M TEST UNTIL YOU DO SOMETHING ABOUT ALL THE EXHAUST LEAKS...
WELL THAT'S THE LAST TIME I BUY "CORNED BEEF & CABBAGE ALPO" JUST BECAUSE IT'S ON SALE...
© TUNDRA 2000
www.tundracomics.com

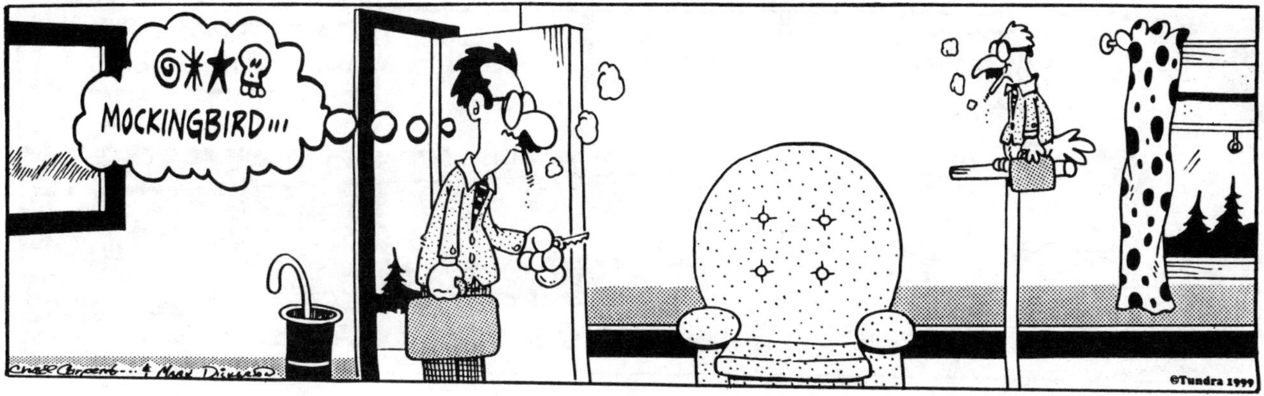
MOCKINGBIRD...
Chad Carpenter & Mark Dickerson
©Tundra 1999

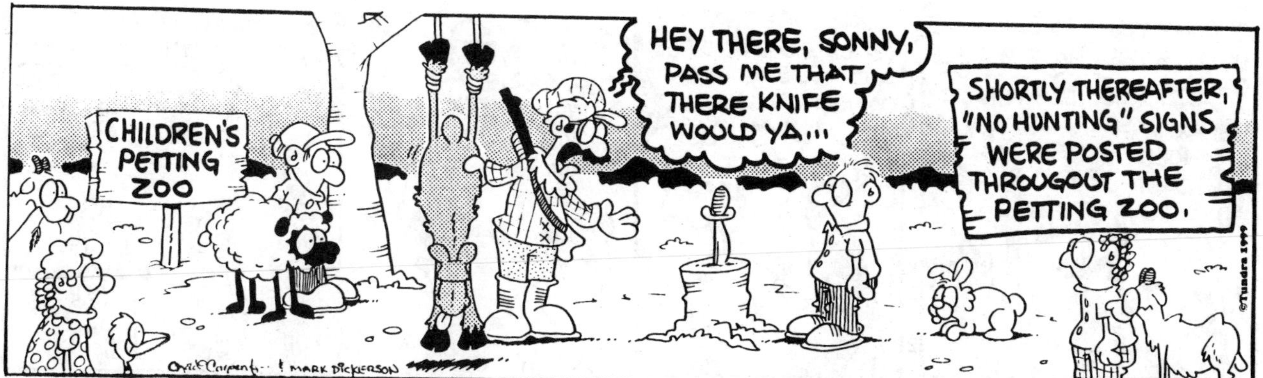
CHILDREN'S PETTING ZOO
HEY THERE, SONNY, PASS ME THAT THERE KNIFE WOULD YA...
SHORTLY THEREAFTER, "NO HUNTING" SIGNS WERE POSTED THROUGOUT THE PETTING ZOO.
Chad Carpenter & MARK DICKERSON
©Tundra 1999

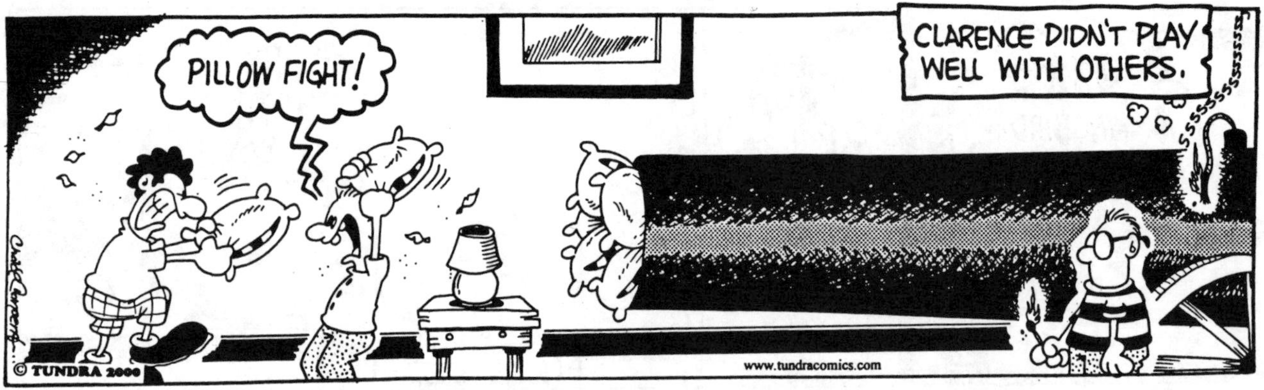
PILLOW FIGHT!
CLARENCE DIDN'T PLAY WELL WITH OTHERS.
SSSSSSSSSSSSSSS
© TUNDRA 2000
www.tundracomics.com

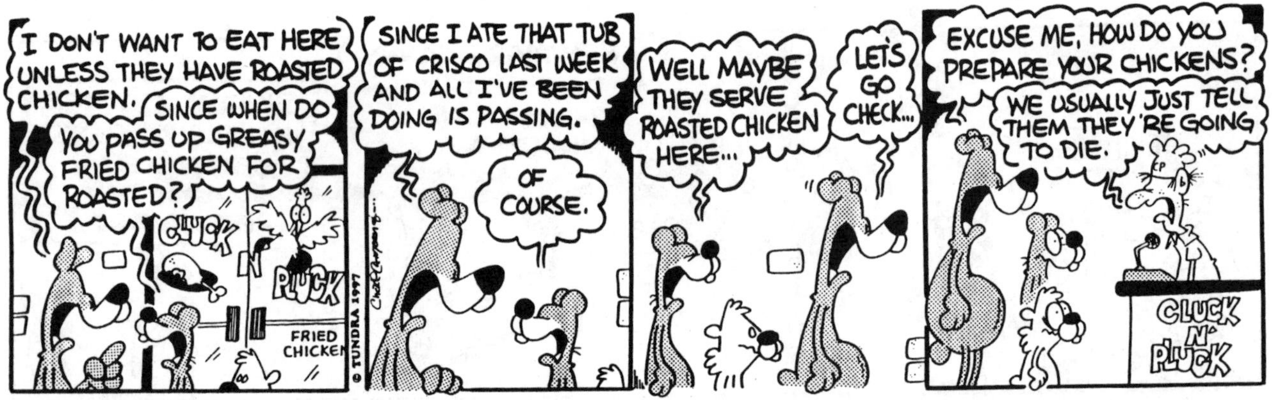
I DON'T WANT TO EAT HERE UNLESS THEY HAVE ROASTED CHICKEN.
SINCE WHEN DO YOU PASS UP GREASY FRIED CHICKEN FOR ROASTED?
CLUCK N PLUCK
FRIED CHICKEN
SINCE I ATE THAT TUB OF CRISCO LAST WEEK AND ALL I'VE BEEN DOING IS PASSING.
OF COURSE.
© TUNDRA 1997
WELL MAYBE THEY SERVE ROASTED CHICKEN HERE...
LET'S GO CHECK...
EXCUSE ME, HOW DO YOU PREPARE YOUR CHICKENS?
WE USUALLY JUST TELL THEM THEY'RE GOING TO DIE.
CLUCK N' PLUCK

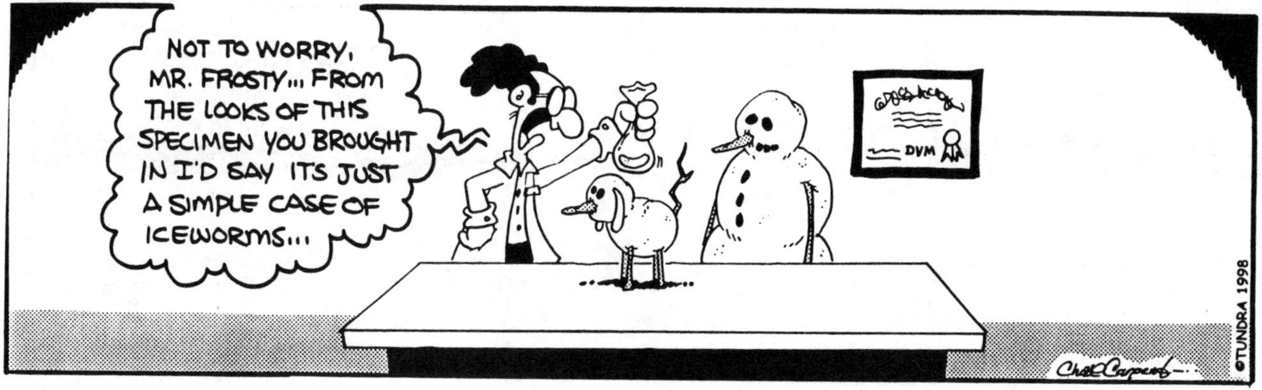
NOT TO WORRY, MR. FROSTY... FROM THE LOOKS OF THIS SPECIMEN YOU BROUGHT IN I'D SAY ITS JUST A SIMPLE CASE OF ICEWORMS...
DVM
©TUNDRA 1998

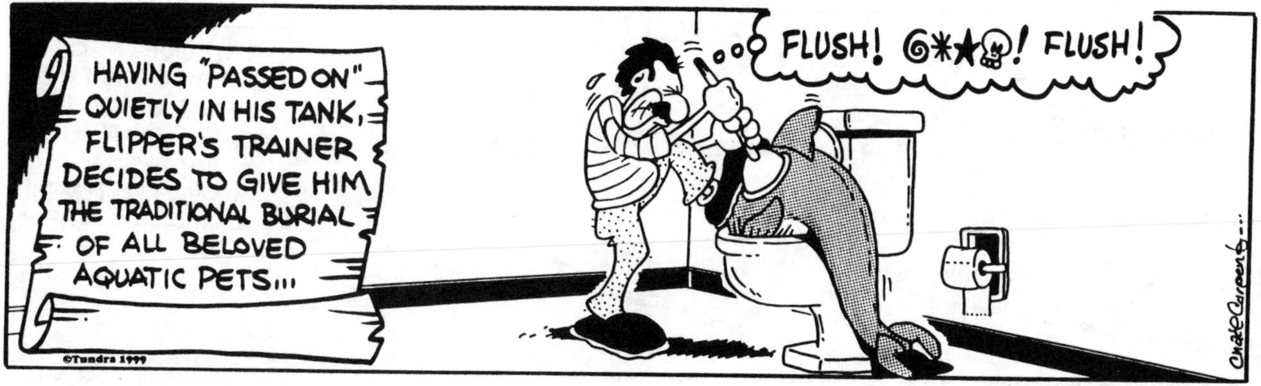
HAVING "PASSED ON" QUIETLY IN HIS TANK, FLIPPER'S TRAINER DECIDES TO GIVE HIM THE TRADITIONAL BURIAL OF ALL BELOVED AQUATIC PETS...
FLUSH! @*★! FLUSH!
©Tundra 1999

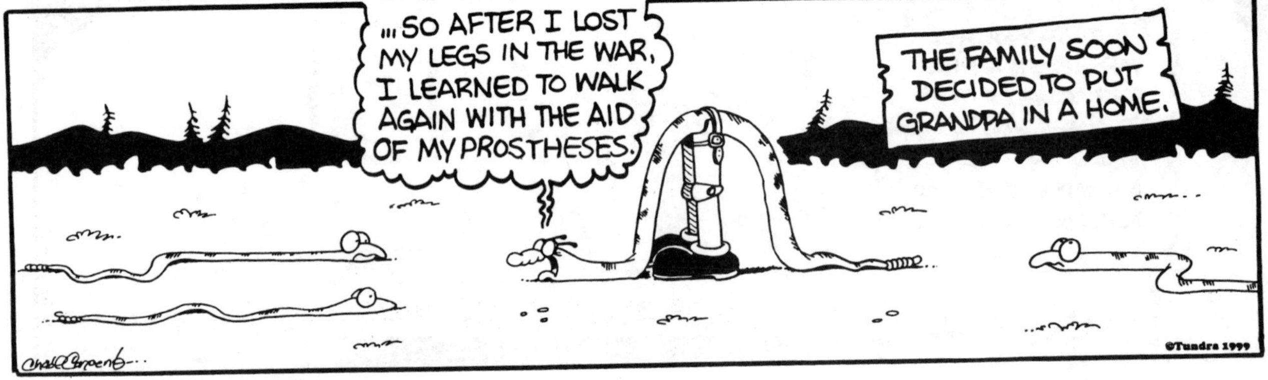
...SO AFTER I LOST MY LEGS IN THE WAR, I LEARNED TO WALK AGAIN WITH THE AID OF MY PROSTHESES.
THE FAMILY SOON DECIDED TO PUT GRANDPA IN A HOME.
©Tundra 1999

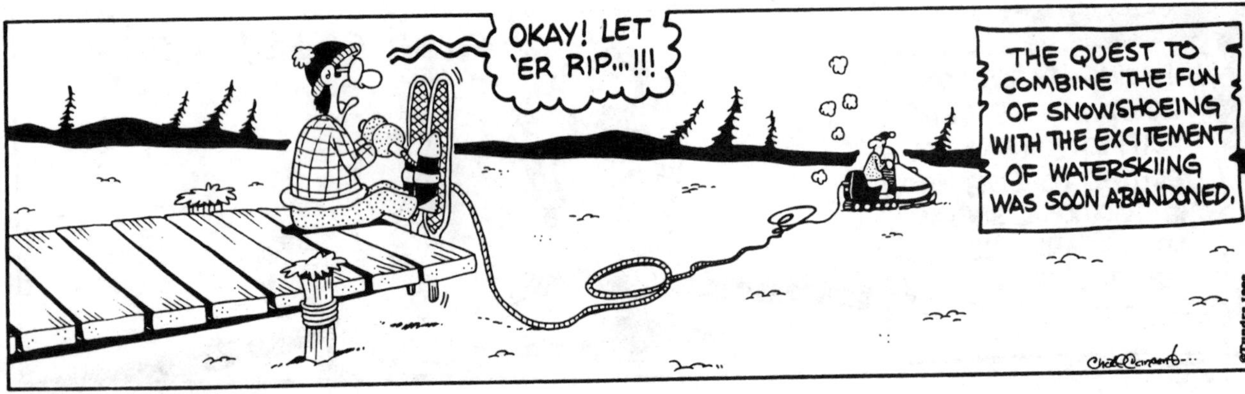
OKAY! LET 'ER RIP...!!!
THE QUEST TO COMBINE THE FUN OF SNOWSHOEING WITH THE EXCITEMENT OF WATERSKIING WAS SOON ABANDONED.
©Tundra 1999

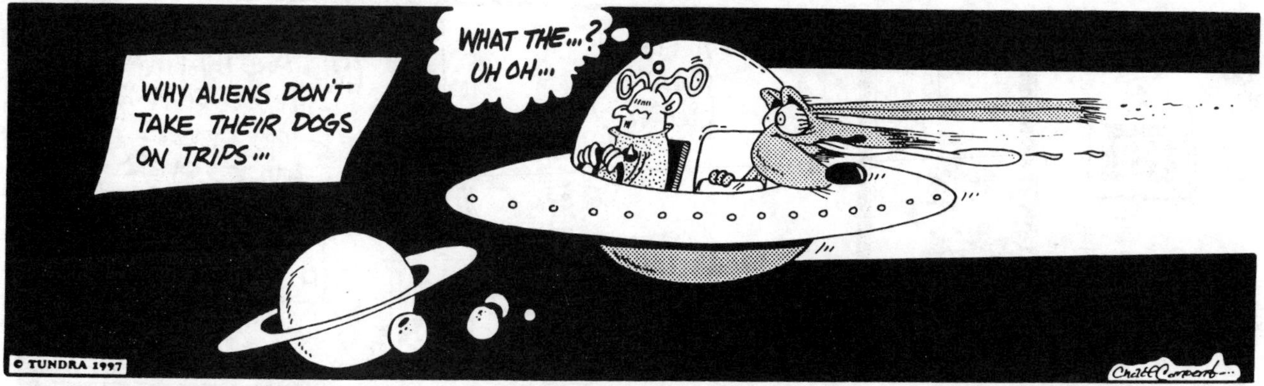
WHY ALIENS DON'T TAKE THEIR DOGS ON TRIPS...
WHAT THE...? UH OH...
© TUNDRA 1997

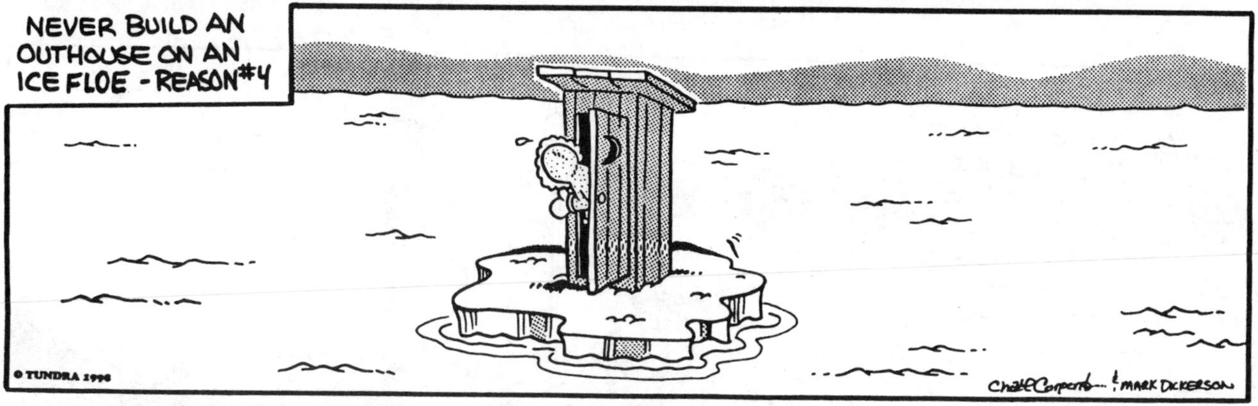
NEVER BUILD AN OUTHOUSE ON AN ICE FLOE - REASON #4
© TUNDRA 1996
MARK DICKERSON

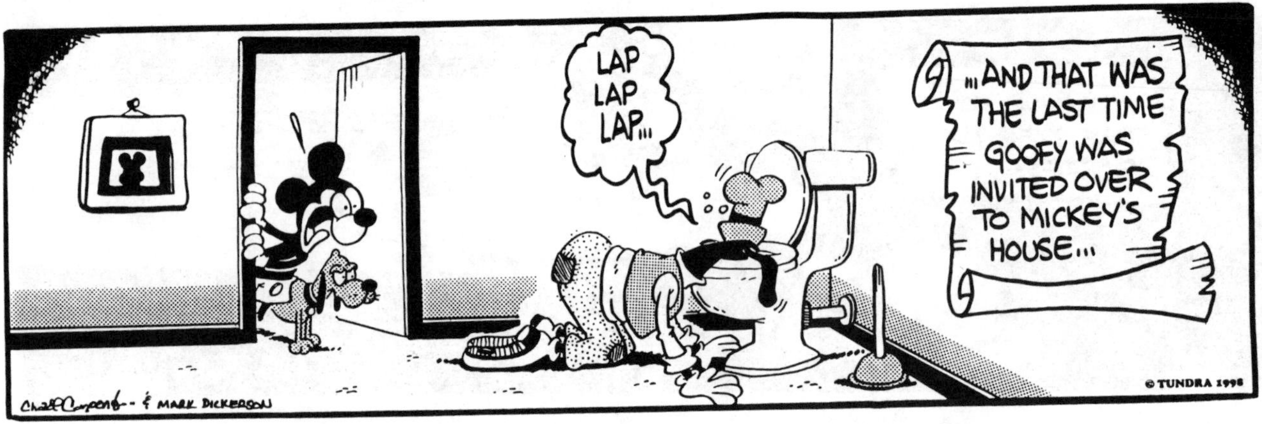
LAP LAP LAP...
...AND THAT WAS THE LAST TIME GOOFY WAS INVITED OVER TO MICKEY'S HOUSE...
© TUNDRA 1998
MARK DICKERSON

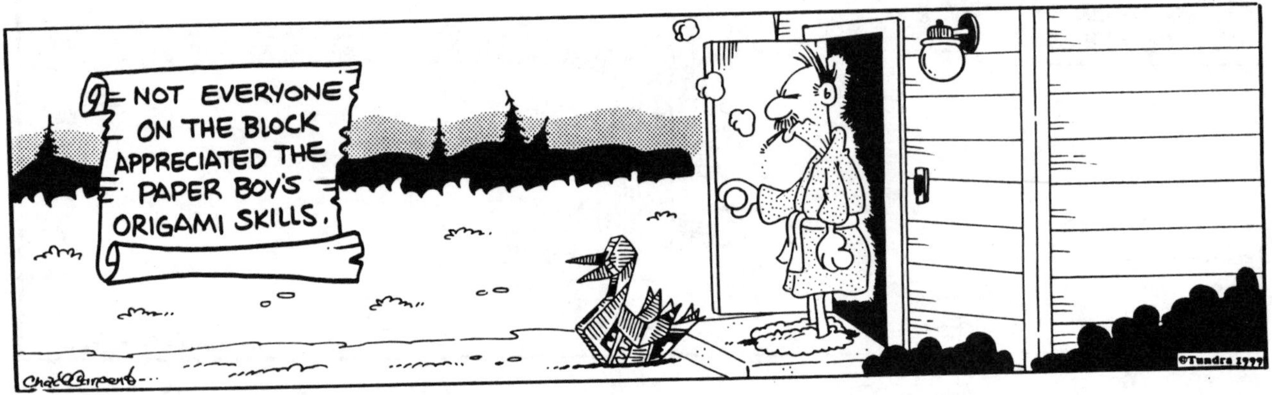
NOT EVERYONE ON THE BLOCK APPRECIATED THE PAPER BOY'S ORIGAMI SKILLS.
©Tundra 1999

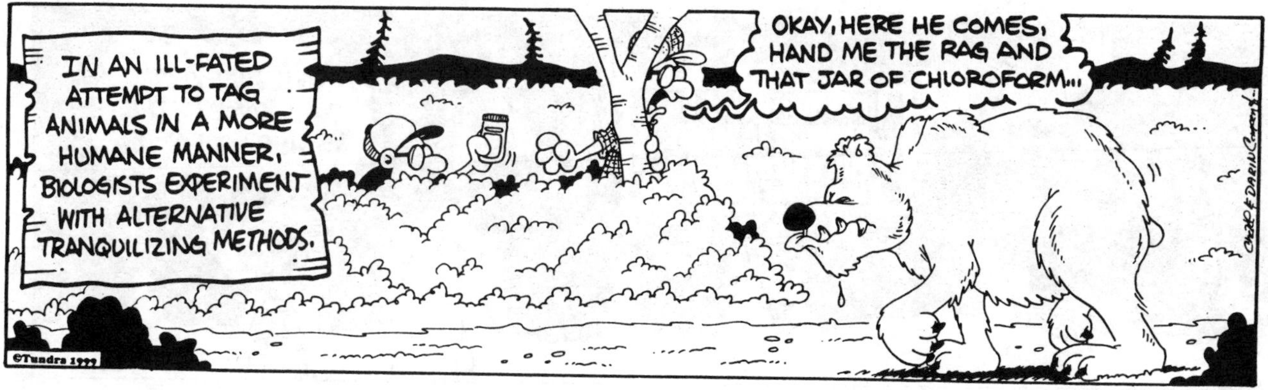
IN AN ILL-FATED ATTEMPT TO TAG ANIMALS IN A MORE HUMANE MANNER, BIOLOGISTS EXPERIMENT WITH ALTERNATIVE TRANQUILIZING METHODS.
OKAY, HERE HE COMES, HAND ME THE RAG AND THAT JAR OF CHLOROFORM...
©Tundra 1999

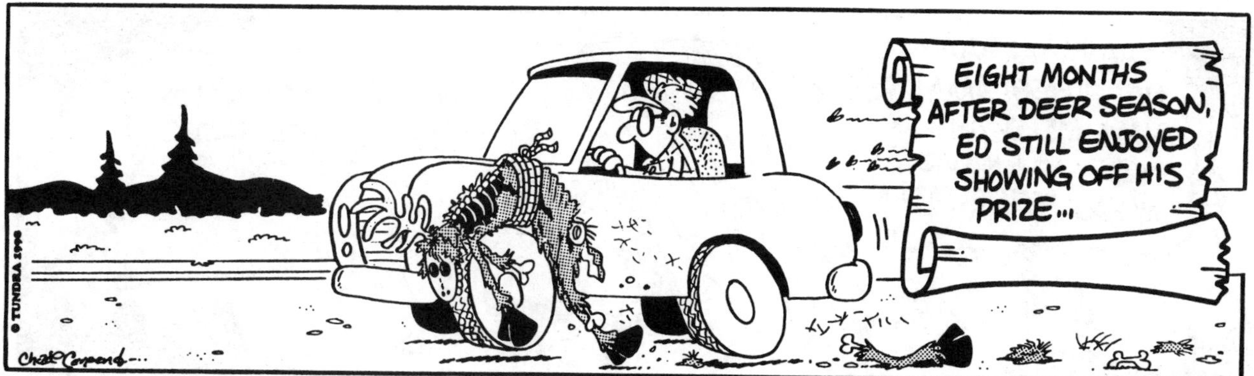
EIGHT MONTHS AFTER DEER SEASON, ED STILL ENJOYED SHOWING OFF HIS PRIZE...
© TUNDRA 1998

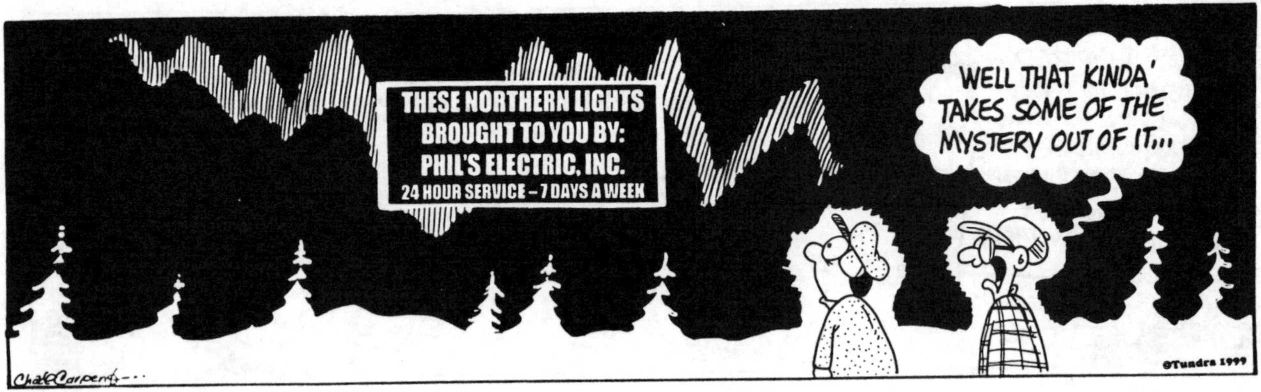
THESE NORTHERN LIGHTS
BROUGHT TO YOU BY:
PHIL'S ELECTRIC, INC.
24 HOUR SERVICE – 7 DAYS A WEEK
WELL THAT KINDA' TAKES SOME OF THE MYSTERY OUT OF IT...
©Tundra 1999

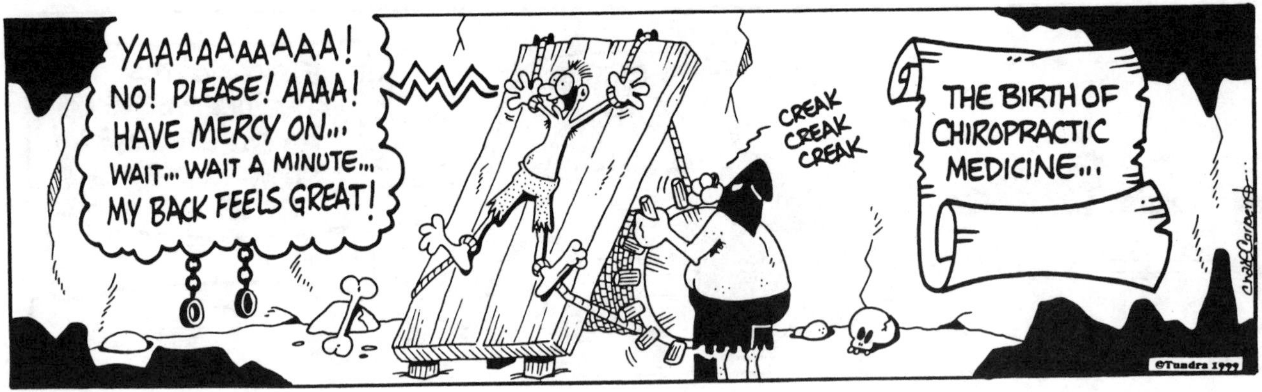
YAAAAAAAAAA! NO! PLEASE! AAAA! HAVE MERCY ON... WAIT... WAIT A MINUTE... MY BACK FEELS GREAT!
CREAK CREAK CREAK
THE BIRTH OF CHIROPRACTIC MEDICINE...
©Tundra 1999

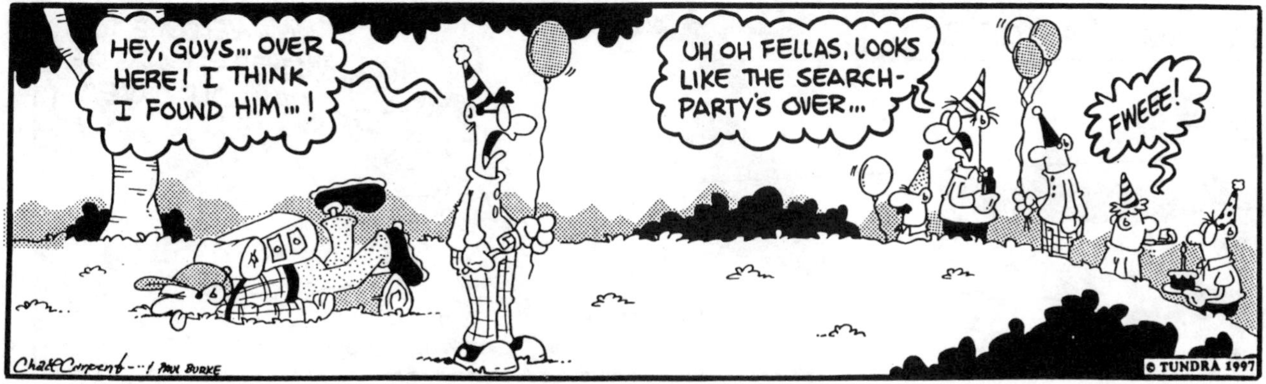
HEY, GUYS... OVER HERE! I THINK I FOUND HIM...!
UH OH FELLAS, LOOKS LIKE THE SEARCH-PARTY'S OVER...
FWEEE!
© TUNDRA 1997

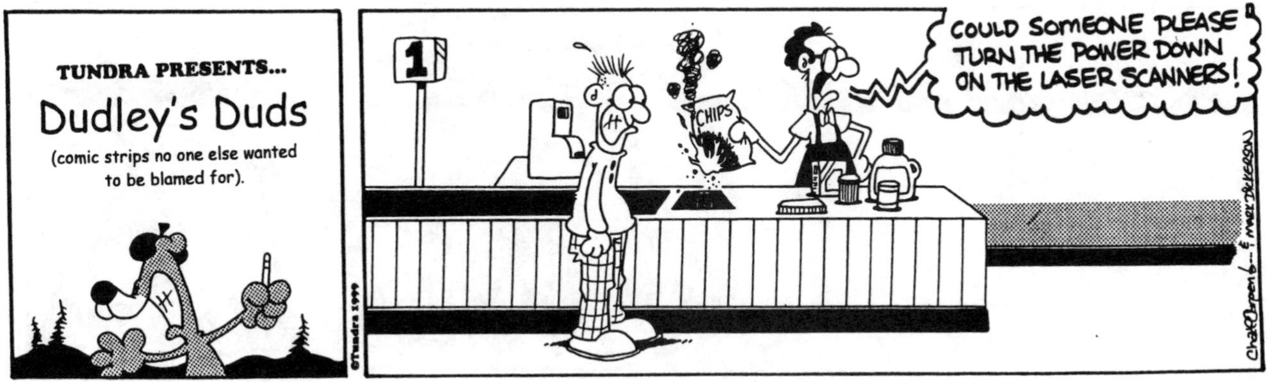
TUNDRA PRESENTS...
Dudley's Duds
(comic strips no one else wanted to be blamed for).
1
CHIPS
COULD SOMEONE PLEASE TURN THE POWER DOWN ON THE LASER SCANNERS!
©Tundra 1999

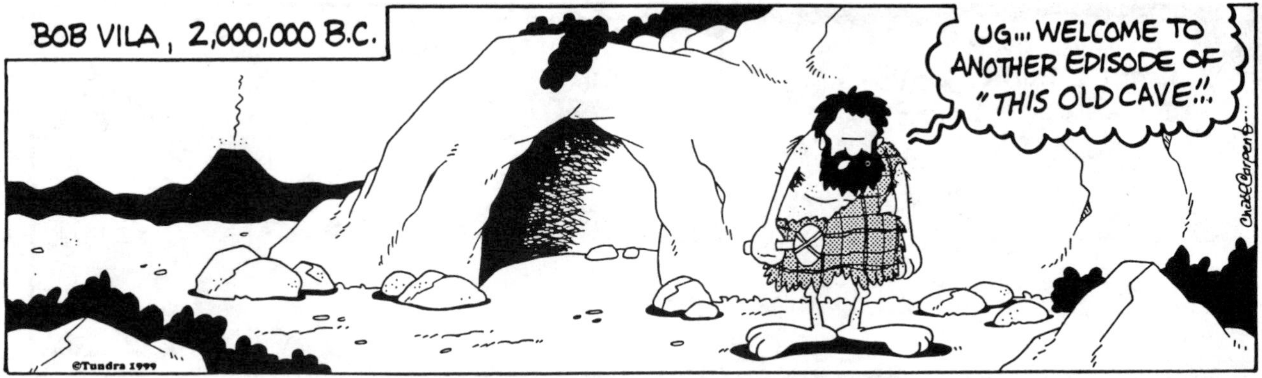
BOB VILA, 2,000,000 B.C.
UG... WELCOME TO ANOTHER EPISODE OF "THIS OLD CAVE"!..
©Tundra 1999

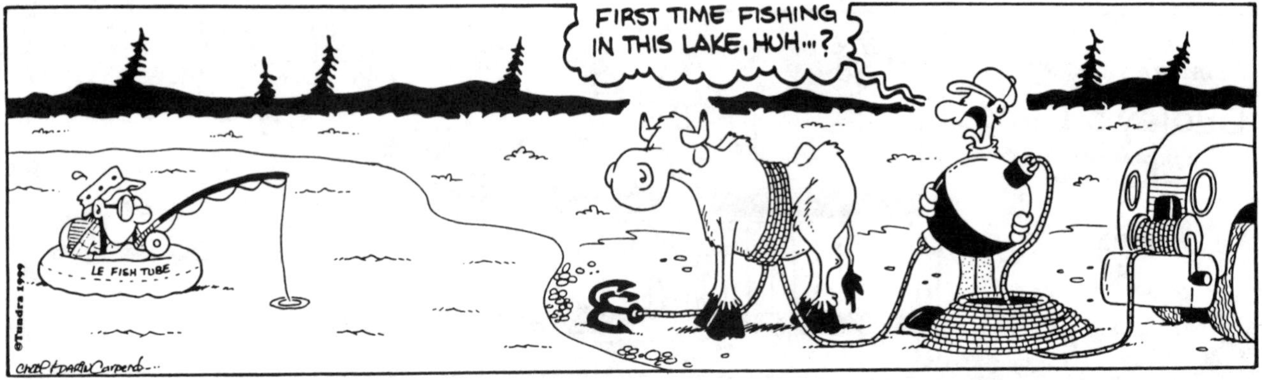
FIRST TIME FISHING IN THIS LAKE, HUH...?
LE FISH TUBE
©Tundra 1999

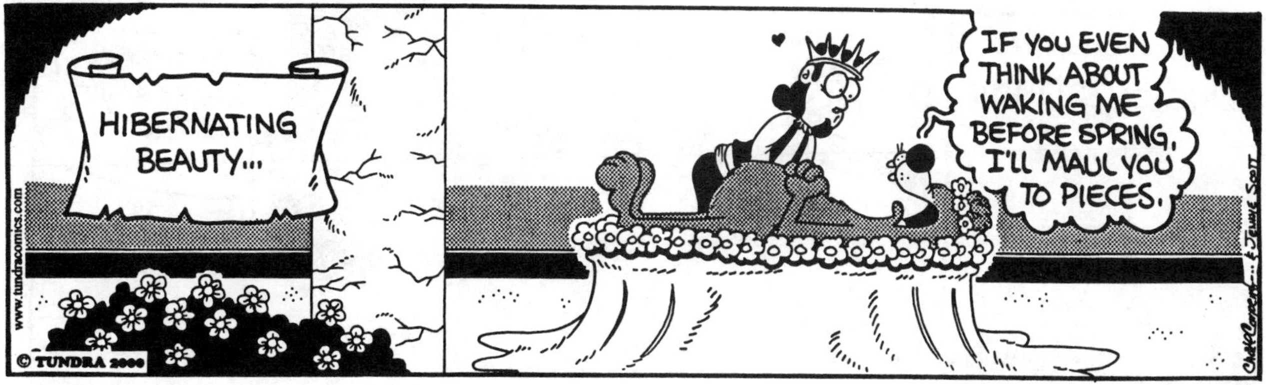
HIBERNATING BEAUTY...
IF YOU EVEN THINK ABOUT WAKING ME BEFORE SPRING, I'LL MAUL YOU TO PIECES.
© TUNDRA 2000
www.tundracomics.com

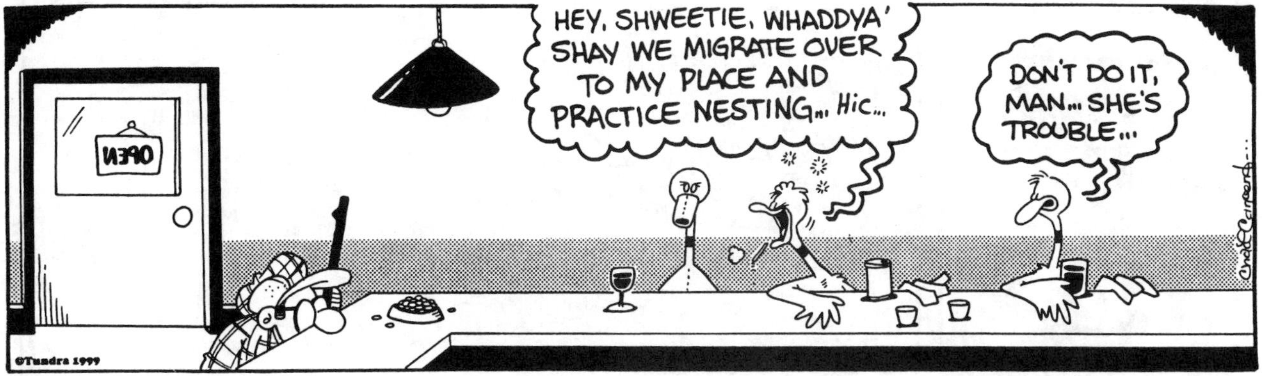
HEY, SHWEETIE, WHADDYA' SHAY WE MIGRATE OVER TO MY PLACE AND PRACTICE NESTING... Hic...
DON'T DO IT, MAN... SHE'S TROUBLE...
OPEN
©Tundra 1999

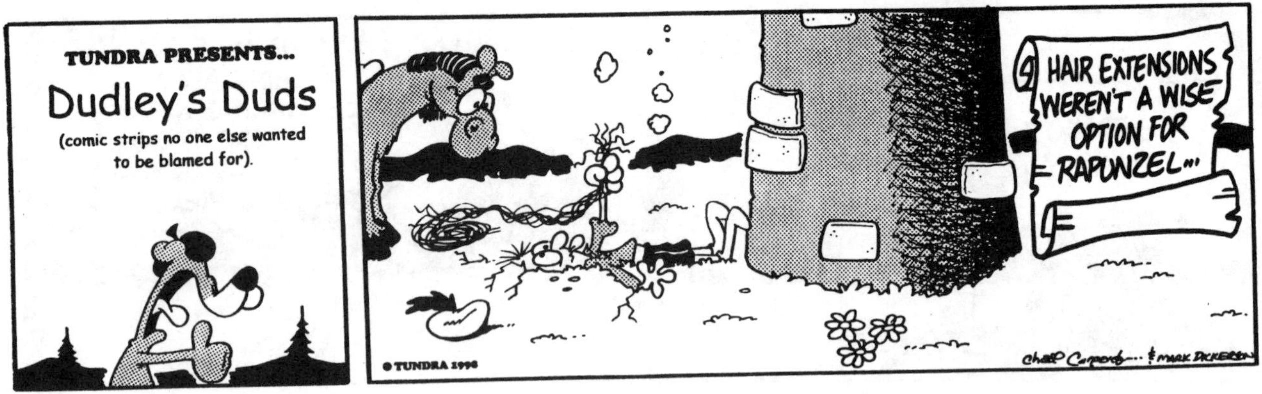
TUNDRA PRESENTS...
Dudley's Duds
(comic strips no one else wanted to be blamed for).
4
HAIR EXTENSIONS WEREN'T A WISE OPTION FOR RAPUNZEL...
© TUNDRA 1998

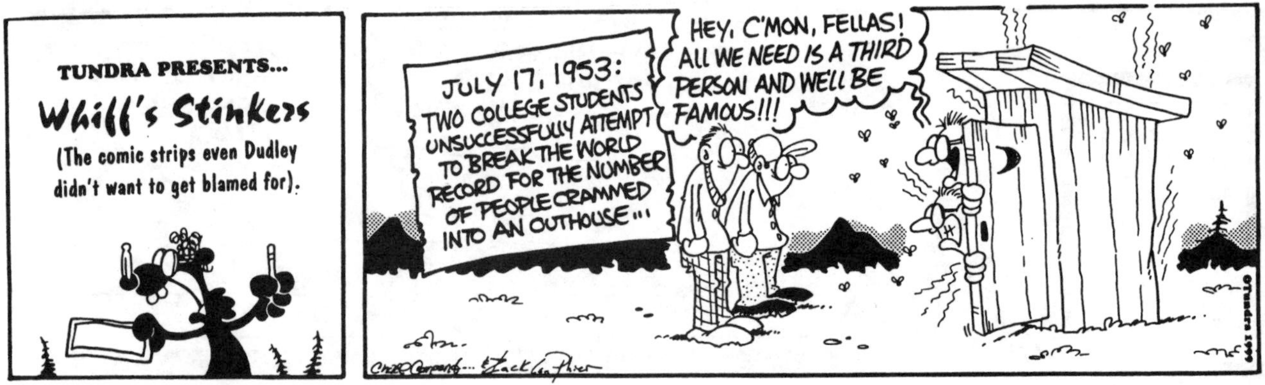
TUNDRA PRESENTS...
Whiff's Stinkers
(The comic strips even Dudley didn't want to get blamed for).
JULY 17, 1953: TWO COLLEGE STUDENTS UNSUCCESSFULLY ATTEMPT TO BREAK THE WORLD RECORD FOR THE NUMBER OF PEOPLE CRAMMED INTO AN OUTHOUSE...
HEY, C'MON, FELLAS! ALL WE NEED IS A THIRD PERSON AND WE'LL BE FAMOUS!!!
©Tundra 1999

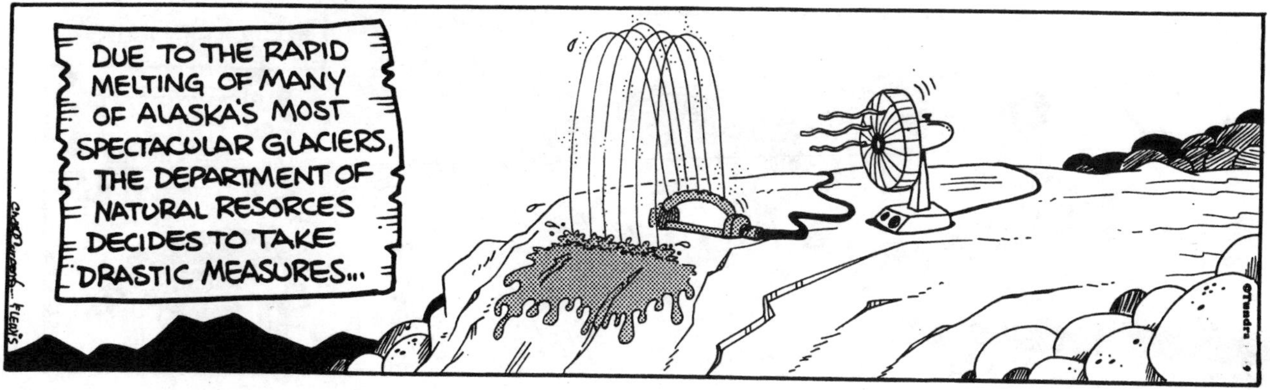
DUE TO THE RAPID MELTING OF MANY OF ALASKA'S MOST SPECTACULAR GLACIERS, THE DEPARTMENT OF NATURAL RESORCES DECIDES TO TAKE DRASTIC MEASURES...
©Tundra

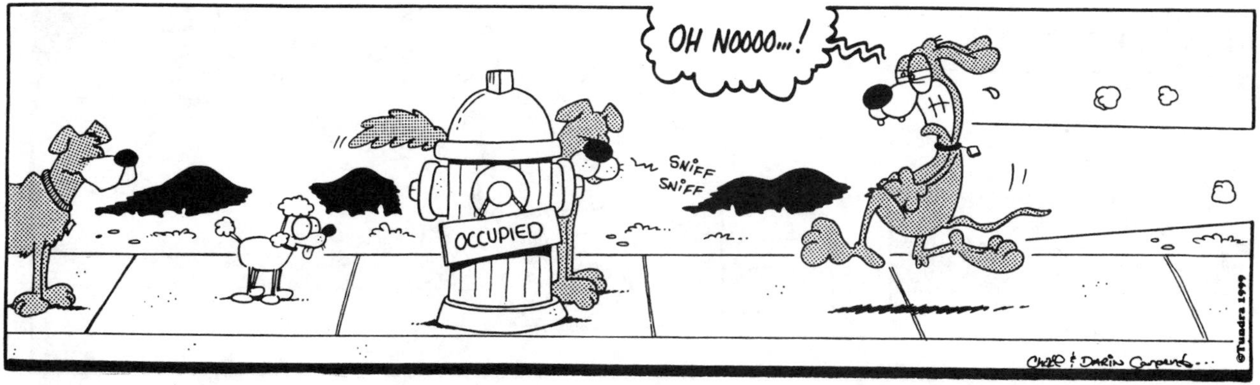
OH NOOOO...!
SNIFF SNIFF
OCCUPIED
©Tundra 1999

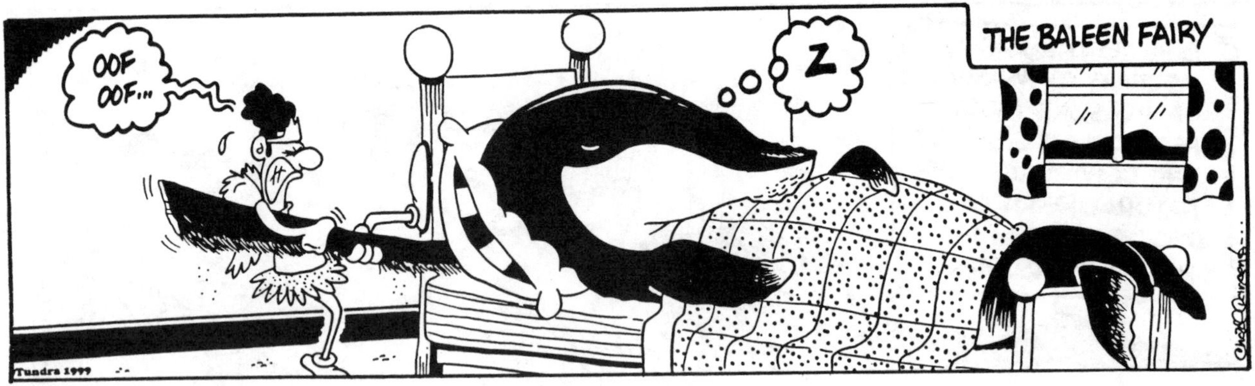
THE BALEEN FAIRY
OOF OOF...
Z
Tundra 1999

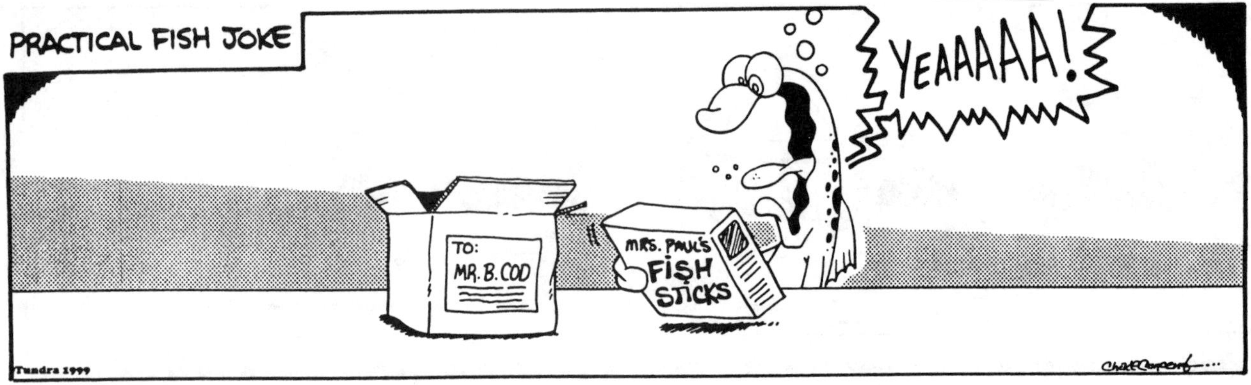
PRACTICAL FISH JOKE
YEAAAAA!
TO: MR. B. COD
MRS. PAUL'S FISH STICKS
Tundra 1999

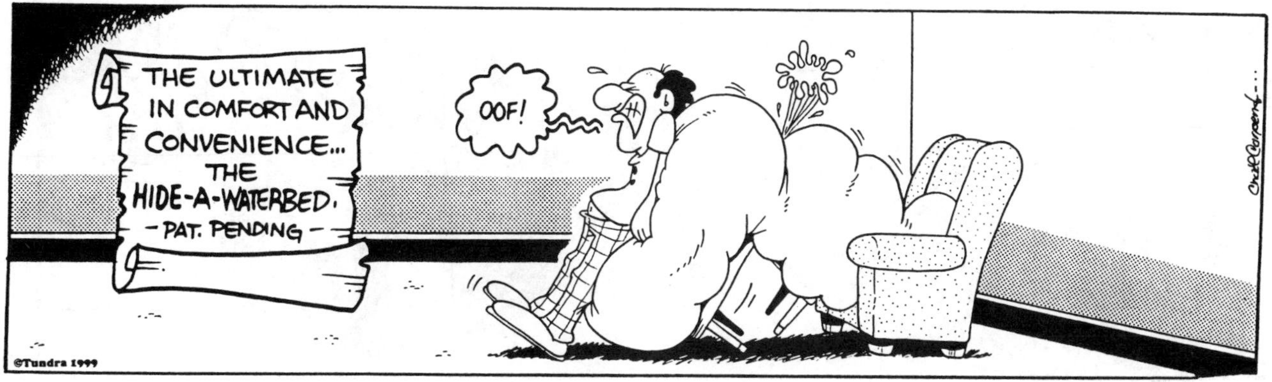
THE ULTIMATE IN COMFORT AND CONVENIENCE... THE HIDE-A-WATERBED. -PAT. PENDING-
OOF!
©Tundra 1999

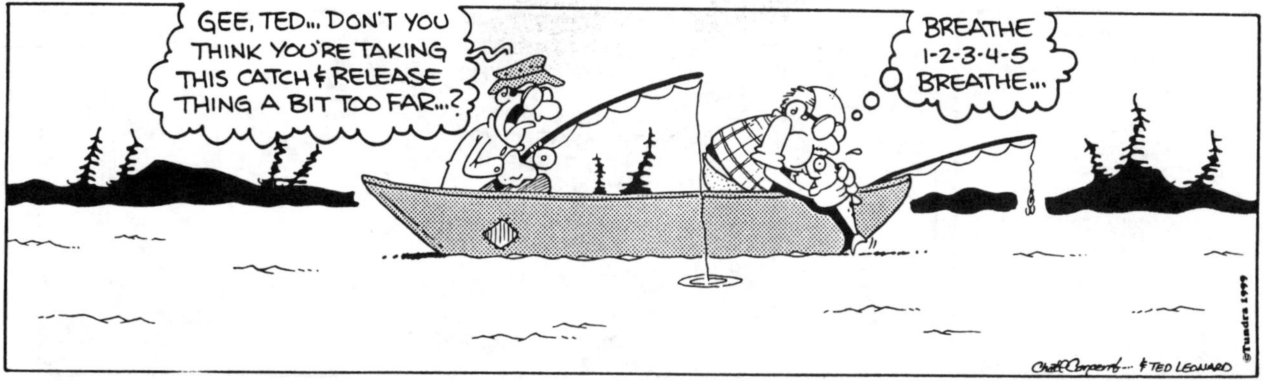
GEE, TED... DON'T YOU THINK YOU'RE TAKING THIS CATCH & RELEASE THING A BIT TOO FAR...?
BREATHE 1-2-3-4-5 BREATHE...
& TED LEONARD
©Tundra 1999

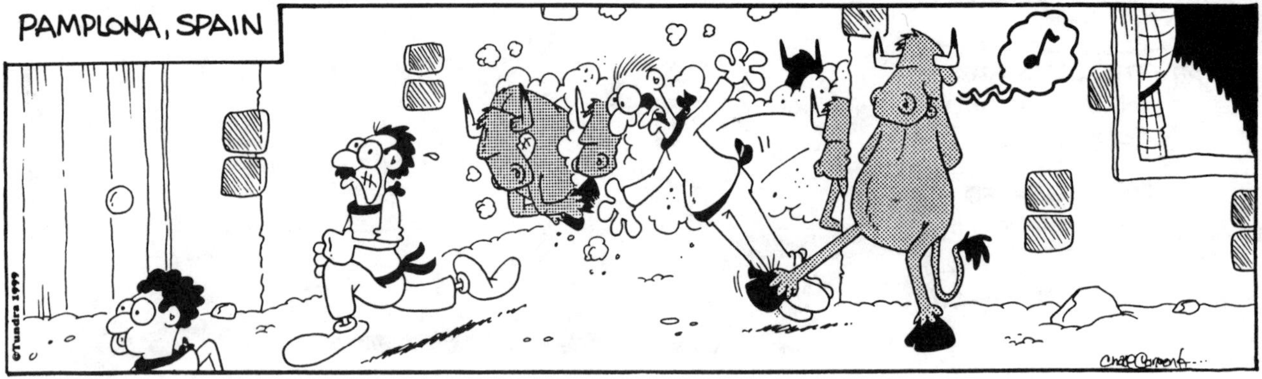
PAMPLONA, SPAIN
©Tundra 1999

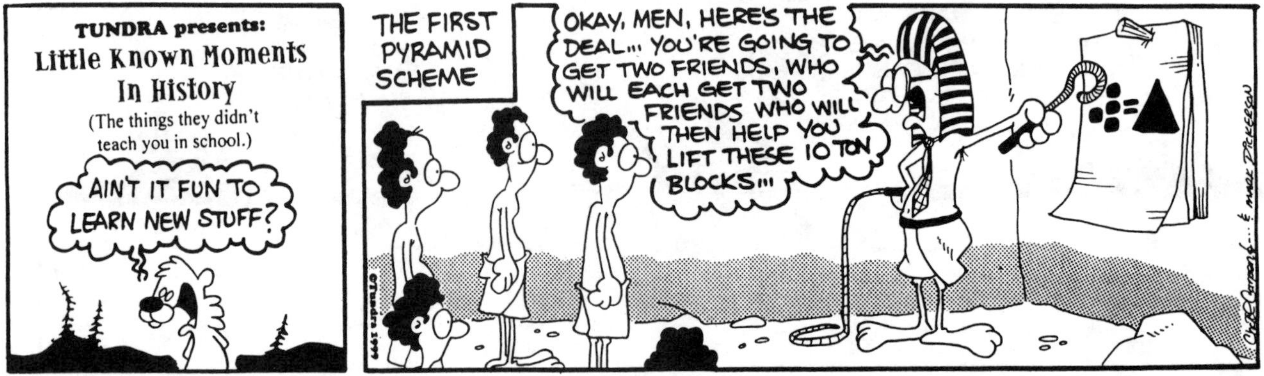
TUNDRA presents:
Little Known Moments In History
(The things they didn't teach you in school.)
AIN'T IT FUN TO LEARN NEW STUFF?
THE FIRST PYRAMID SCHEME
OKAY, MEN, HERE'S THE DEAL... YOU'RE GOING TO GET TWO FRIENDS, WHO WILL EACH GET TWO FRIENDS WHO WILL THEN HELP YOU LIFT THESE 10 TON BLOCKS...
©Tundra 1999

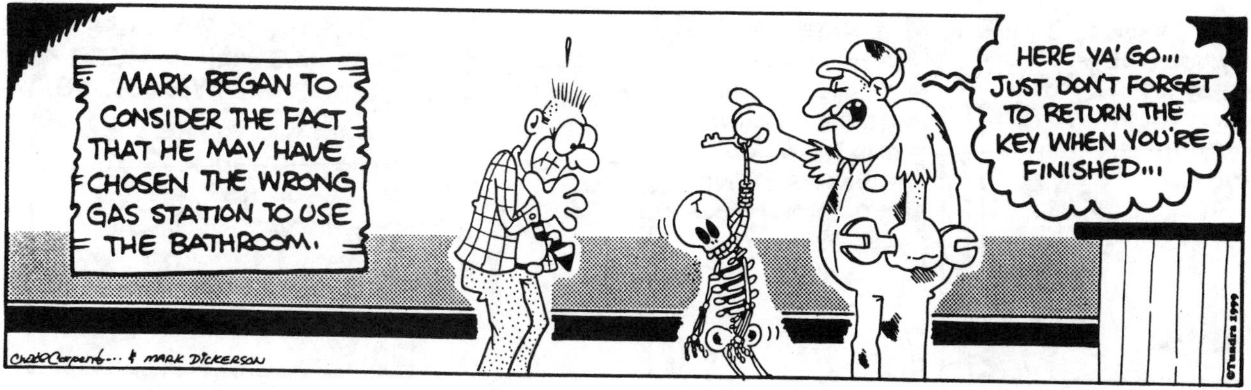
MARK BEGAN TO CONSIDER THE FACT THAT HE MAY HAVE CHOSEN THE WRONG GAS STATION TO USE THE BATHROOM.
HERE YA' GO... JUST DON'T FORGET TO RETURN THE KEY WHEN YOU'RE FINISHED...
& MARK DICKERSON
©Tundra 1999

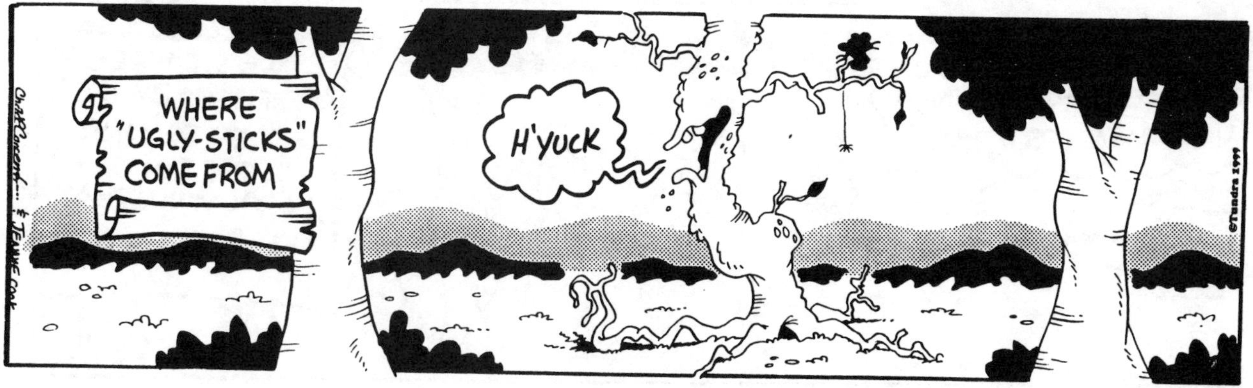
WHERE "UGLY-STICKS" COME FROM
H'YUCK
©Tundra 1999

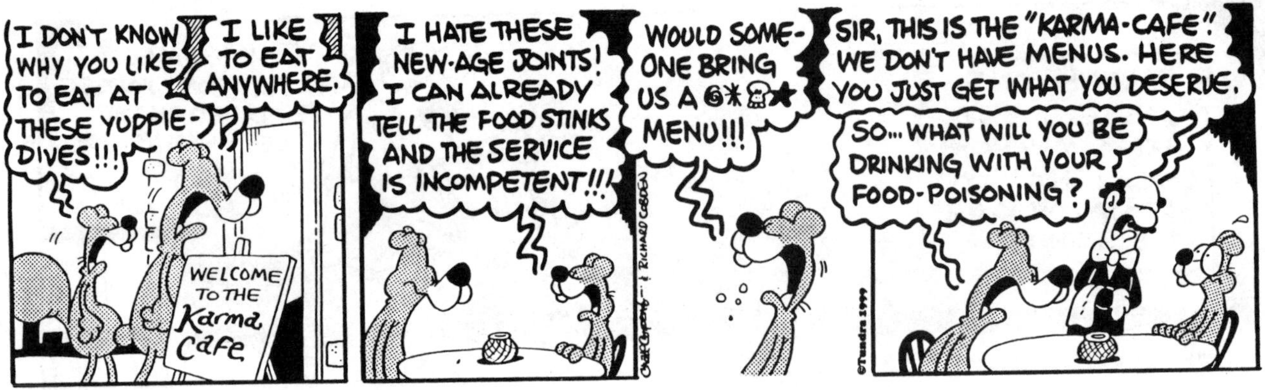
I DON'T KNOW WHY YOU LIKE TO EAT AT THESE YUPPIE-DIVES!!!
I LIKE TO EAT ANYWHERE.
WELCOME TO THE Karma Cafe
I HATE THESE NEW-AGE JOINTS! I CAN ALREADY TELL THE FOOD STINKS AND THE SERVICE IS INCOMPETENT!!!
WOULD SOME-ONE BRING US A @*☠★ MENU!!!
SIR, THIS IS THE "KARMA-CAFE"! WE DON'T HAVE MENUS. HERE YOU JUST GET WHAT YOU DESERVE.
SO... WHAT WILL YOU BE DRINKING WITH YOUR FOOD-POISONING?
©Tundra 1999

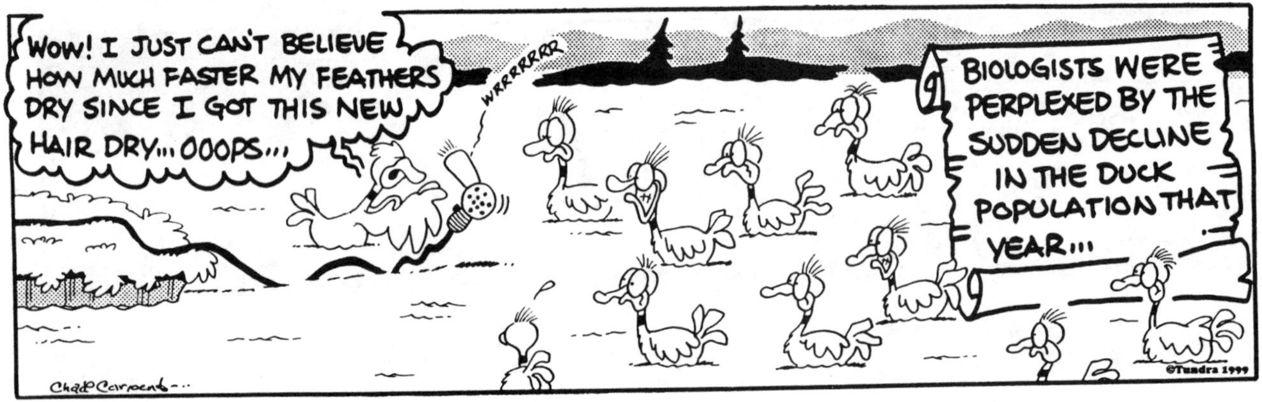
WOW! I JUST CAN'T BELIEVE HOW MUCH FASTER MY FEATHERS DRY SINCE I GOT THIS NEW HAIR DRY... OOOPS...
WRRRRRRR
BIOLOGISTS WERE PERPLEXED BY THE SUDDEN DECLINE IN THE DUCK POPULATION THAT YEAR...
©Tundra 1999

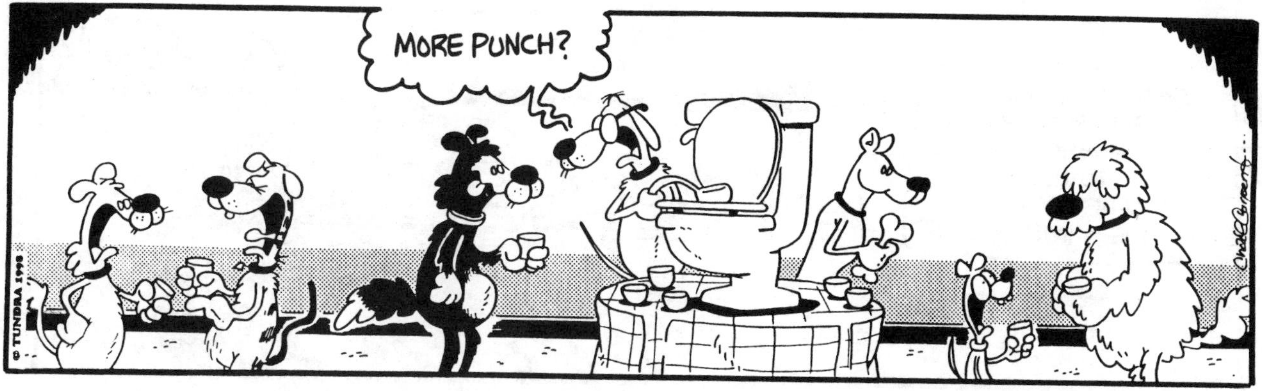
MORE PUNCH?
© TUNDRA 1998

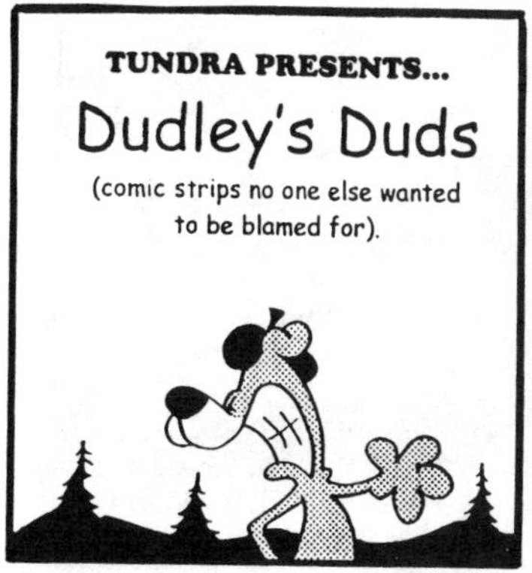
TUNDRA PRESENTS...
Dudley's Duds
(comic strips no one else wanted to be blamed for).

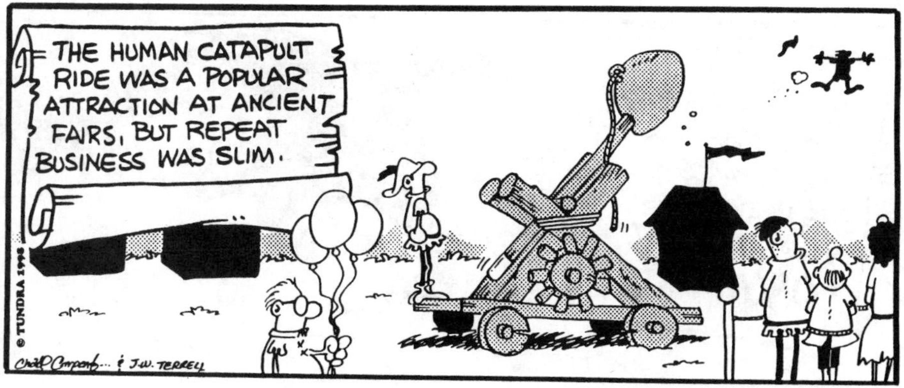
THE HUMAN CATAPULT RIDE WAS A POPULAR ATTRACTION AT ANCIENT FAIRS, BUT REPEAT BUSINESS WAS SLIM.
© TUNDRA 1998
J.W. TERRELL

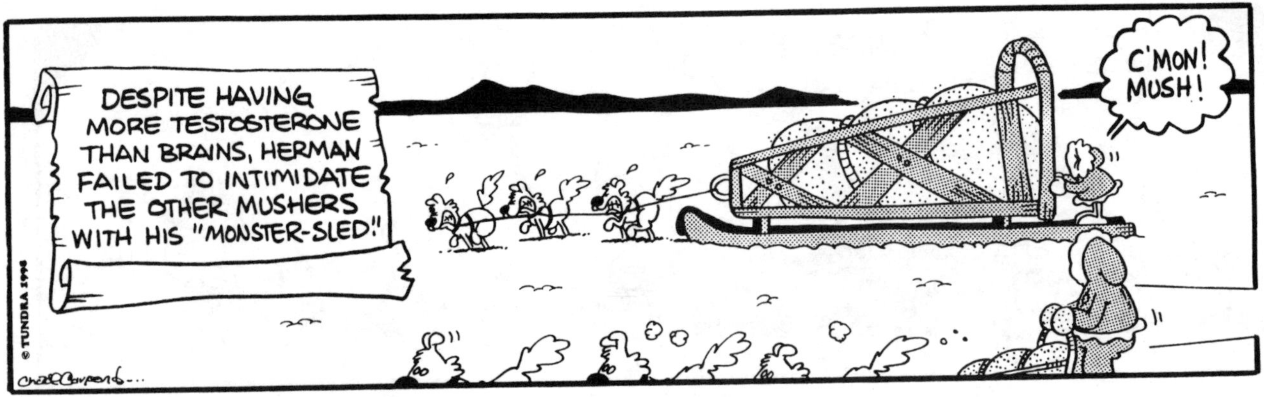
DESPITE HAVING MORE TESTOSTERONE THAN BRAINS, HERMAN FAILED TO INTIMIDATE THE OTHER MUSHERS WITH HIS "MONSTER-SLED!"
C'MON! MUSH!
© TUNDRA 1998

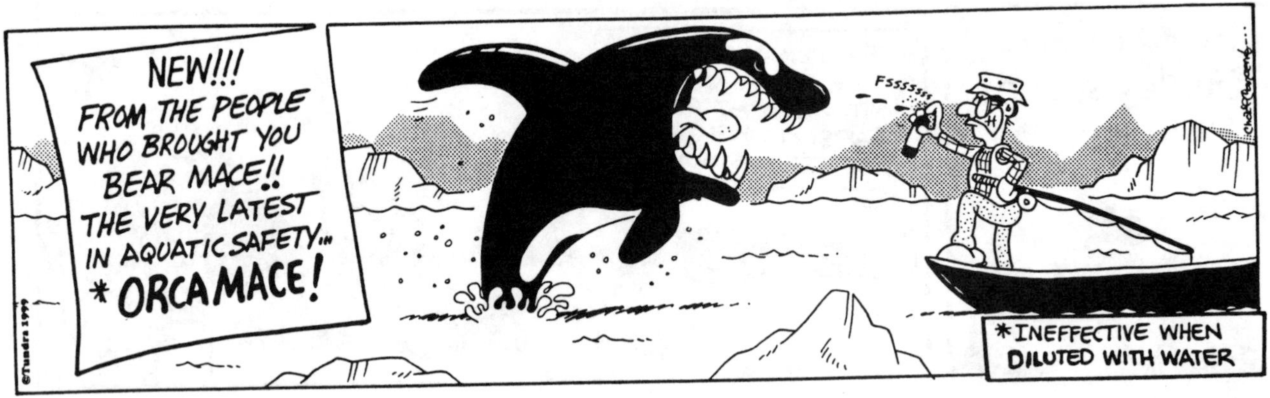
NEW!!! FROM THE PEOPLE WHO BROUGHT YOU BEAR MACE!! THE VERY LATEST IN AQUATIC SAFETY... *ORCAMACE!
FSSSSSSS
*INEFFECTIVE WHEN DILUTED WITH WATER
©Tundra 1999

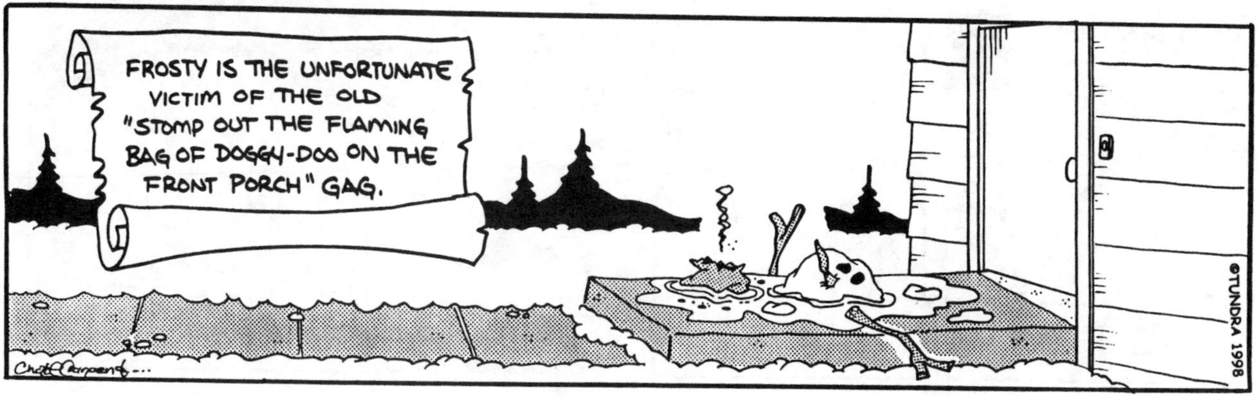
FROSTY IS THE UNFORTUNATE VICTIM OF THE OLD "STOMP OUT THE FLAMING BAG OF DOGGY-DOO ON THE FRONT PORCH" GAG.
©TUNDRA 1998

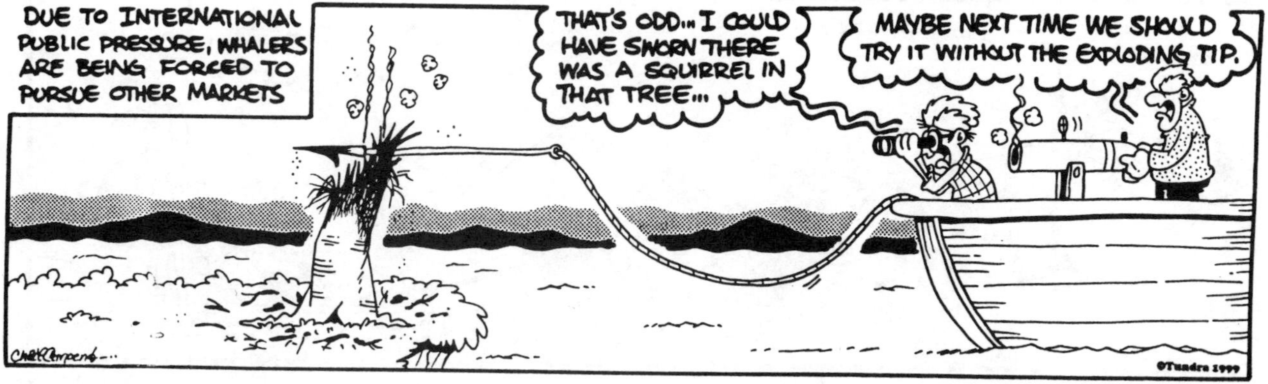
DUE TO INTERNATIONAL PUBLIC PRESSURE, WHALERS ARE BEING FORCED TO PURSUE OTHER MARKETS
THAT'S ODD... I COULD HAVE SWORN THERE WAS A SQUIRREL IN THAT TREE...
MAYBE NEXT TIME WE SHOULD TRY IT WITHOUT THE EXPLODING TIP.
©Tundra 1999

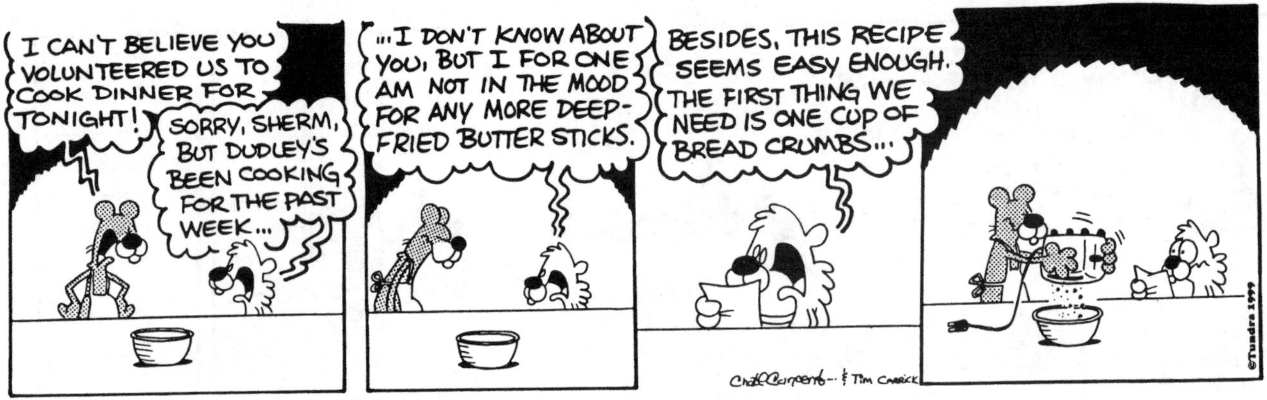
I CAN'T BELIEVE YOU VOLUNTEERED US TO COOK DINNER FOR TONIGHT!
SORRY, SHERM, BUT DUDLEY'S BEEN COOKING FOR THE PAST WEEK...
...I DON'T KNOW ABOUT YOU, BUT I FOR ONE AM NOT IN THE MOOD FOR ANY MORE DEEP-FRIED BUTTER STICKS.
BESIDES, THIS RECIPE SEEMS EASY ENOUGH. THE FIRST THING WE NEED IS ONE CUP OF BREAD CRUMBS...
©Tundra 1999
Chad Carpenter... & TIM CARRICK

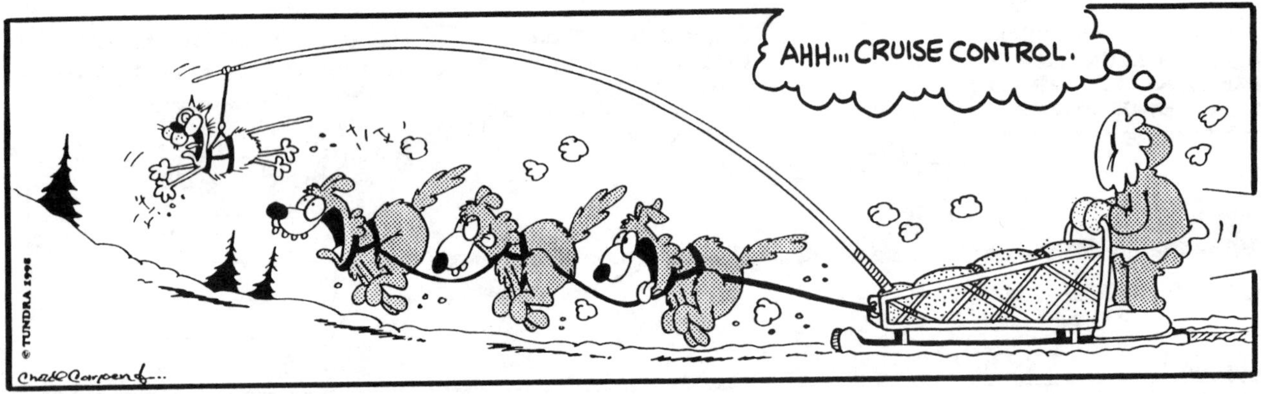
AHH... CRUISE CONTROL.
© TUNDRA 1998
Chad Carpenter...

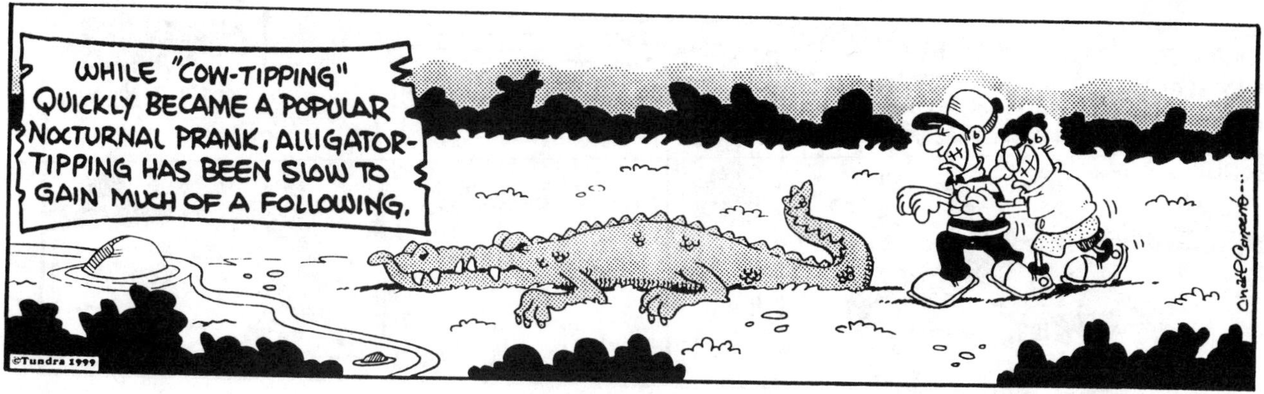
WHILE "COW-TIPPING" QUICKLY BECAME A POPULAR NOCTURNAL PRANK, ALLIGATOR-TIPPING HAS BEEN SLOW TO GAIN MUCH OF A FOLLOWING.
©Tundra 1999

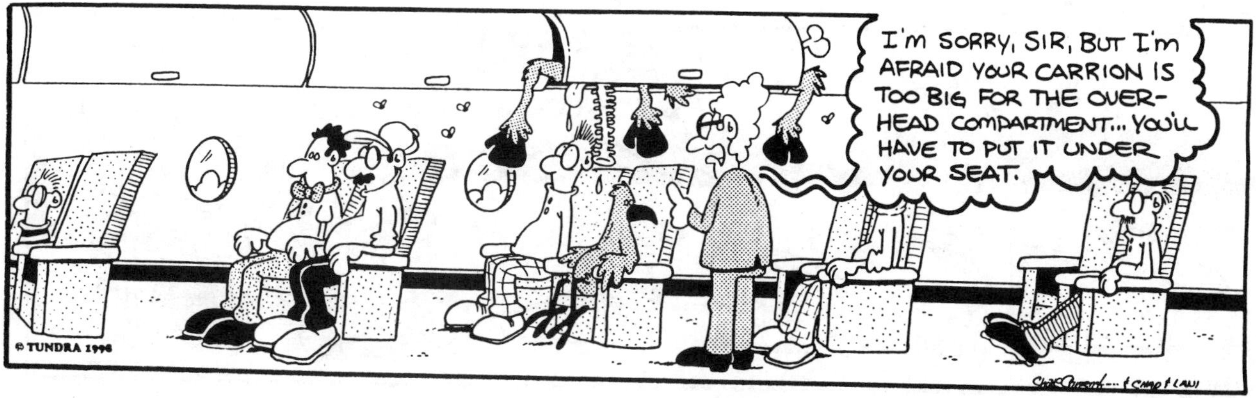
I'M SORRY, SIR, BUT I'M AFRAID YOUR CARRION IS TOO BIG FOR THE OVERHEAD COMPARTMENT... YOU'LL HAVE TO PUT IT UNDER YOUR SEAT.
© TUNDRA 1998

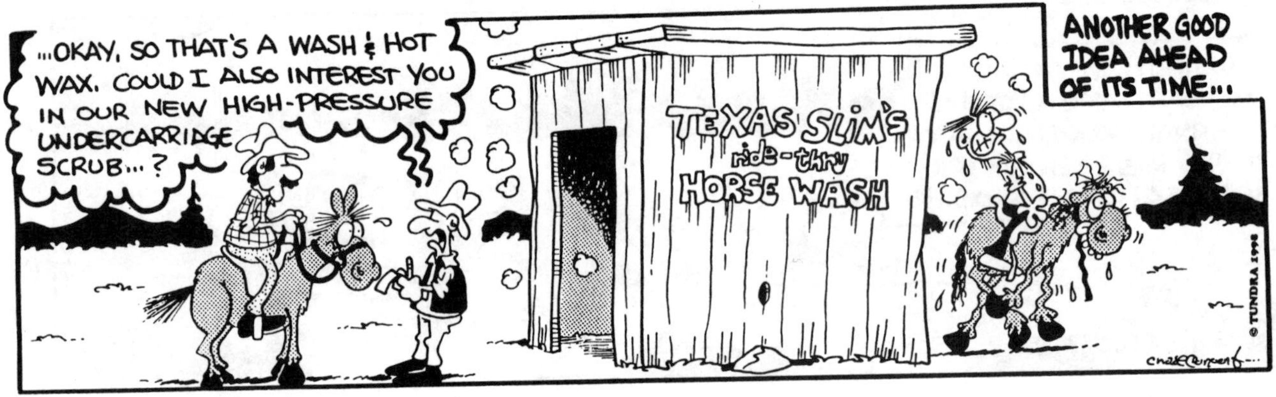
...OKAY, SO THAT'S A WASH & HOT WAX. COULD I ALSO INTEREST YOU IN OUR NEW HIGH-PRESSURE UNDERCARRIAGE SCRUB...?
TEXAS SLIM'S ride-thru HORSE WASH
ANOTHER GOOD IDEA AHEAD OF ITS TIME...
© TUNDRA 1998

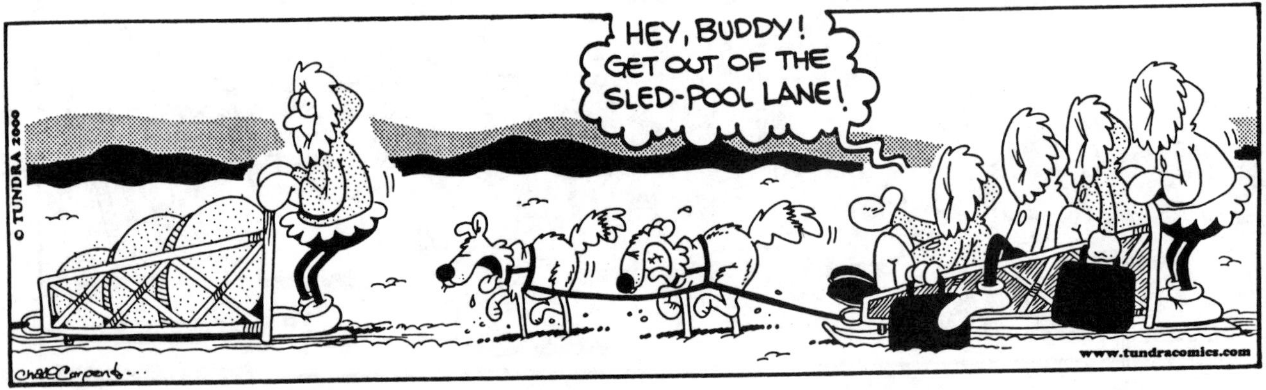
HEY, BUDDY! GET OUT OF THE SLED-POOL LANE!
© TUNDRA 2000
www.tundracomics.com

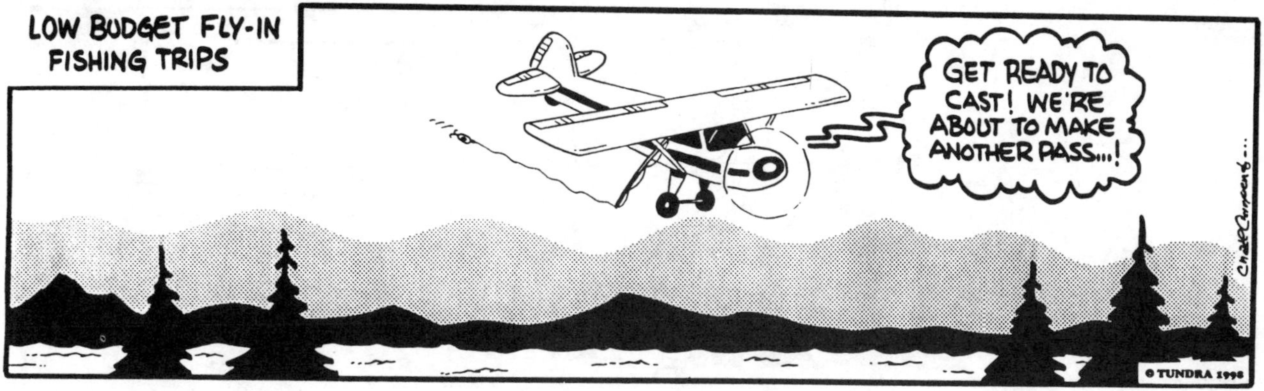
LOW BUDGET FLY-IN FISHING TRIPS
GET READY TO CAST! WE'RE ABOUT TO MAKE ANOTHER PASS...!
© TUNDRA 1998

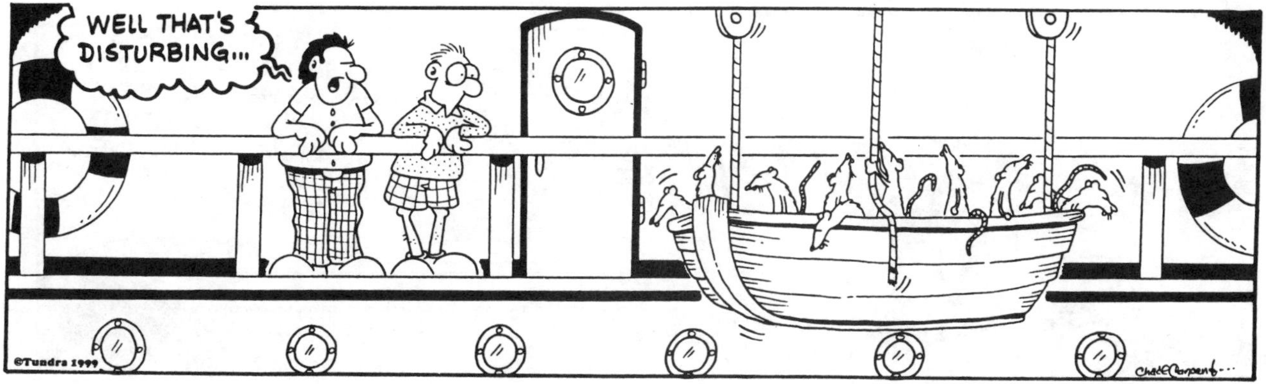
WELL THAT'S DISTURBING...
©Tundra 1999

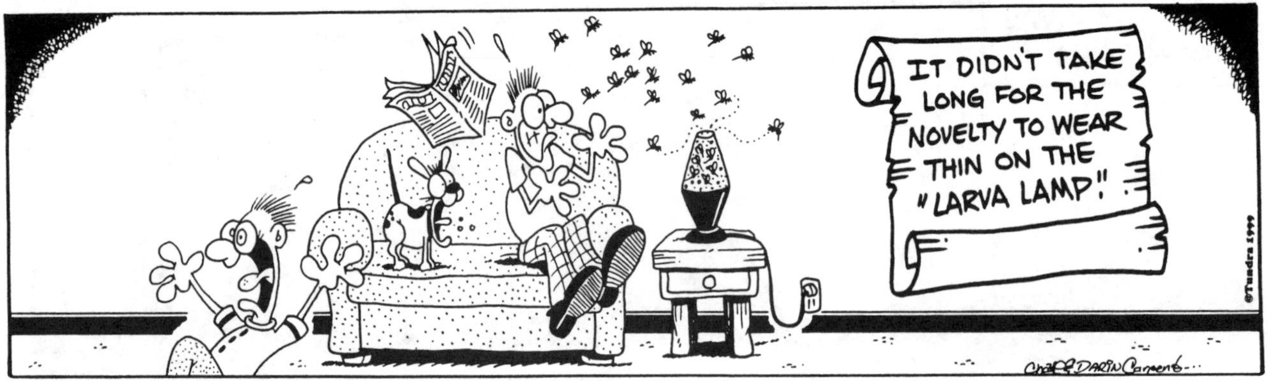
IT DIDN'T TAKE LONG FOR THE NOVELTY TO WEAR THIN ON THE "LARVA LAMP."
©Tundra 1999

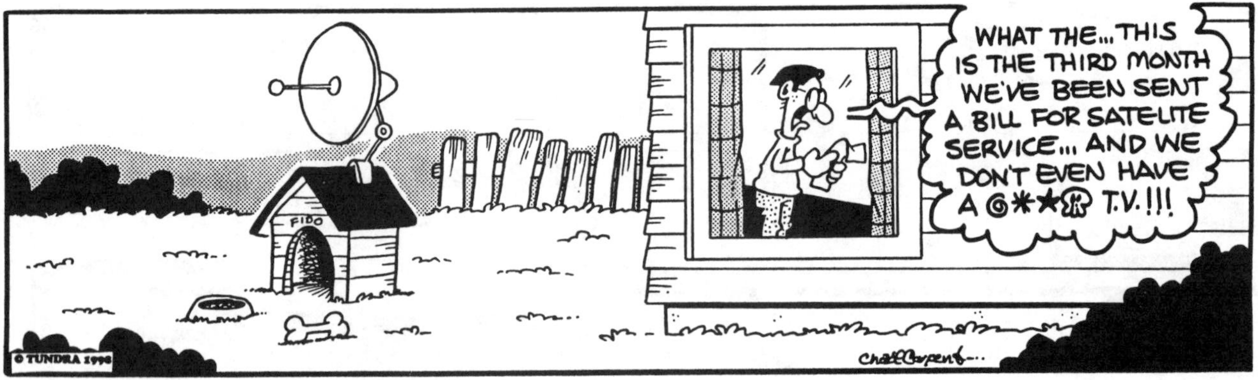
FIDO
WHAT THE... THIS IS THE THIRD MONTH WE'VE BEEN SENT A BILL FOR SATELLITE SERVICE... AND WE DON'T EVEN HAVE A @✱★ T.V.!!!
© TUNDRA 1998

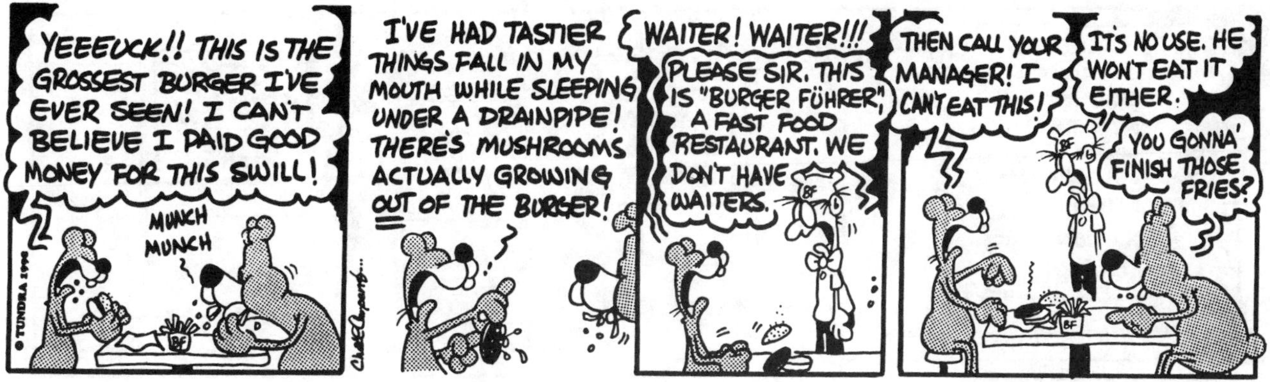
YEEEUCK!! THIS IS THE GROSSEST BURGER I'VE EVER SEEN! I CAN'T BELIEVE I PAID GOOD MONEY FOR THIS SWILL!
MUNCH MUNCH
© TUNDRA 1998
I'VE HAD TASTIER THINGS FALL IN MY MOUTH WHILE SLEEPING UNDER A DRAINPIPE! THERE'S MUSHROOMS ACTUALLY GROWING OUT OF THE BURGER!
WAITER! WAITER!!!
PLEASE SIR. THIS IS "BURGER FÜHRER", A FAST FOOD RESTAURANT. WE DON'T HAVE WAITERS.
BF
THEN CALL YOUR MANAGER! I CAN'T EAT THIS!
IT'S NO USE. HE WON'T EAT IT EITHER.
YOU GONNA' FINISH THOSE FRIES?
BF

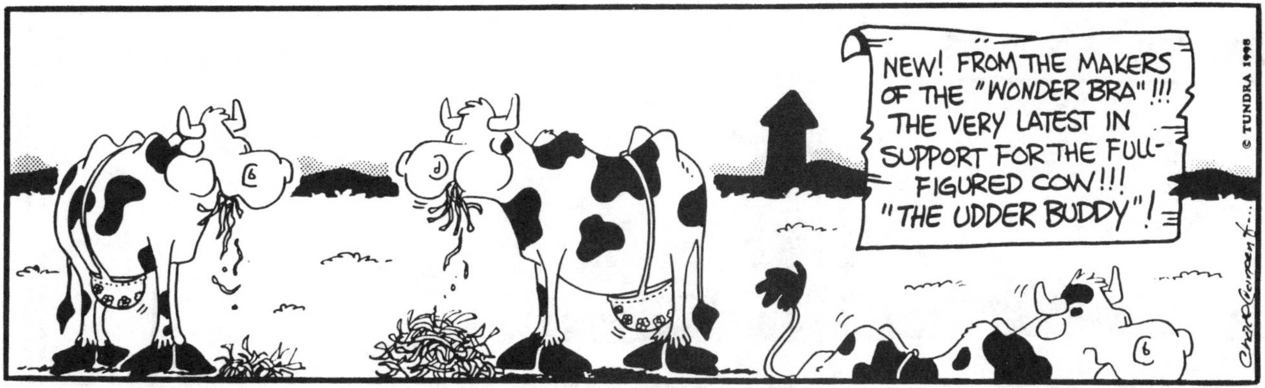
NEW! FROM THE MAKERS OF THE "WONDER BRA"!!! THE VERY LATEST IN SUPPORT FOR THE FULL-FIGURED COW!!! "THE UDDER BUDDY"!
© TUNDRA 1998

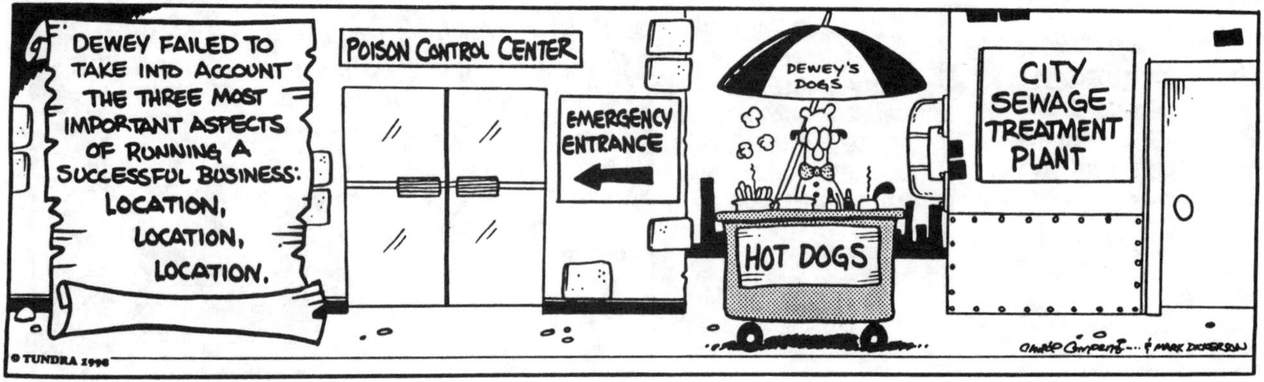
DEWEY FAILED TO TAKE INTO ACCOUNT THE THREE MOST IMPORTANT ASPECTS OF RUNNING A SUCCESSFUL BUSINESS: LOCATION, LOCATION, LOCATION.
POISON CONTROL CENTER
EMERGENCY ENTRANCE
DEWEY'S DOGS
HOT DOGS
CITY SEWAGE TREATMENT PLANT
© TUNDRA 1998

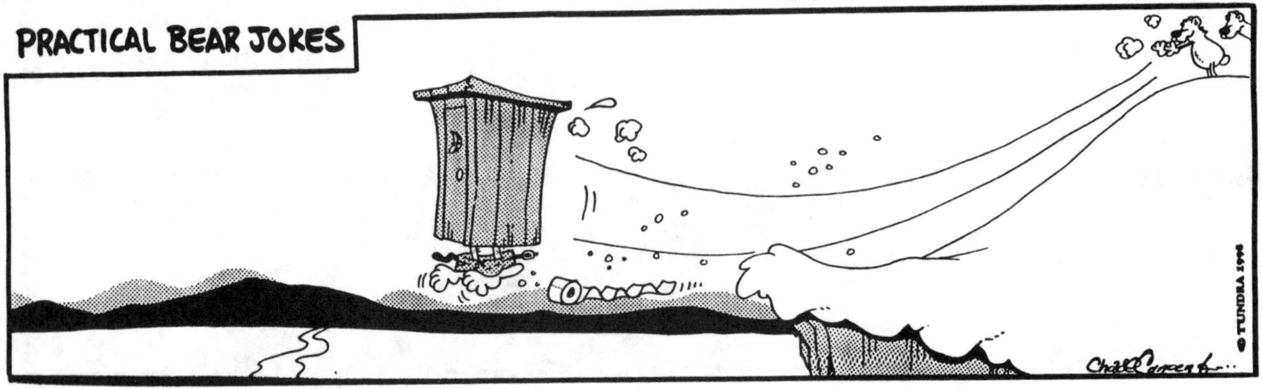
PRACTICAL BEAR JOKES

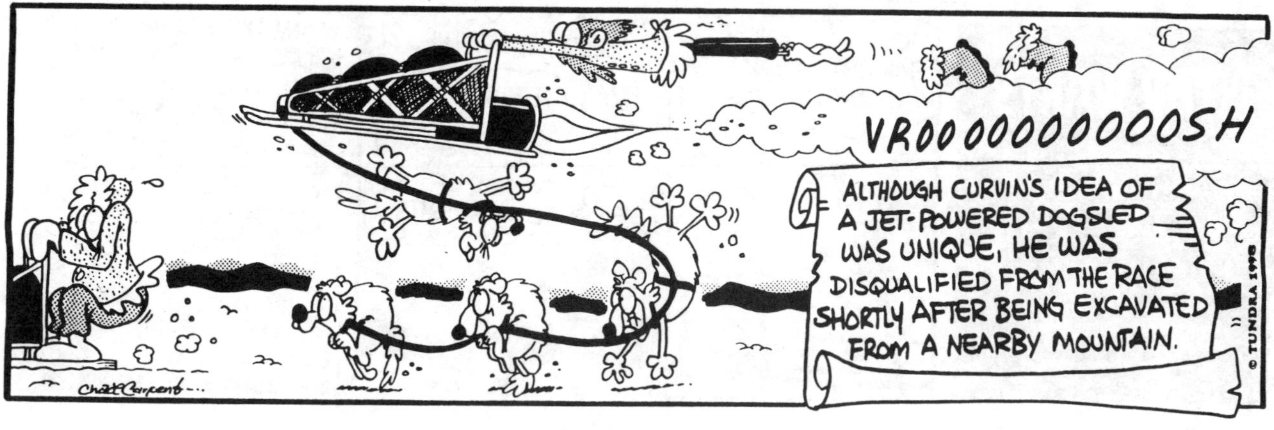
VROOOOOOOOOOOSH
ALTHOUGH CURVIN'S IDEA OF A JET-POWERED DOGSLED WAS UNIQUE, HE WAS DISQUALIFIED FROM THE RACE SHORTLY AFTER BEING EXCAVATED FROM A NEARBY MOUNTAIN.
© TUNDRA 1998

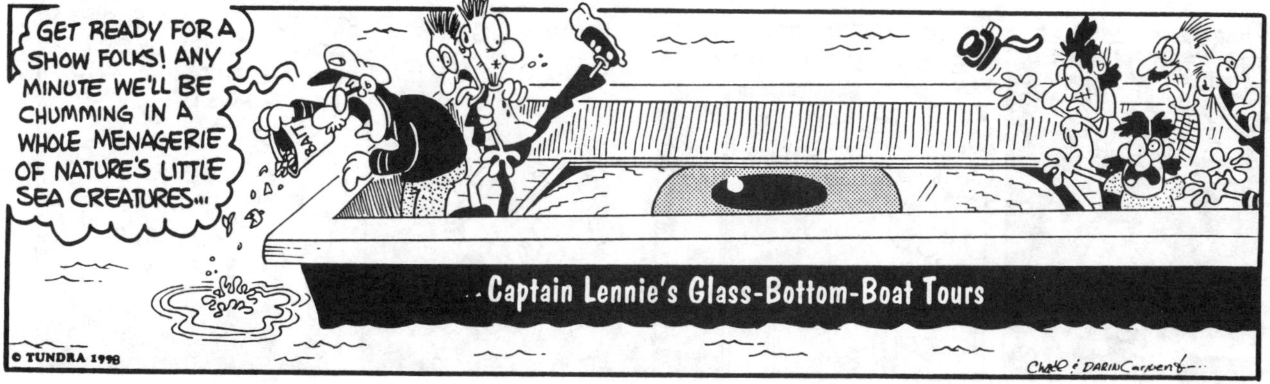
GET READY FOR A SHOW FOLKS! ANY MINUTE WE'LL BE CHUMMING IN A WHOLE MENAGERIE OF NATURE'S LITTLE SEA CREATURES...
BAIT
Captain Lennie's Glass-Bottom-Boat Tours
© TUNDRA 1998

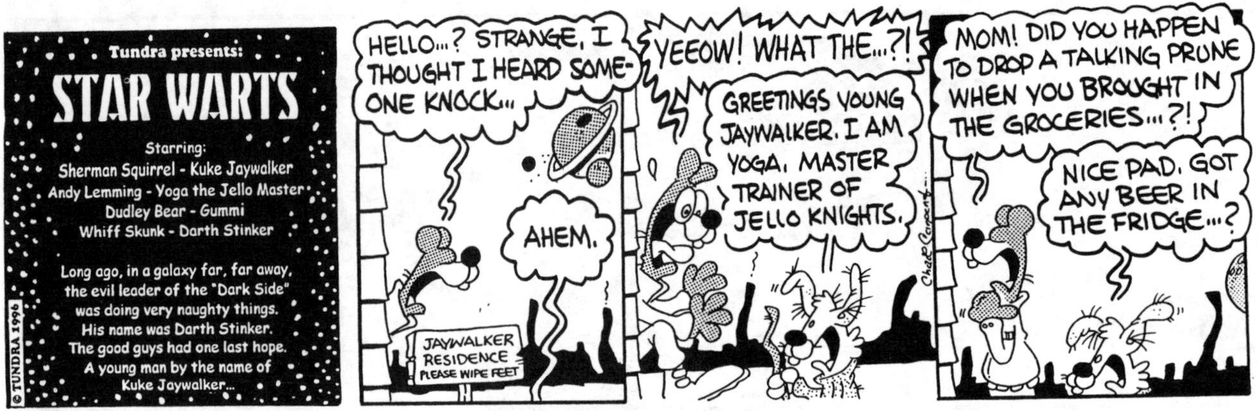
Tundra presents:
STAR WARTS
Starring:
Sherman Squirrel - Kuke Jaywalker
Andy Lemming - Yoga the Jello Master
Dudley Bear - Gummi
Whiff Skunk - Darth Stinker
Long ago, in a galaxy far, far away, the evil leader of the "Dark Side" was doing very naughty things. His name was Darth Stinker. The good guys had one last hope. A young man by the name of Kuke Jaywalker...
© TUNDRA 1996
HELLO...? STRANGE, I THOUGHT I HEARD SOME-ONE KNOCK...
AHEM.
JAYWALKER RESIDENCE PLEASE WIPE FEET
YEEOW! WHAT THE...?!
GREETINGS YOUNG JAYWALKER. I AM YOGA, MASTER TRAINER OF JELLO KNIGHTS.
MOM! DID YOU HAPPEN TO DROP A TALKING PRUNE WHEN YOU BROUGHT IN THE GROCERIES...?!
NICE PAD. GOT ANY BEER IN THE FRIDGE...?

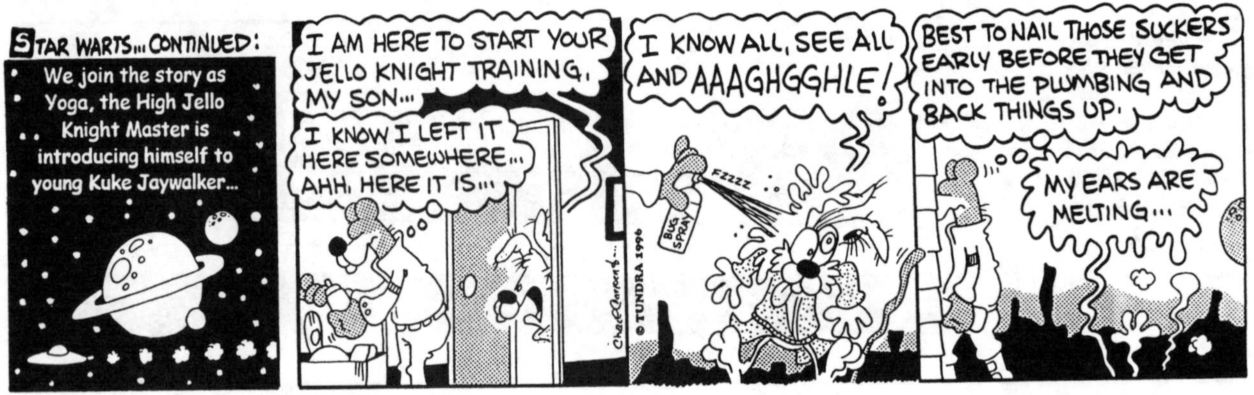
STAR WARTS... CONTINUED:
We join the story as Yoga, the High Jello Knight Master is introducing himself to young Kuke Jaywalker...
I AM HERE TO START YOUR JELLO KNIGHT TRAINING, MY SON...
I KNOW I LEFT IT HERE SOMEWHERE... AHH, HERE IT IS...
I KNOW ALL, SEE ALL AND AAAGHGGHLE!
FZZZZ
BUG SPRAY
© TUNDRA 1996
BEST TO NAIL THOSE SUCKERS EARLY BEFORE THEY GET INTO THE PLUMBING AND BACK THINGS UP.
MY EARS ARE MELTING...

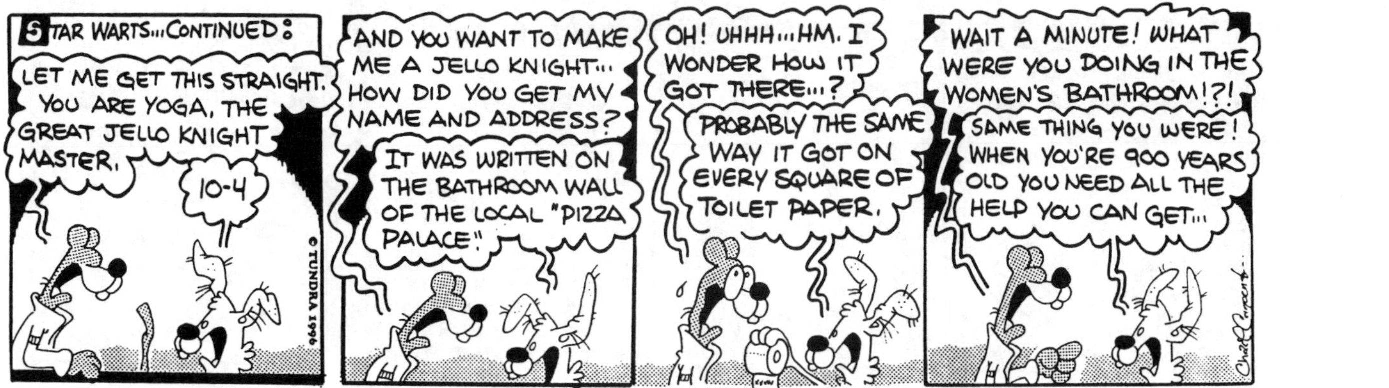
STAR WARTS... CONTINUED:
LET ME GET THIS STRAIGHT. YOU ARE YOGA, THE GREAT JELLO KNIGHT MASTER.
10-4
© TUNDRA 1996
AND YOU WANT TO MAKE ME A JELLO KNIGHT... HOW DID YOU GET MY NAME AND ADDRESS?
IT WAS WRITTEN ON THE BATHROOM WALL OF THE LOCAL "PIZZA PALACE"!
OH! UHHH...HM. I WONDER HOW IT GOT THERE...?
PROBABLY THE SAME WAY IT GOT ON EVERY SQUARE OF TOILET PAPER.
WAIT A MINUTE! WHAT WERE YOU DOING IN THE WOMEN'S BATHROOM!?!
SAME THING YOU WERE! WHEN YOU'RE 900 YEARS OLD YOU NEED ALL THE HELP YOU CAN GET...

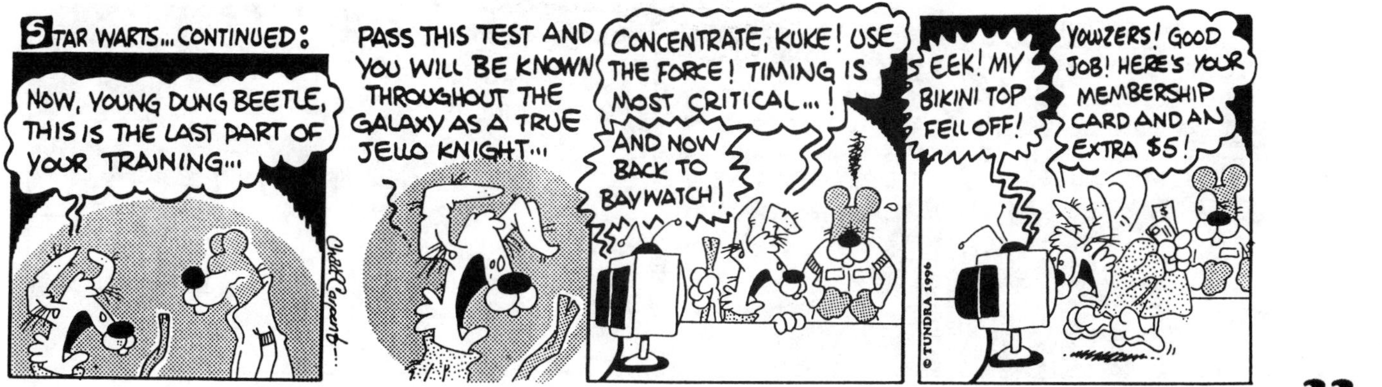
STAR WARTS... CONTINUED:
NOW, YOUNG DUNG BEETLE, THIS IS THE LAST PART OF YOUR TRAINING...
PASS THIS TEST AND YOU WILL BE KNOWN THROUGHOUT THE GALAXY AS A TRUE JELLO KNIGHT...
CONCENTRATE, KUKE! USE THE FORCE! TIMING IS MOST CRITICAL...!
AND NOW BACK TO BAYWATCH!
EEK! MY BIKINI TOP FELL OFF!
YOWZERS! GOOD JOB! HERE'S YOUR MEMBERSHIP CARD AND AN EXTRA $5!
© TUNDRA 1996

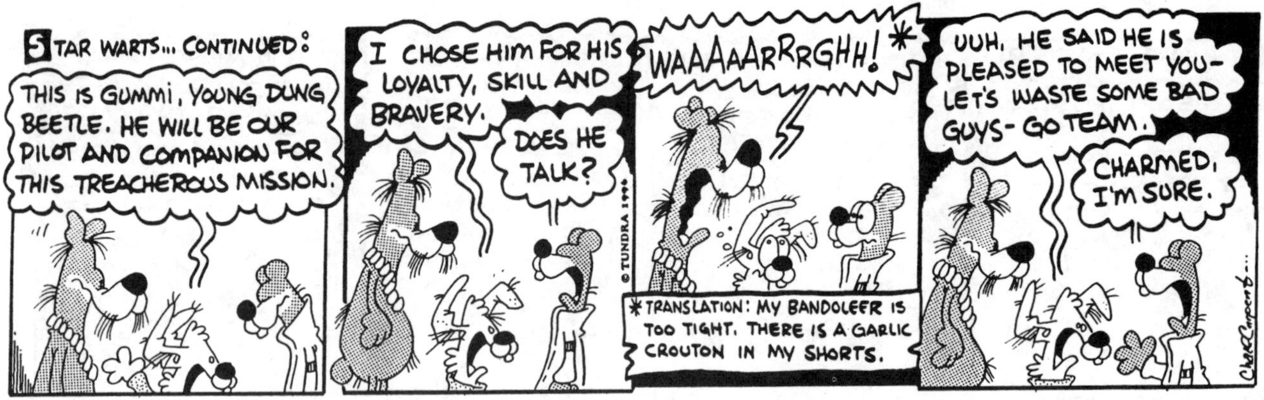
STAR WARTS... CONTINUED:
THIS IS GUMMI, YOUNG DUNG BEETLE. HE WILL BE OUR PILOT AND COMPANION FOR THIS TREACHEROUS MISSION.
I CHOSE HIM FOR HIS LOYALTY, SKILL AND BRAVERY.
DOES HE TALK?
© TUNDRA 1996
WAAAAARRRGHH! *
* TRANSLATION: MY BANDOLEER IS TOO TIGHT. THERE IS A GARLIC CROUTON IN MY SHORTS.
UUH, HE SAID HE IS PLEASED TO MEET YOU-LET'S WASTE SOME BAD GUYS- GO TEAM.
CHARMED, I'M SURE.

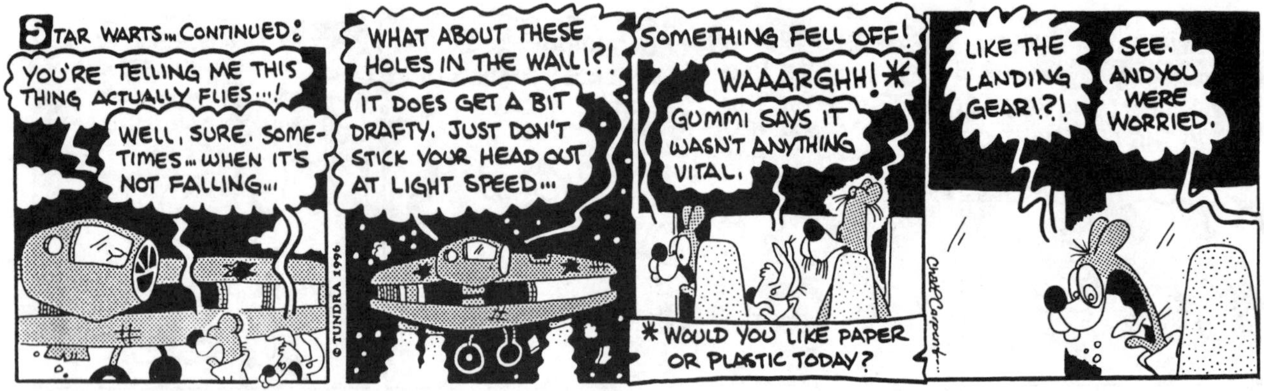
STAR WARTS... CONTINUED:
YOU'RE TELLING ME THIS THING ACTUALLY FLIES...!
WELL, SURE. SOMETIMES... WHEN IT'S NOT FALLING...
© TUNDRA 1996
WHAT ABOUT THESE HOLES IN THE WALL!?!
IT DOES GET A BIT DRAFTY. JUST DON'T STICK YOUR HEAD OUT AT LIGHT SPEED...
SOMETHING FELL OFF!
WAAARGHH! *
GUMMI SAYS IT WASN'T ANYTHING VITAL.
* WOULD YOU LIKE PAPER OR PLASTIC TODAY?
LIKE THE LANDING GEAR!?!
SEE. AND YOU WERE WORRIED.

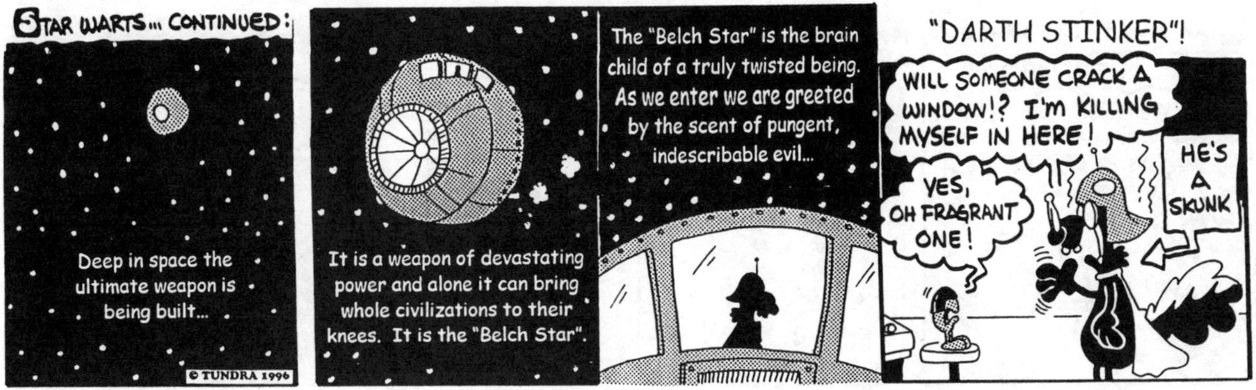
STAR WARTS... CONTINUED:
Deep in space the ultimate weapon is being built...
© TUNDRA 1996
It is a weapon of devastating power and alone it can bring whole civilizations to their knees. It is the "Belch Star".
The "Belch Star" is the brain child of a truly twisted being. As we enter we are greeted by the scent of pungent, indescribable evil...
"DARTH STINKER"!
WILL SOMEONE CRACK A WINDOW!? I'M KILLING MYSELF IN HERE!
YES, OH FRAGRANT ONE!
HE'S A SKUNK

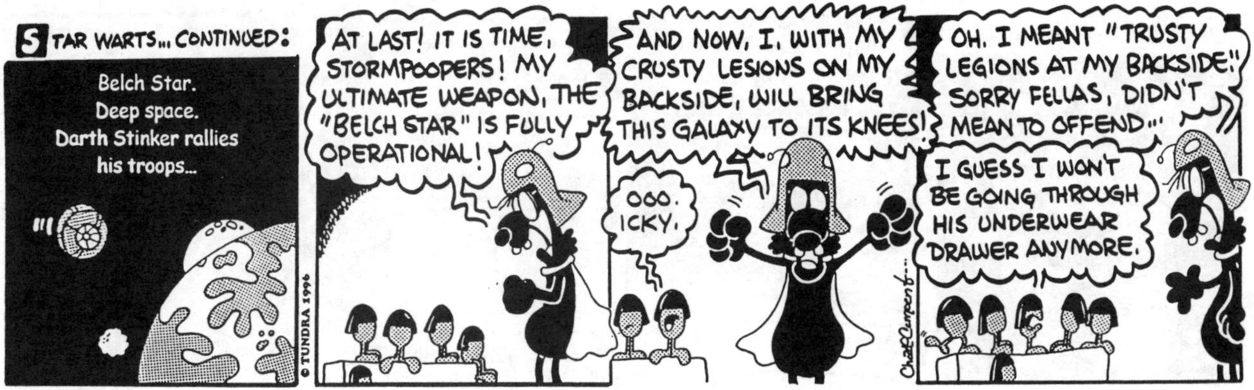
STAR WARTS... CONTINUED:
Belch Star. Deep space. Darth Stinker rallies his troops...
© TUNDRA 1996
AT LAST! IT IS TIME, STORMPOOPERS! MY ULTIMATE WEAPON, THE "BELCH STAR" IS FULLY OPERATIONAL!
AND NOW, I, WITH MY CRUSTY LESIONS ON MY BACKSIDE, WILL BRING THIS GALAXY TO ITS KNEES!
OOO. ICKY.
OH. I MEANT "TRUSTY LEGIONS AT MY BACKSIDE!" SORRY FELLAS, DIDN'T MEAN TO OFFEND...
I GUESS I WON'T BE GOING THROUGH HIS UNDERWEAR DRAWER ANYMORE.

STAR WARTS... CONTINUED:

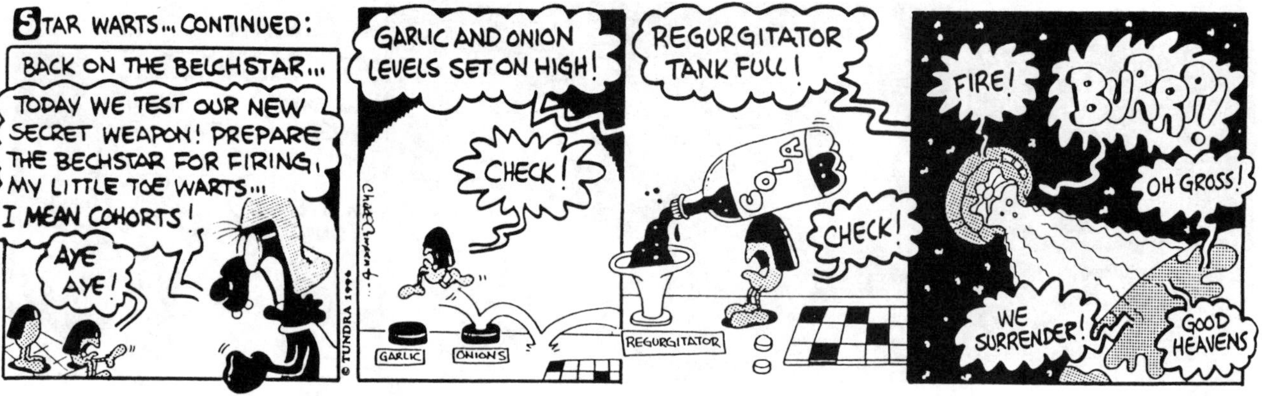
BACK ON THE BELCHSTAR...
TODAY WE TEST OUR NEW SECRET WEAPON! PREPARE THE BECHSTAR FOR FIRING, MY LITTLE TOE WARTS... I MEAN COHORTS!
AYE AYE!
© TUNDRA 1996
GARLIC AND ONION LEVELS SET ON HIGH!
CHECK!
GARLIC
ONIONS
REGURGITATOR TANK FULL!
COLA
CHECK!
REGURGITATOR
FIRE!
BURP!
OH GROSS!
WE SURRENDER!
GOOD HEAVENS

STAR WARTS... CONTINUED:

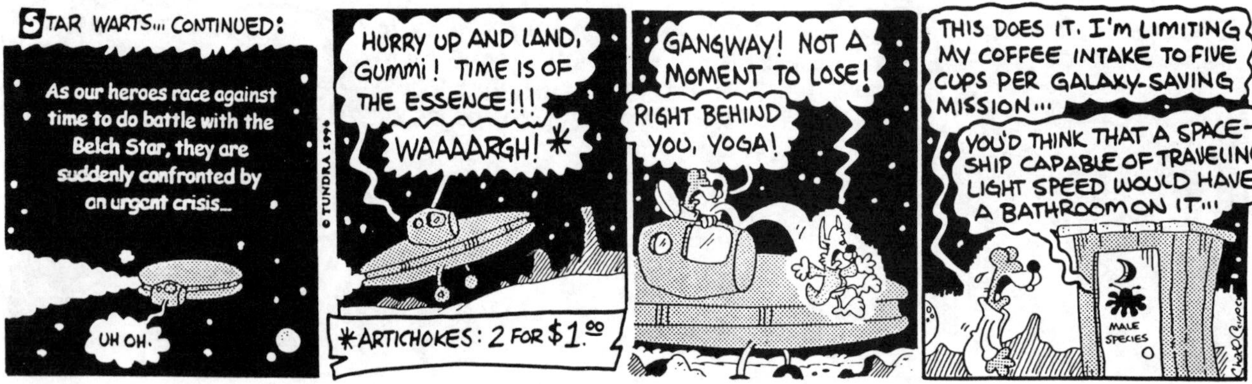
As our heroes race against time to do battle with the Belch Star, they are suddenly confronted by an urgent crisis...
UH OH.
© TUNDRA 1996
HURRY UP AND LAND, GUMMI! TIME IS OF THE ESSENCE!!!
WAAAARGH! *
*ARTICHOKES: 2 FOR $1.00
GANGWAY! NOT A MOMENT TO LOSE!
RIGHT BEHIND YOU, YOGA!
THIS DOES IT. I'M LIMITING MY COFFEE INTAKE TO FIVE CUPS PER GALAXY-SAVING MISSION...
YOU'D THINK THAT A SPACE-SHIP CAPABLE OF TRAVELING LIGHT SPEED WOULD HAVE A BATHROOM ON IT...
MALE SPECIES

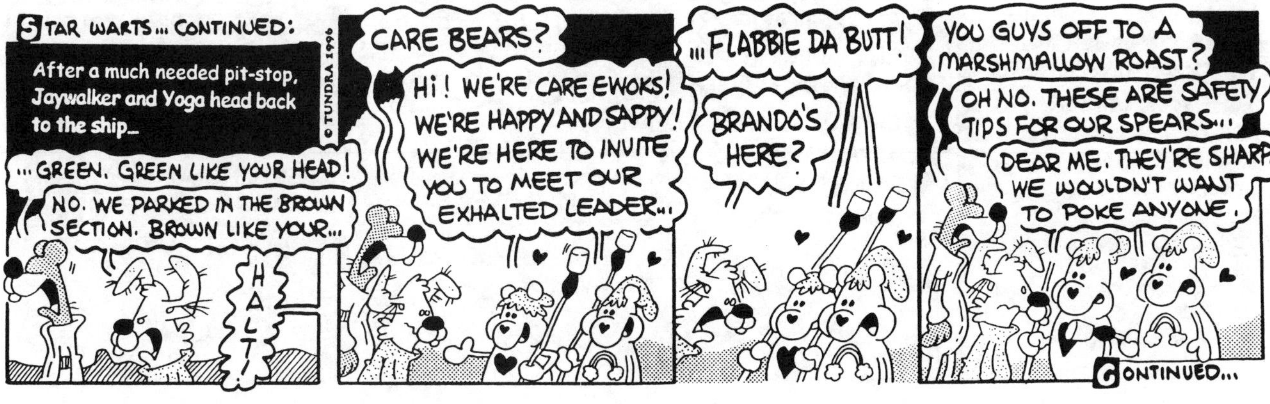
STAR WARTS... CONTINUED:
After a much needed pit-stop, Jaywalker and Yoga head back to the ship...
© TUNDRA 1996
...GREEN. GREEN LIKE YOUR HEAD!
NO. WE PARKED IN THE BROWN SECTION. BROWN LIKE YOUR...
HALT!
CARE BEARS?
Hi! WE'RE CARE EWOKS! WE'RE HAPPY AND SAPPY! WE'RE HERE TO INVITE YOU TO MEET OUR EXHALTED LEADER...
...FLABBIE DA BUTT!
BRANDO'S HERE?
YOU GUYS OFF TO A MARSHMALLOW ROAST?
OH NO. THESE ARE SAFETY TIPS FOR OUR SPEARS...
DEAR ME. THEY'RE SHARP. WE WOULDN'T WANT TO POKE ANYONE.
CONTINUED...

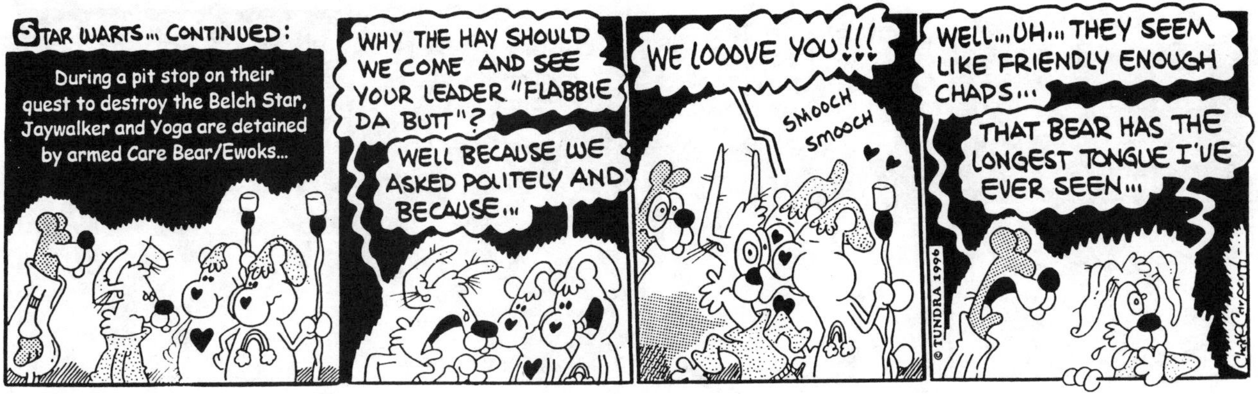
STAR WARTS... CONTINUED:
During a pit stop on their quest to destroy the Belch Star, Jaywalker and Yoga are detained by armed Care Bear/Ewoks...
WHY THE HAY SHOULD WE COME AND SEE YOUR LEADER "FLABBIE DA BUTT"?
WELL BECAUSE WE ASKED POLITELY AND BECAUSE...
WE LOOOVE YOU!!!
SMOOCH SMOOCH
© TUNDRA 1996
WELL... UH... THEY SEEM LIKE FRIENDLY ENOUGH CHAPS...
THAT BEAR HAS THE LONGEST TONGUE I'VE EVER SEEN...

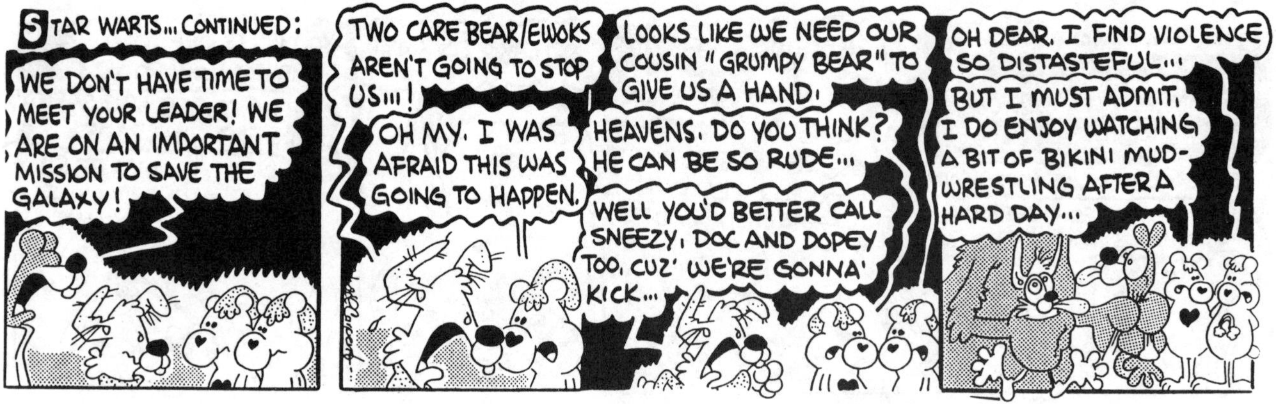
STAR WARTS... CONTINUED:
WE DON'T HAVE TIME TO MEET YOUR LEADER! WE ARE ON AN IMPORTANT MISSION TO SAVE THE GALAXY!
TWO CARE BEAR/EWOKS AREN'T GOING TO STOP US...!
OH MY. I WAS AFRAID THIS WAS GOING TO HAPPEN.
LOOKS LIKE WE NEED OUR COUSIN "GRUMPY BEAR" TO GIVE US A HAND.
HEAVENS. DO YOU THINK? HE CAN BE SO RUDE...
WELL YOU'D BETTER CALL SNEEZY, DOC AND DOPEY TOO, CUZ' WE'RE GONNA' KICK...
OH DEAR. I FIND VIOLENCE SO DISTASTEFUL...
BUT I MUST ADMIT, I DO ENJOY WATCHING A BIT OF BIKINI MUD-WRESTLING AFTER A HARD DAY...

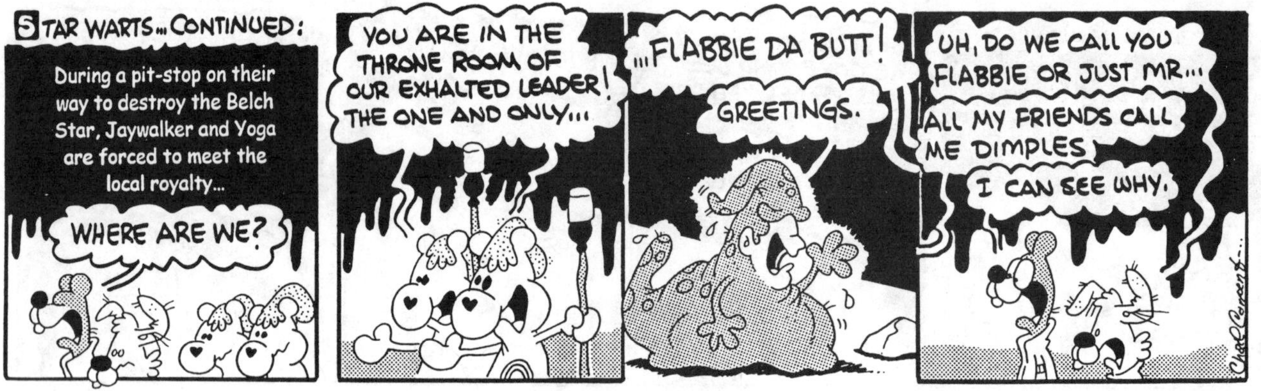
STAR WARTS... CONTINUED:
During a pit-stop on their way to destroy the Belch Star, Jaywalker and Yoga are forced to meet the local royalty...
WHERE ARE WE?
YOU ARE IN THE THRONE ROOM OF OUR EXHALTED LEADER! THE ONE AND ONLY...
...FLABBIE DA BUTT!
GREETINGS.
UH, DO WE CALL YOU FLABBIE OR JUST MR...
ALL MY FRIENDS CALL ME DIMPLES.
I CAN SEE WHY.

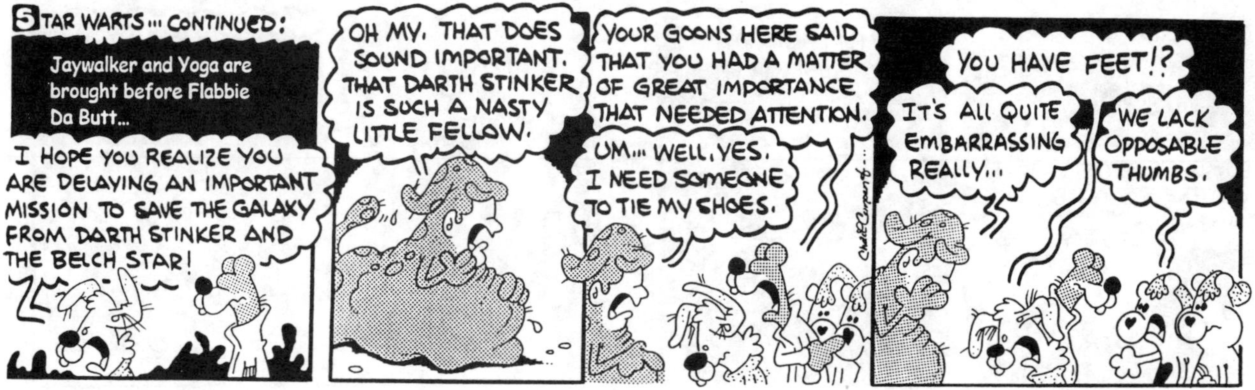
STAR WARTS... CONTINUED:
Jaywalker and Yoga are brought before Flabbie Da Butt...
I HOPE YOU REALIZE YOU ARE DELAYING AN IMPORTANT MISSION TO SAVE THE GALAXY FROM DARTH STINKER AND THE BELCH STAR!
OH MY. THAT DOES SOUND IMPORTANT. THAT DARTH STINKER IS SUCH A NASTY LITTLE FELLOW.
YOUR GOONS HERE SAID THAT YOU HAD A MATTER OF GREAT IMPORTANCE THAT NEEDED ATTENTION.
UM... WELL, YES. I NEED SOMEONE TO TIE MY SHOES.
YOU HAVE FEET!?
IT'S ALL QUITE EMBARRASSING REALLY...
WE LACK OPPOSABLE THUMBS.

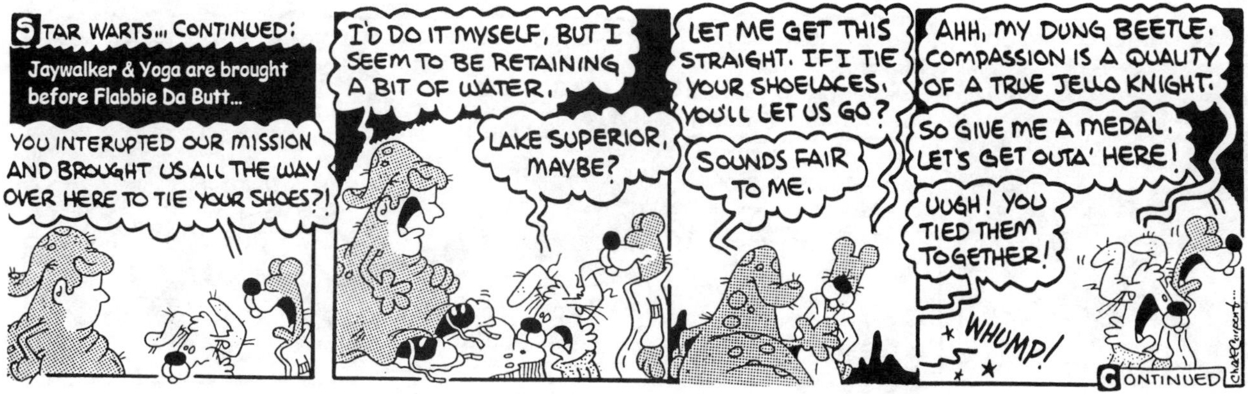
STAR WARTS... CONTINUED:
Jaywalker & Yoga are brought before Flabbie Da Butt...
YOU INTERUPTED OUR MISSION AND BROUGHT US ALL THE WAY OVER HERE TO TIE YOUR SHOES?!
I'D DO IT MYSELF, BUT I SEEM TO BE RETAINING A BIT OF WATER.
LAKE SUPERIOR, MAYBE?
LET ME GET THIS STRAIGHT. IF I TIE YOUR SHOELACES, YOU'LL LET US GO?
SOUNDS FAIR TO ME.
AHH, MY DUNG BEETLE. COMPASSION IS A QUALITY OF A TRUE JELLO KNIGHT.
SO GIVE ME A MEDAL. LET'S GET OUTA' HERE!
UUGH! YOU TIED THEM TOGETHER!
WHUMP!
CONTINUED

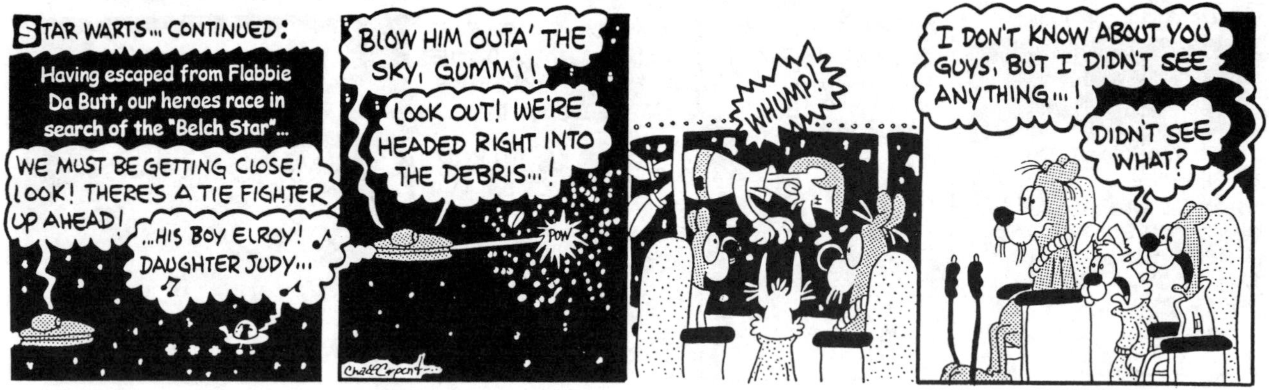
STAR WARTS... CONTINUED:
Having escaped from Flabbie Da Butt, our heroes race in search of the "Belch Star"...
WE MUST BE GETTING CLOSE! LOOK! THERE'S A TIE FIGHTER UP AHEAD!
...HIS BOY ELROY! DAUGHTER JUDY...
BLOW HIM OUTA' THE SKY, GUMMI!
LOOK OUT! WE'RE HEADED RIGHT INTO THE DEBRIS...!
POW
WHUMP!
I DON'T KNOW ABOUT YOU GUYS, BUT I DIDN'T SEE ANYTHING...!
DIDN'T SEE WHAT?

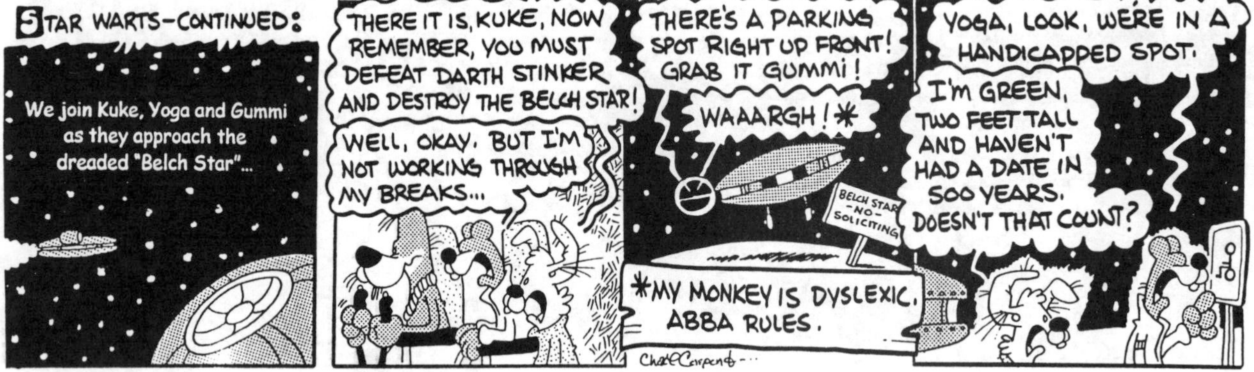
STAR WARTS–CONTINUED:
We join Kuke, Yoga and Gummi as they approach the dreaded "Belch Star"...
THERE IT IS, KUKE, NOW REMEMBER, YOU MUST DEFEAT DARTH STINKER AND DESTROY THE BELCH STAR!
WELL, OKAY. BUT I'M NOT WORKING THROUGH MY BREAKS...
THERE'S A PARKING SPOT RIGHT UP FRONT! GRAB IT GUMMI!
WAAARGH! *
BELCH STAR -NO- SOLICITING
*MY MONKEY IS DYSLEXIC. ABBA RULES.
YOGA, LOOK, WE'RE IN A HANDICAPPED SPOT.
I'M GREEN, TWO FEET TALL AND HAVEN'T HAD A DATE IN 500 YEARS. DOESN'T THAT COUNT?

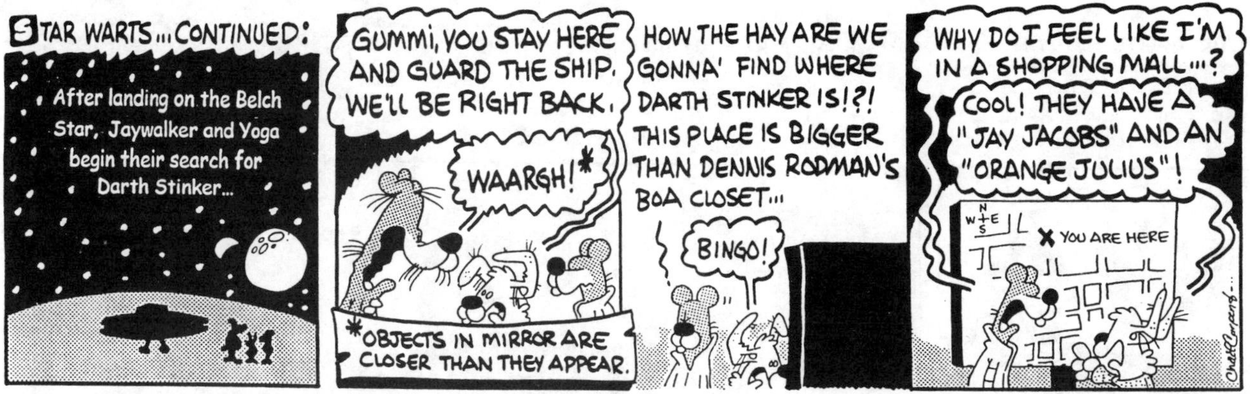
STAR WARTS... CONTINUED:
After landing on the Belch Star, Jaywalker and Yoga begin their search for Darth Stinker...
GUMMI, YOU STAY HERE AND GUARD THE SHIP. WE'LL BE RIGHT BACK.
WAARGH!*
*OBJECTS IN MIRROR ARE CLOSER THAN THEY APPEAR.
HOW THE HAY ARE WE GONNA' FIND WHERE DARTH STINKER IS!?! THIS PLACE IS BIGGER THAN DENNIS RODMAN'S BOA CLOSET...
BINGO!
WHY DO I FEEL LIKE I'M IN A SHOPPING MALL...?
COOL! THEY HAVE A "JAY JACOBS" AND AN "ORANGE JULIUS"!
YOU ARE HERE

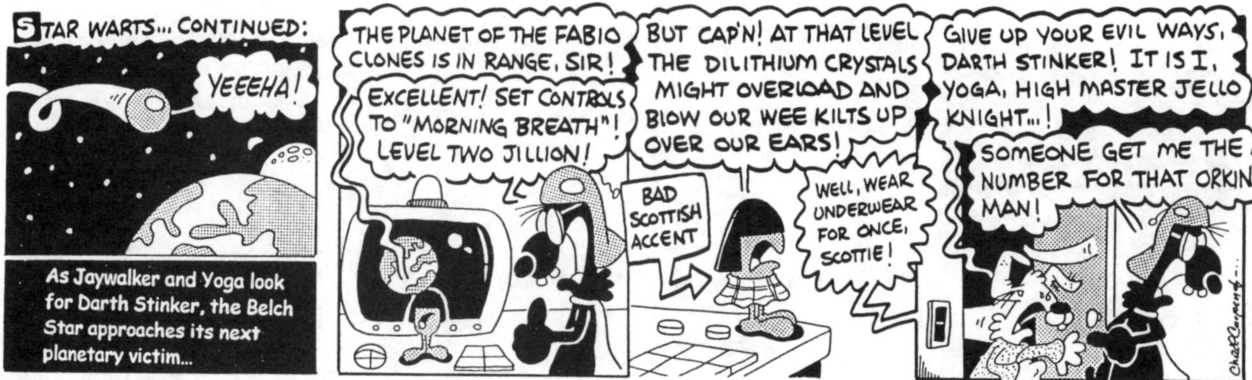
STAR WARTS... CONTINUED:
YEEEHA!
As Jaywalker and Yoga look for Darth Stinker, the Belch Star approaches its next planetary victim...
THE PLANET OF THE FABIO CLONES IS IN RANGE, SIR!
EXCELLENT! SET CONTROLS TO "MORNING BREATH"! LEVEL TWO JILLION!
BUT CAP'N! AT THAT LEVEL THE DILITHIUM CRYSTALS MIGHT OVERLOAD AND BLOW OUR WEE KILTS UP OVER OUR EARS!
BAD SCOTTISH ACCENT
WELL, WEAR UNDERWEAR FOR ONCE, SCOTTIE!
GIVE UP YOUR EVIL WAYS, DARTH STINKER! IT IS I, YOGA, HIGH MASTER JELLO KNIGHT...!
SOMEONE GET ME THE NUMBER FOR THAT ORKIN MAN!

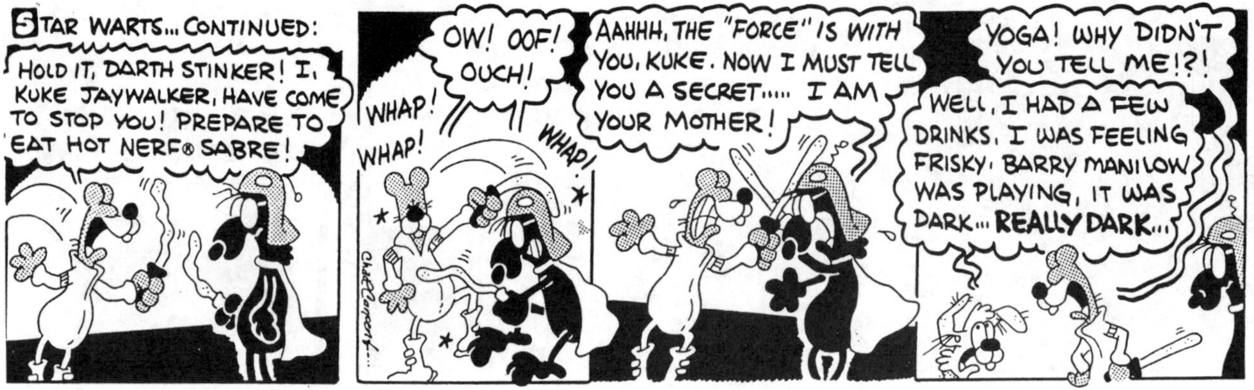
STAR WARTS... CONTINUED:
HOLD IT, DARTH STINKER! I, KUKE JAYWALKER, HAVE COME TO STOP YOU! PREPARE TO EAT HOT NERF® SABRE!
OW! OOF! OUCH!
WHAP!
WHAP!
WHAP!
AAHHH, THE "FORCE" IS WITH YOU, KUKE. NOW I MUST TELL YOU A SECRET..... I AM YOUR MOTHER!
YOGA! WHY DIDN'T YOU TELL ME!?!
WELL, I HAD A FEW DRINKS, I WAS FEELING FRISKY, BARRY MANILOW WAS PLAYING, IT WAS DARK... REALLY DARK...

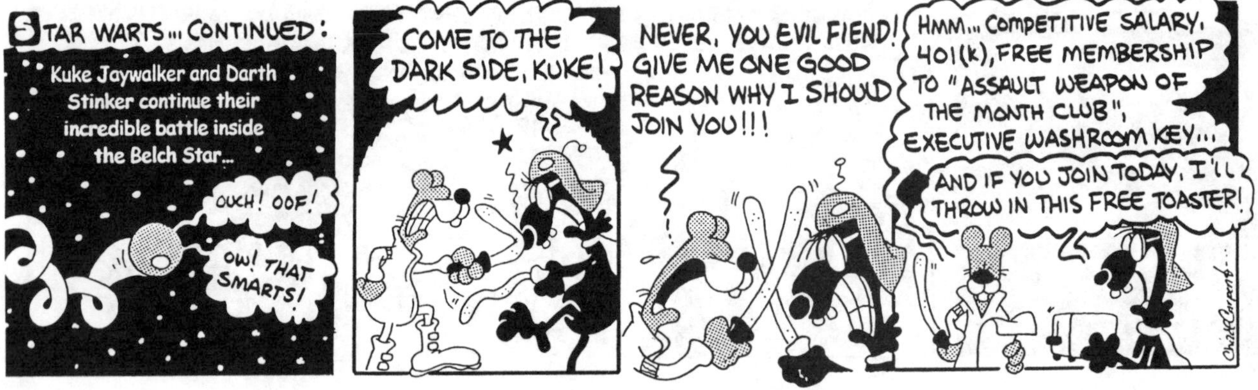
STAR WARTS... CONTINUED:
Kuke Jaywalker and Darth Stinker continue their incredible battle inside the Belch Star...
OUCH! OOF!
OW! THAT SMARTS!
COME TO THE DARK SIDE, KUKE!
NEVER, YOU EVIL FIEND! GIVE ME ONE GOOD REASON WHY I SHOULD JOIN YOU!!!
HMM... COMPETITIVE SALARY, 401(k), FREE MEMBERSHIP TO "ASSAULT WEAPON OF THE MONTH CLUB", EXECUTIVE WASHROOM KEY...
AND IF YOU JOIN TODAY, I'LL THROW IN THIS FREE TOASTER!

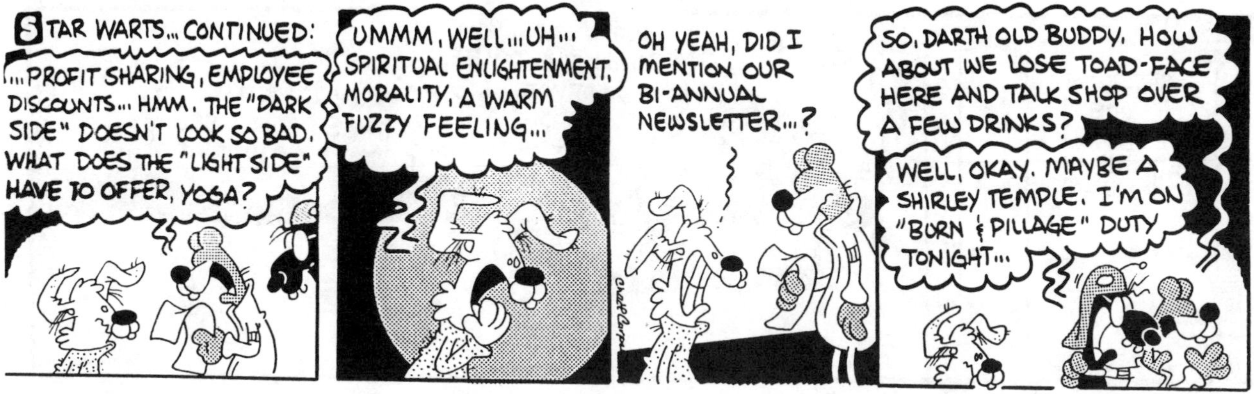
STAR WARTS... CONTINUED:
...PROFIT SHARING, EMPLOYEE DISCOUNTS... HMM. THE "DARK SIDE" DOESN'T LOOK SO BAD. WHAT DOES THE "LIGHT SIDE" HAVE TO OFFER, YOGA?
UMMM, WELL... UH... SPIRITUAL ENLIGHTENMENT, MORALITY, A WARM FUZZY FEELING...
OH YEAH, DID I MENTION OUR BI-ANNUAL NEWSLETTER...?
SO, DARTH OLD BUDDY, HOW ABOUT WE LOSE TOAD-FACE HERE AND TALK SHOP OVER A FEW DRINKS?
WELL, OKAY. MAYBE A SHIRLEY TEMPLE. I'M ON "BURN & PILLAGE" DUTY TONIGHT...

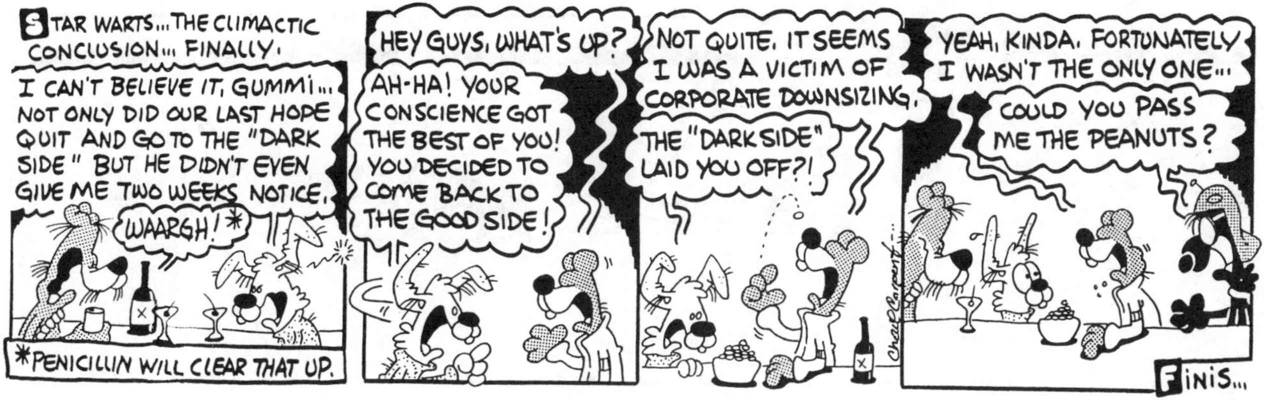
STAR WARTS... THE CLIMACTIC CONCLUSION... FINALLY.
I CAN'T BELIEVE IT, GUMMI... NOT ONLY DID OUR LAST HOPE QUIT AND GO TO THE "DARK SIDE" BUT HE DIDN'T EVEN GIVE ME TWO WEEKS NOTICE.
WAARGH!*
*PENICILLIN WILL CLEAR THAT UP.
HEY GUYS, WHAT'S UP?
AH-HA! YOUR CONSCIENCE GOT THE BEST OF YOU! YOU DECIDED TO COME BACK TO THE GOOD SIDE!
NOT QUITE. IT SEEMS I WAS A VICTIM OF CORPORATE DOWNSIZING.
THE "DARK SIDE" LAID YOU OFF?!
YEAH, KINDA. FORTUNATELY I WASN'T THE ONLY ONE...
COULD YOU PASS ME THE PEANUTS?
FINIS...

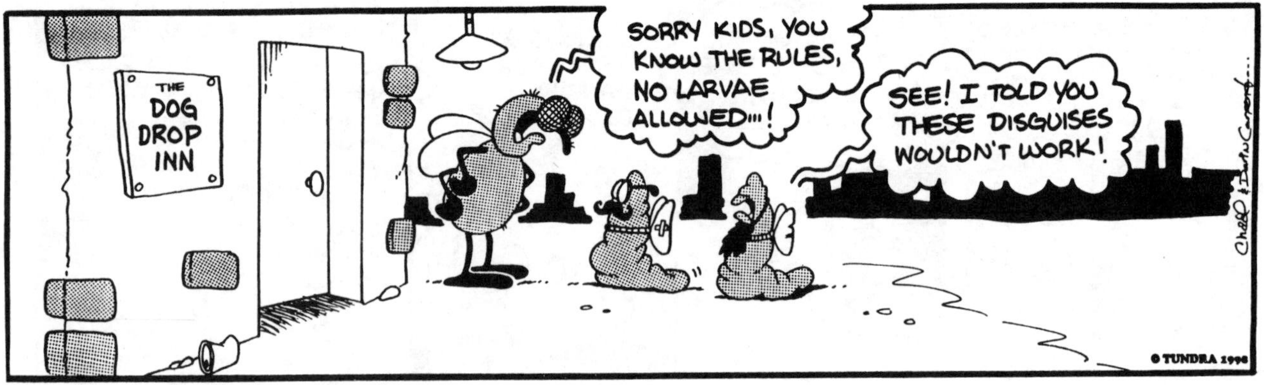
THE DOG DROP INN
SORRY KIDS, YOU KNOW THE RULES, NO LARVAE ALLOWED!!!!
SEE! I TOLD YOU THESE DISGUISES WOULDN'T WORK!
© TUNDRA 1998

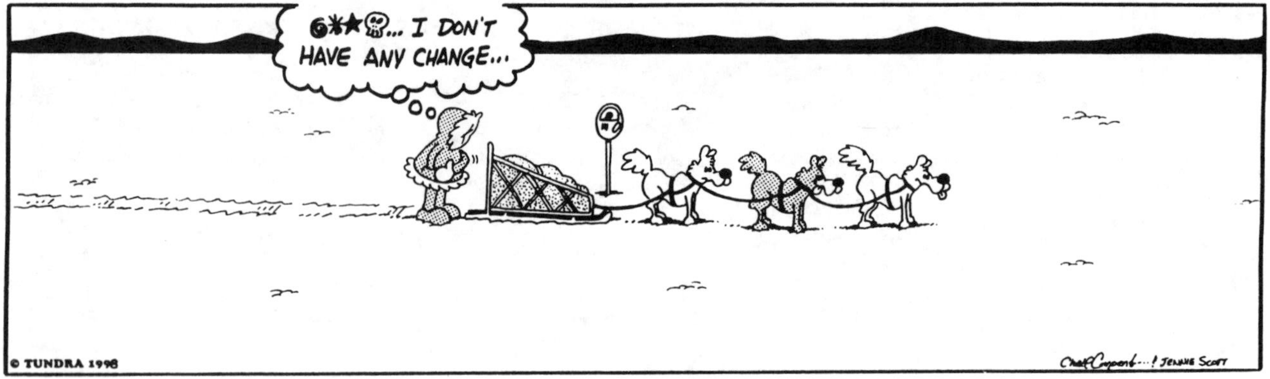
@*★☠... I DON'T HAVE ANY CHANGE...
© TUNDRA 1998
JENNIE SCOTT

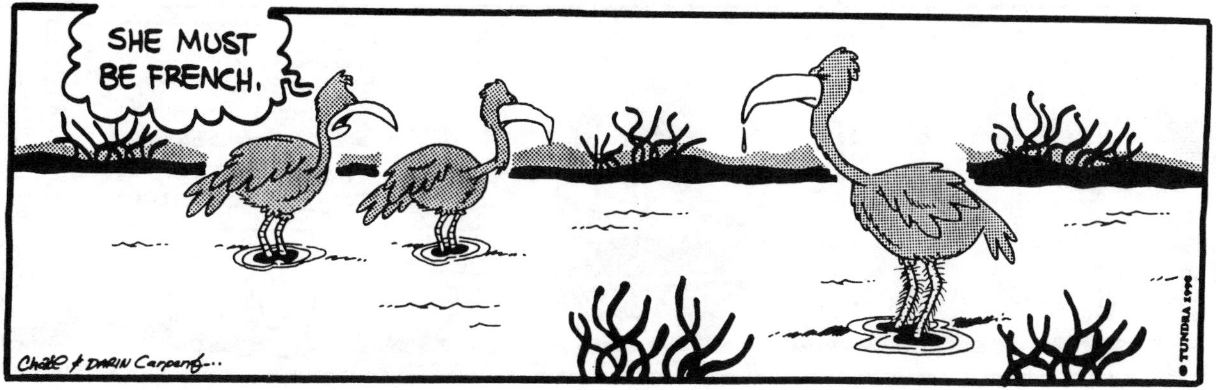
SHE MUST BE FRENCH.
Chaz & DARIN Carpenter...
© TUNDRA 1998

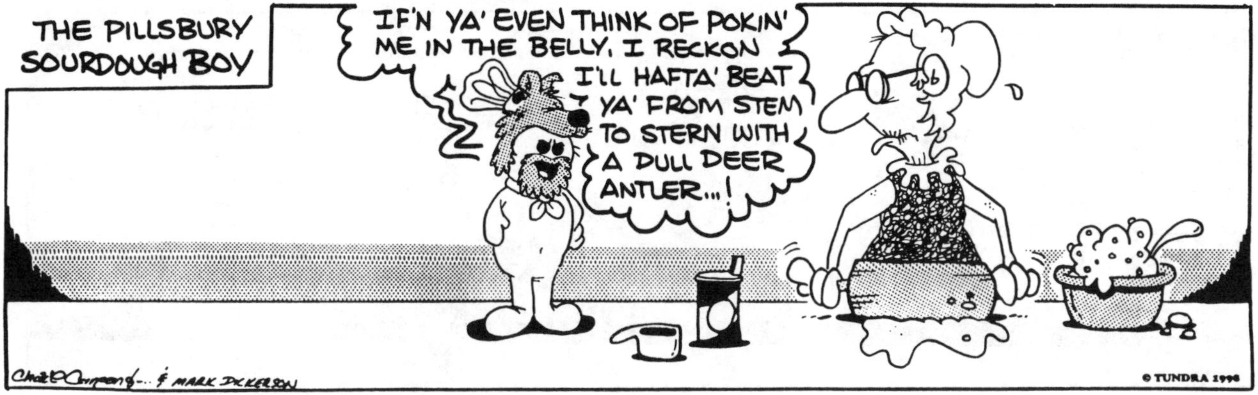
THE PILLSBURY SOURDOUGH BOY
IF'N YA' EVEN THINK OF POKIN' ME IN THE BELLY, I RECKON I'LL HAFTA' BEAT YA' FROM STEM TO STERN WITH A DULL DEER ANTLER...!
© TUNDRA 1998

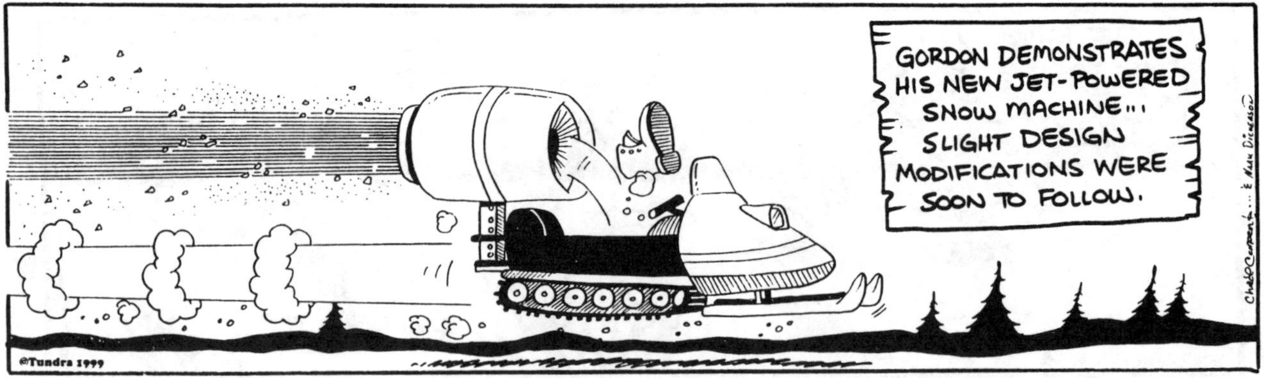
GORDON DEMONSTRATES HIS NEW JET-POWERED SNOW MACHINE... SLIGHT DESIGN MODIFICATIONS WERE SOON TO FOLLOW.
©Tundra 1999

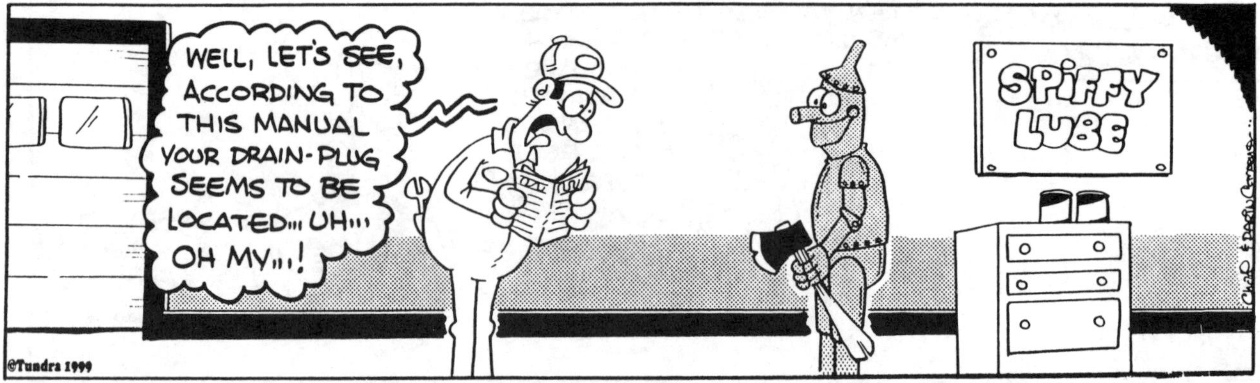
WELL, LET'S SEE, ACCORDING TO THIS MANUAL YOUR DRAIN-PLUG SEEMS TO BE LOCATED... UH... OH MY...!
SPIFFY LUBE
©Tundra 1999

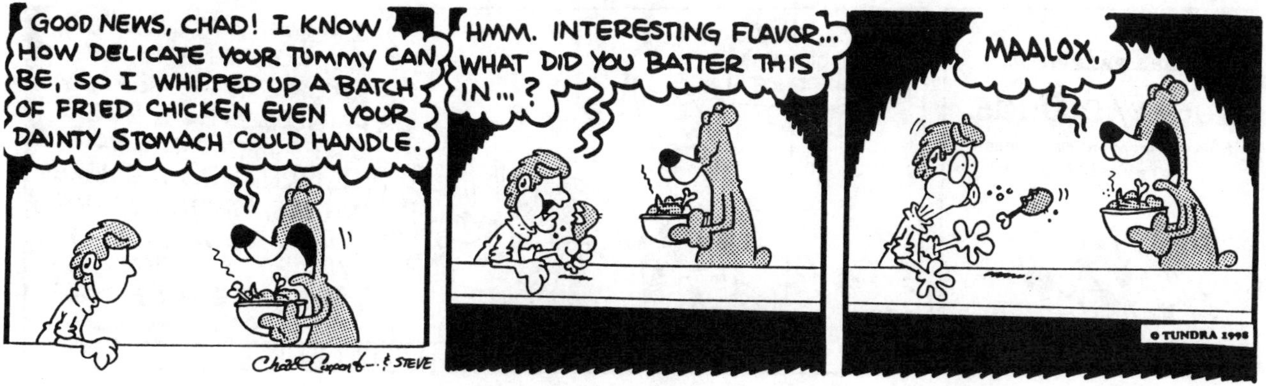
GOOD NEWS, CHAD! I KNOW HOW DELICATE YOUR TUMMY CAN BE, SO I WHIPPED UP A BATCH OF FRIED CHICKEN EVEN YOUR DAINTY STOMACH COULD HANDLE.
HMM. INTERESTING FLAVOR... WHAT DID YOU BATTER THIS IN... ?
MAALOX.
© TUNDRA 1998

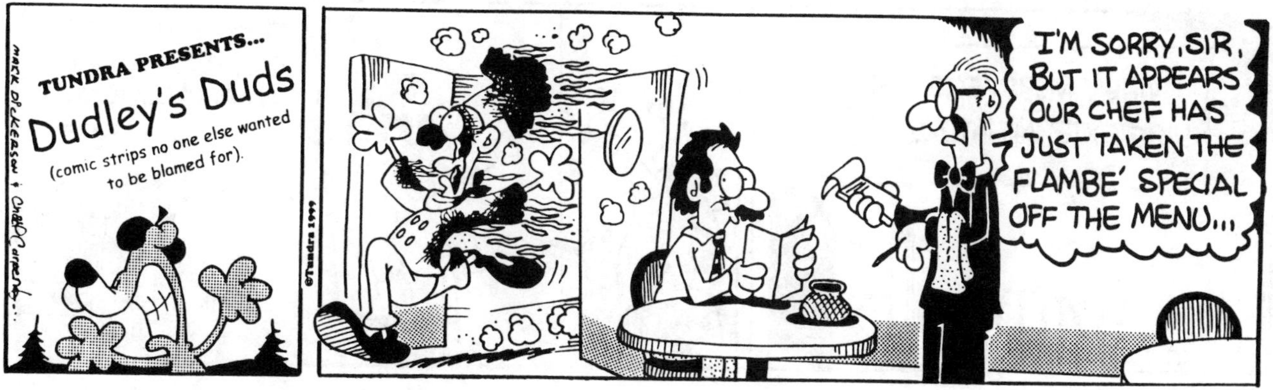
TUNDRA PRESENTS...
Dudley's Duds
(comic strips no one else wanted to be blamed for).
I'M SORRY, SIR, BUT IT APPEARS OUR CHEF HAS JUST TAKEN THE FLAMBE' SPECIAL OFF THE MENU...

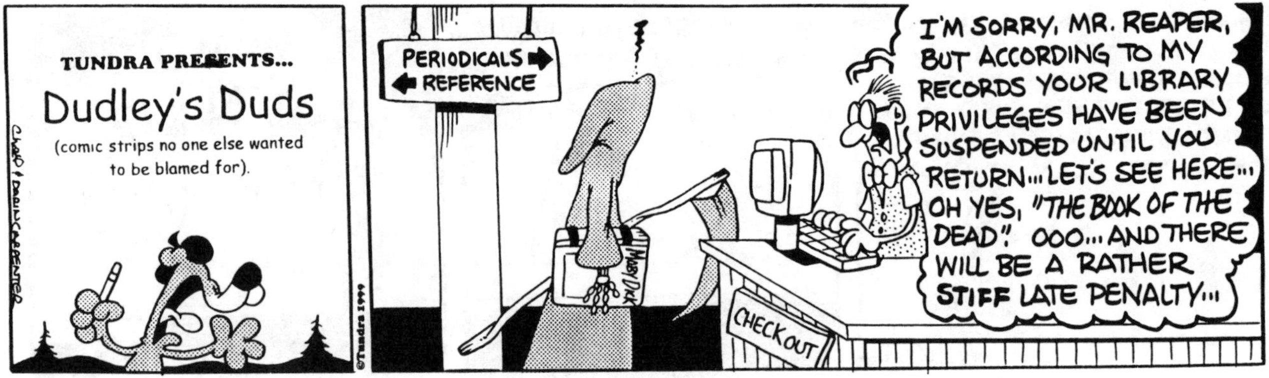
TUNDRA PRESENTS...
Dudley's Duds
(comic strips no one else wanted to be blamed for).
©Tundra 1999
PERIODICALS
REFERENCE
MOBY DICK
CHECK OUT
I'M SORRY, MR. REAPER, BUT ACCORDING TO MY RECORDS YOUR LIBRARY PRIVILEGES HAVE BEEN SUSPENDED UNTIL YOU RETURN... LET'S SEE HERE... OH YES, "THE BOOK OF THE DEAD". OOO... AND THERE WILL BE A RATHER STIFF LATE PENALTY...

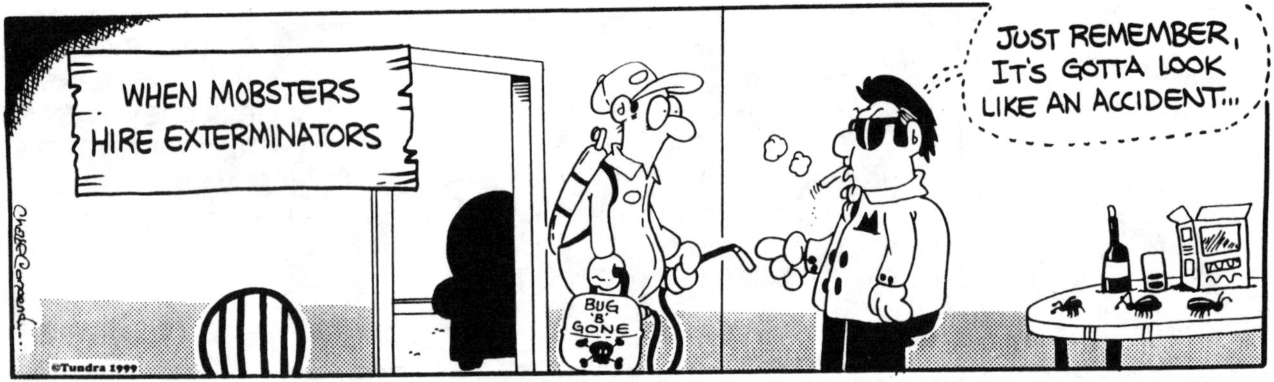
WHEN MOBSTERS HIRE EXTERMINATORS
BUG 'B' GONE
©Tundra 1999
JUST REMEMBER, IT'S GOTTA LOOK LIKE AN ACCIDENT...

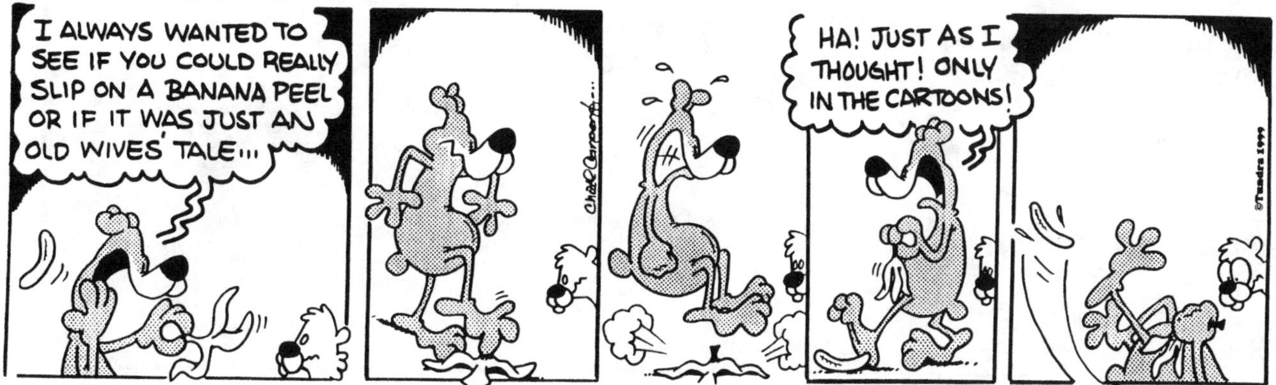
I ALWAYS WANTED TO SEE IF YOU COULD REALLY SLIP ON A BANANA PEEL OR IF IT WAS JUST AN OLD WIVES' TALE...
HA! JUST AS I THOUGHT! ONLY IN THE CARTOONS!
©Tundra 1999

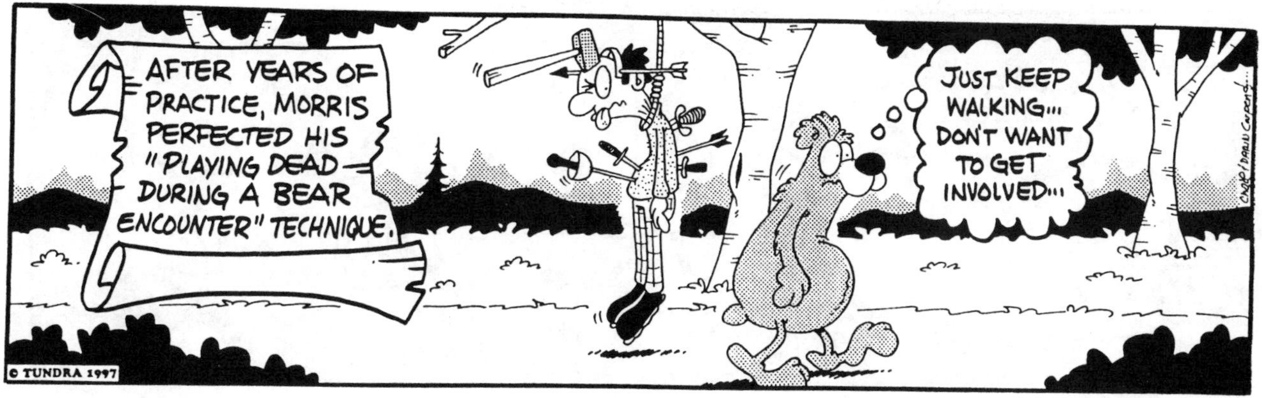
AFTER YEARS OF PRACTICE, MORRIS PERFECTED HIS "PLAYING DEAD DURING A BEAR ENCOUNTER" TECHNIQUE.
JUST KEEP WALKING... DON'T WANT TO GET INVOLVED...
© TUNDRA 1997

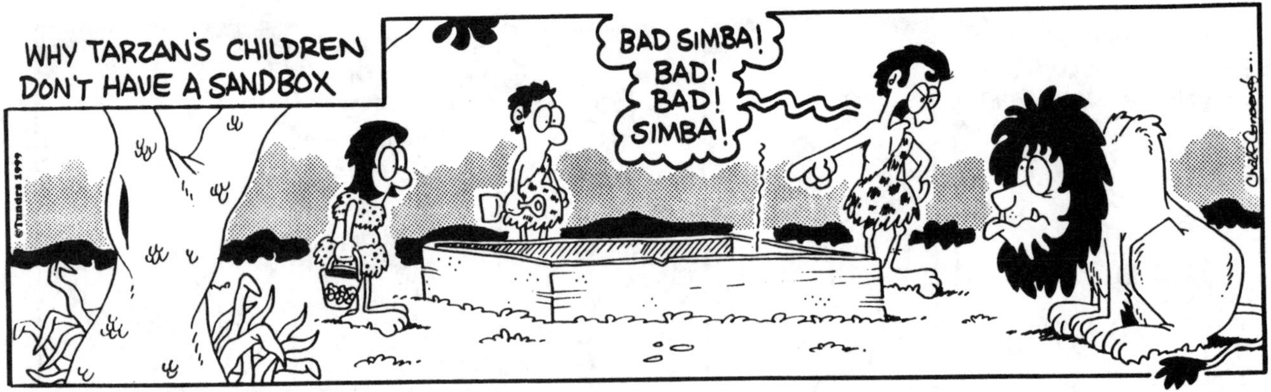
WHY TARZAN'S CHILDREN DON'T HAVE A SANDBOX
BAD SIMBA! BAD! BAD! SIMBA!
©Tundra 1999

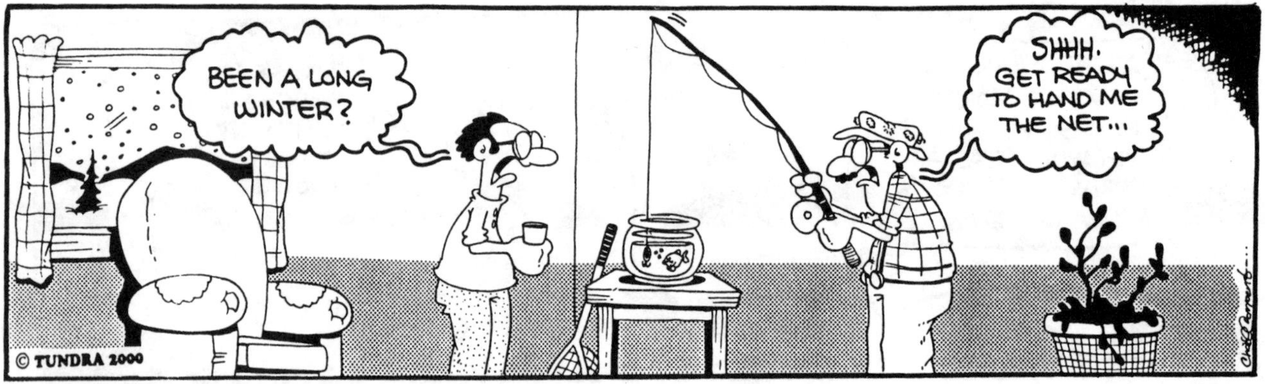
BEEN A LONG WINTER?
SHHH. GET READY TO HAND ME THE NET...
© TUNDRA 2000

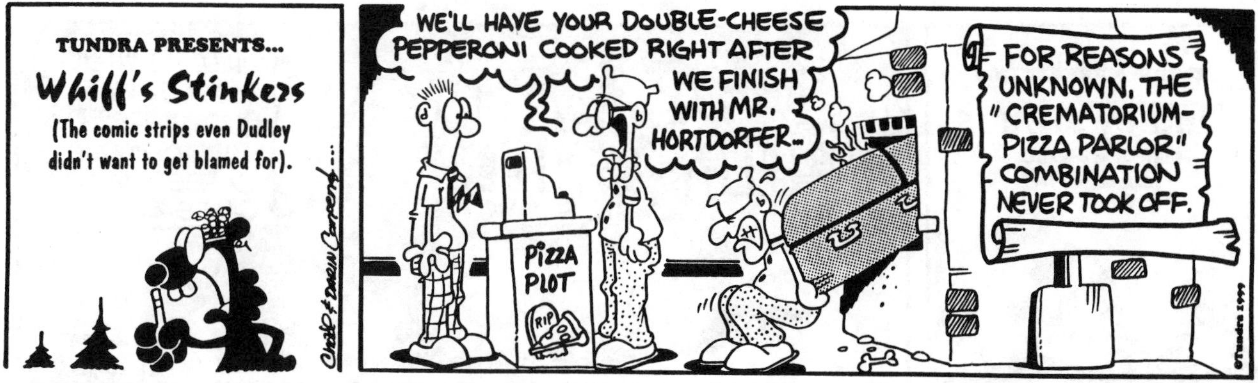
TUNDRA PRESENTS...
Whiff's Stinkers
(The comic strips even Dudley didn't want to get blamed for).
WE'LL HAVE YOUR DOUBLE-CHEESE PEPPERONI COOKED RIGHT AFTER WE FINISH WITH MR. HORTDORFER...
PIZZA PLOT
RIP
FOR REASONS UNKNOWN, THE "CREMATORIUM-PIZZA PARLOR" COMBINATION NEVER TOOK OFF.
©Tundra 1999

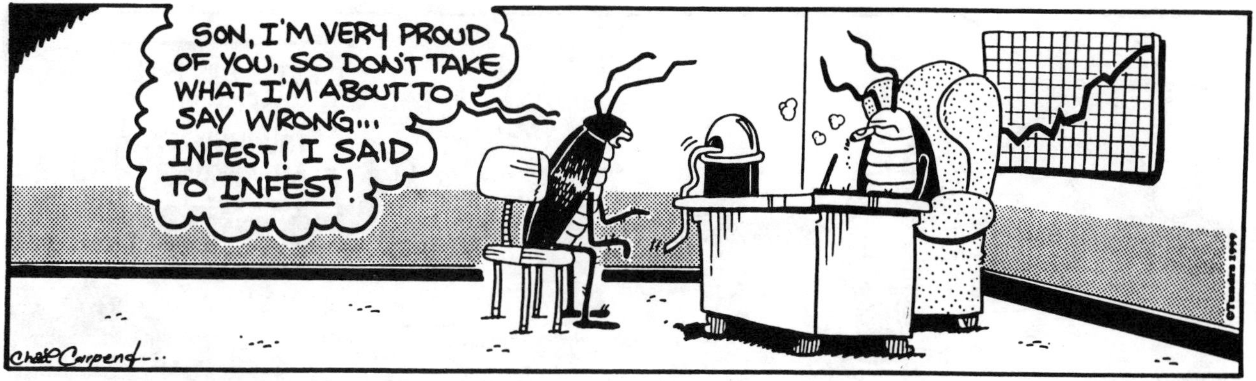
SON, I'M VERY PROUD OF YOU, SO DON'T TAKE WHAT I'M ABOUT TO SAY WRONG... INFEST! I SAID TO INFEST!
©Tundra 1999

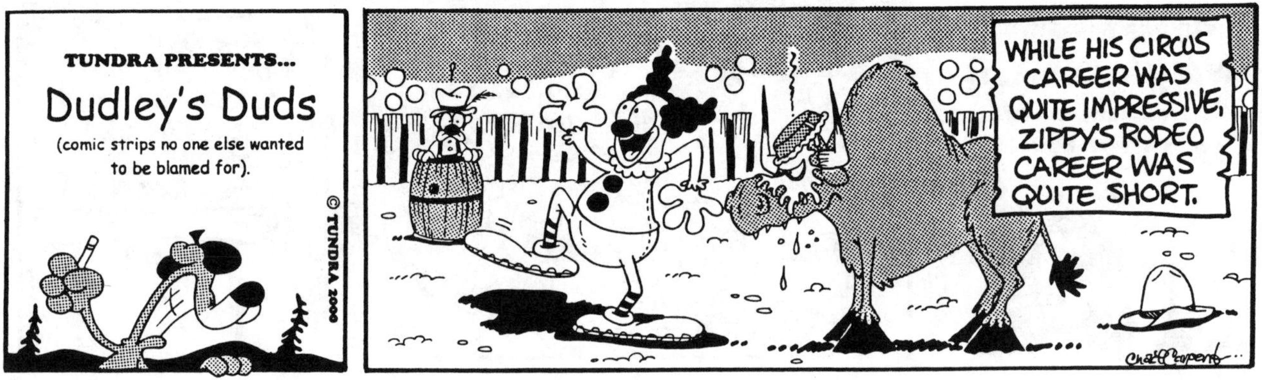
TUNDRA PRESENTS...
Dudley's Duds
(comic strips no one else wanted to be blamed for).
© TUNDRA 2000
WHILE HIS CIRCUS CAREER WAS QUITE IMPRESSIVE, ZIPPY'S RODEO CAREER WAS QUITE SHORT.

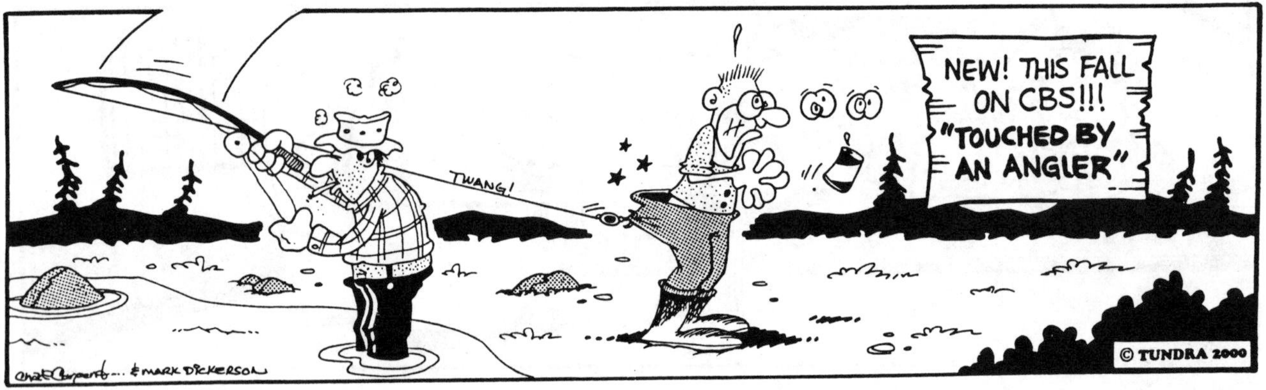
TWANG!
NEW! THIS FALL ON CBS!!!
"TOUCHED BY AN ANGLER"
© TUNDRA 2000

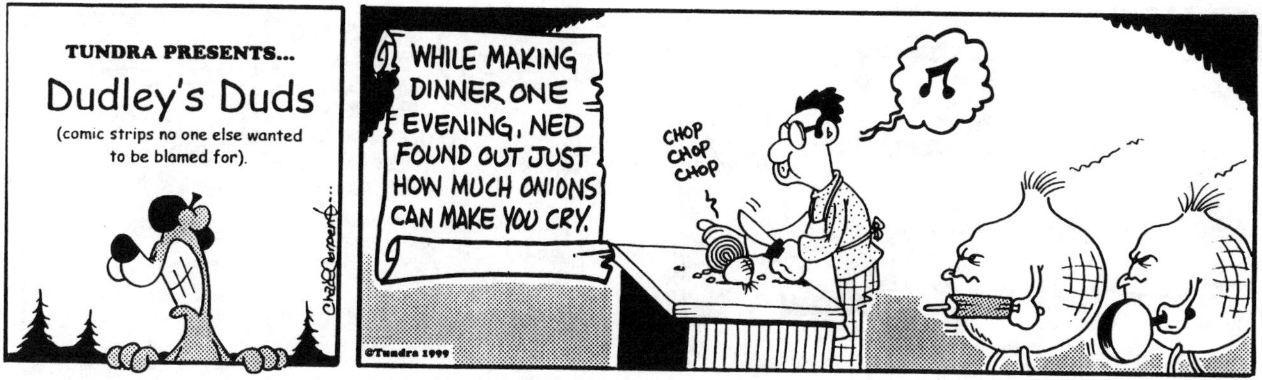
TUNDRA PRESENTS...
Dudley's Duds
(comic strips no one else wanted to be blamed for).
WHILE MAKING DINNER ONE EVENING, NED FOUND OUT JUST HOW MUCH ONIONS CAN MAKE YOU CRY.
CHOP CHOP CHOP
©Tundra 1999

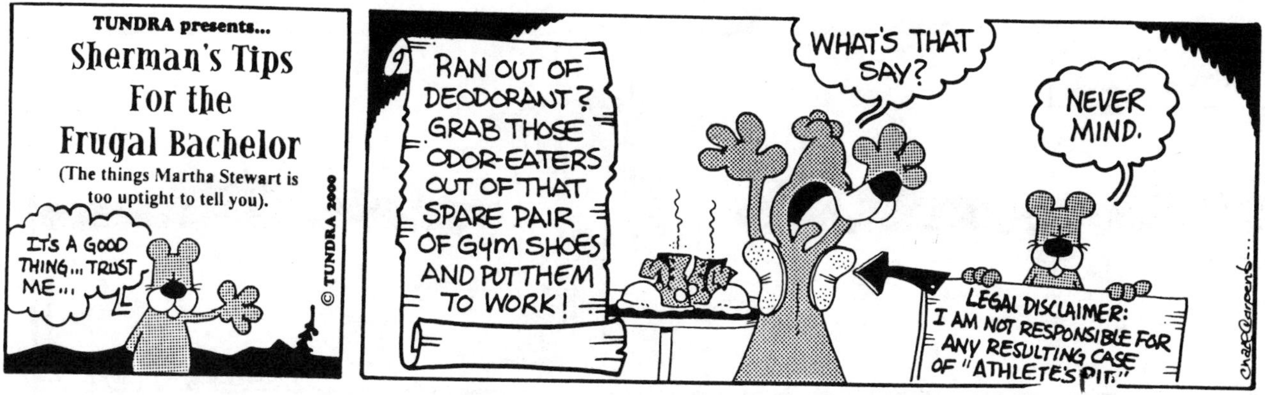
TUNDRA presents...
Sherman's Tips For the Frugal Bachelor
(The things Martha Stewart is too uptight to tell you).
IT'S A GOOD THING... TRUST ME...
© TUNDRA 2000
RAN OUT OF DEODORANT? GRAB THOSE ODOR-EATERS OUT OF THAT SPARE PAIR OF GYM SHOES AND PUT THEM TO WORK!
WHAT'S THAT SAY?
NEVER MIND.
LEGAL DISCLAIMER: I AM NOT RESPONSIBLE FOR ANY RESULTING CASE OF "ATHLETE'S PIT."

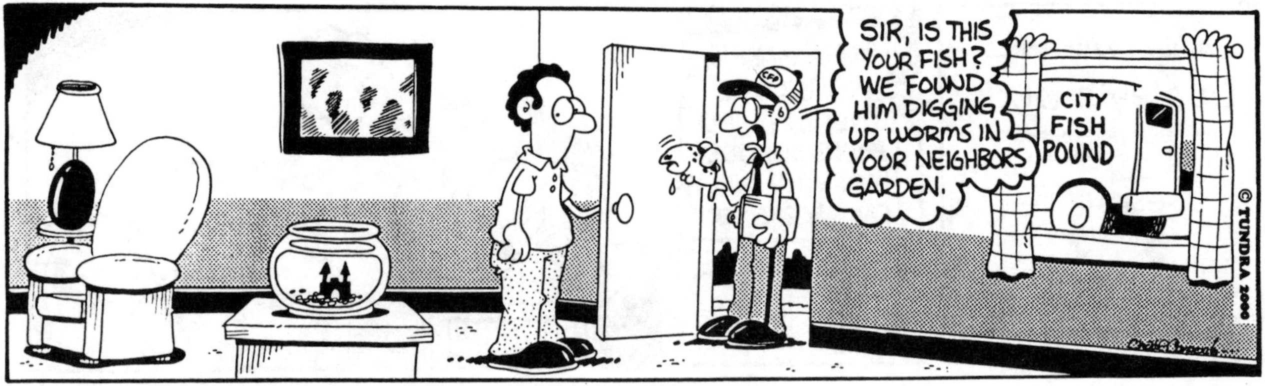
SIR, IS THIS YOUR FISH? WE FOUND HIM DIGGING UP WORMS IN YOUR NEIGHBORS GARDEN.
CITY FISH POUND
© TUNDRA 2000

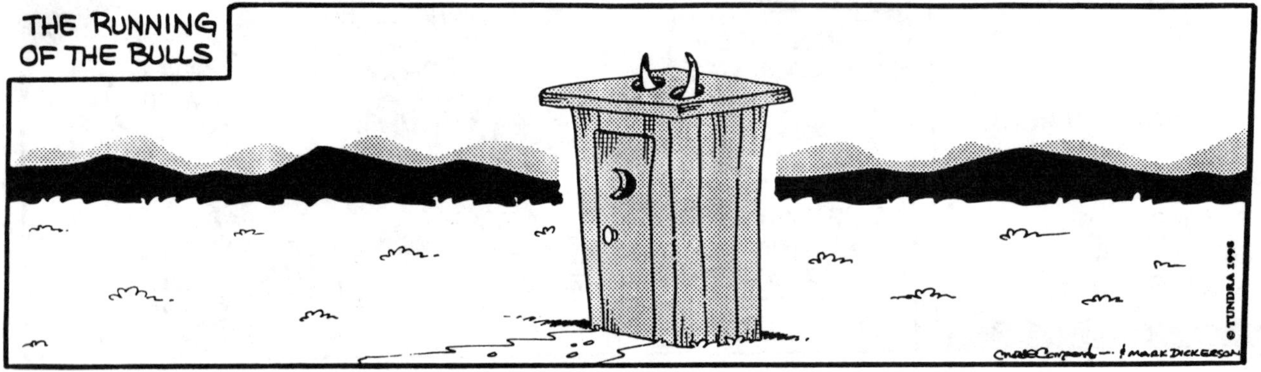
THE RUNNING OF THE BULLS
© TUNDRA 1998

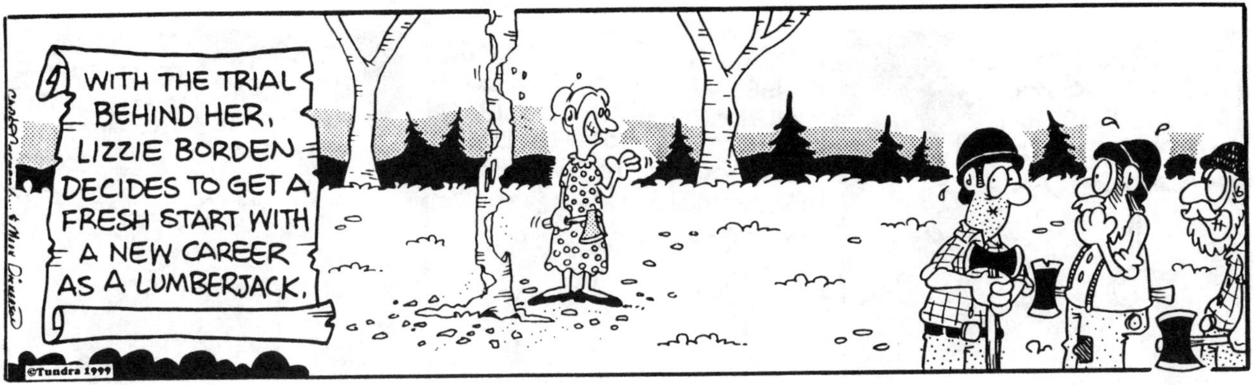
4
WITH THE TRIAL BEHIND HER, LIZZIE BORDEN DECIDES TO GET A FRESH START WITH A NEW CAREER AS A LUMBERJACK.
©Tundra 1999

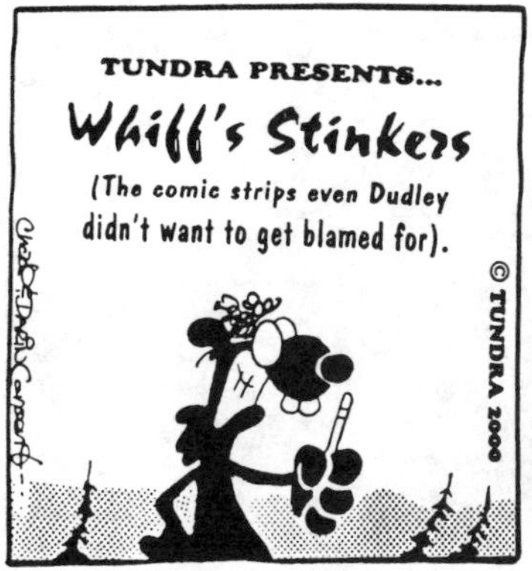
TUNDRA PRESENTS...
Whiff's Stinkers
(The comic strips even Dudley didn't want to get blamed for).
© TUNDRA 2000

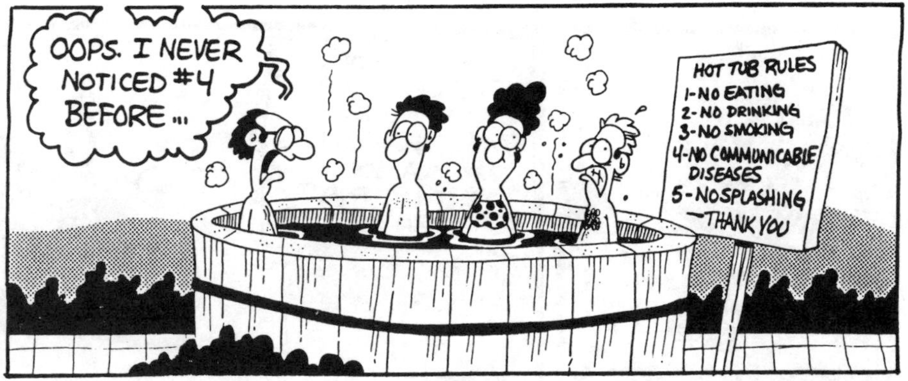
OOPS. I NEVER NOTICED #4 BEFORE...
HOT TUB RULES
1-NO EATING
2-NO DRINKING
3-NO SMOKING
4-NO COMMUNICABLE DISEASES
5-NO SPLASHING
—THANK YOU

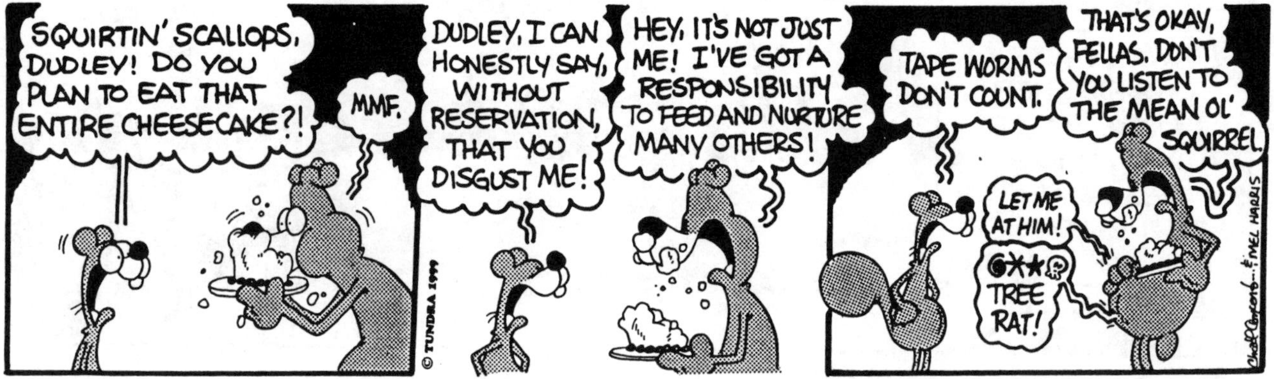
SQUIRTIN' SCALLOPS, DUDLEY! DO YOU PLAN TO EAT THAT ENTIRE CHEESECAKE?!
MMF.
© TUNDRA 1999
DUDLEY, I CAN HONESTLY SAY, WITHOUT RESERVATION, THAT YOU DISGUST ME!
HEY, IT'S NOT JUST ME! I'VE GOT A RESPONSIBILITY TO FEED AND NURTURE MANY OTHERS!
TAPE WORMS DON'T COUNT.
THAT'S OKAY, FELLAS. DON'T YOU LISTEN TO THE MEAN OL' SQUIRREL.
LET ME AT HIM!
TREE RAT!

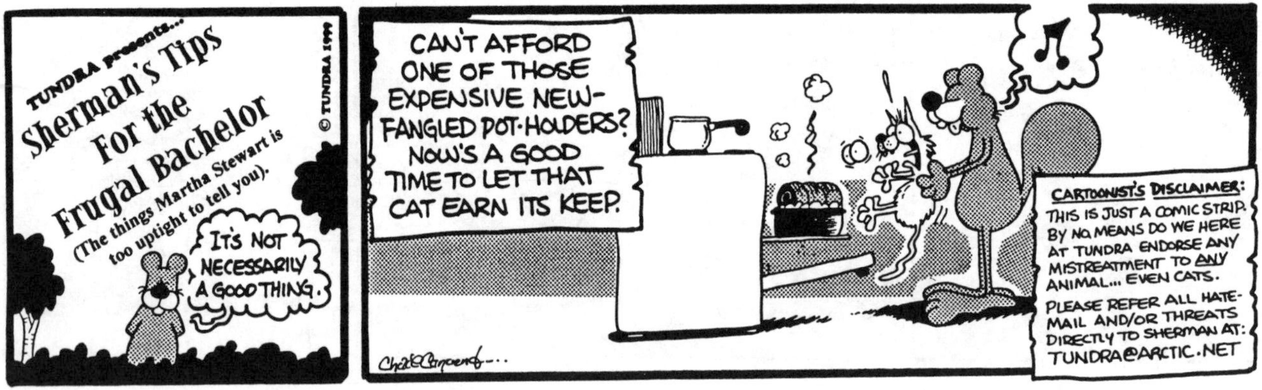
TUNDRA presents...
Sherman's Tips For the Frugal Bachelor
(The things Martha Stewart is too uptight to tell you).
© TUNDRA 1999
IT'S NOT NECESSARILY A GOOD THING.
CAN'T AFFORD ONE OF THOSE EXPENSIVE NEW-FANGLED POT-HOLDERS? NOW'S A GOOD TIME TO LET THAT CAT EARN ITS KEEP.
CARTOONIST'S DISCLAIMER:
THIS IS JUST A COMIC STRIP. BY NO MEANS DO WE HERE AT TUNDRA ENDORSE ANY MISTREATMENT TO ANY ANIMAL... EVEN CATS.
PLEASE REFER ALL HATE-MAIL AND/OR THREATS DIRECTLY TO SHERMAN AT: TUNDRA@ARCTIC.NET

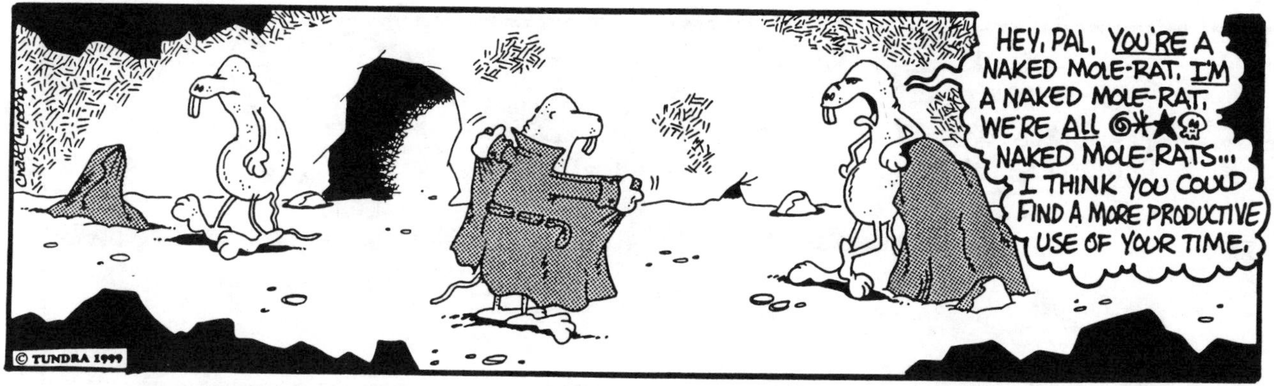
HEY, PAL, YOU'RE A NAKED MOLE-RAT, I'M A NAKED MOLE-RAT, WE'RE ALL @*★☠ NAKED MOLE-RATS... I THINK YOU COULD FIND A MORE PRODUCTIVE USE OF YOUR TIME.
© TUNDRA 1999

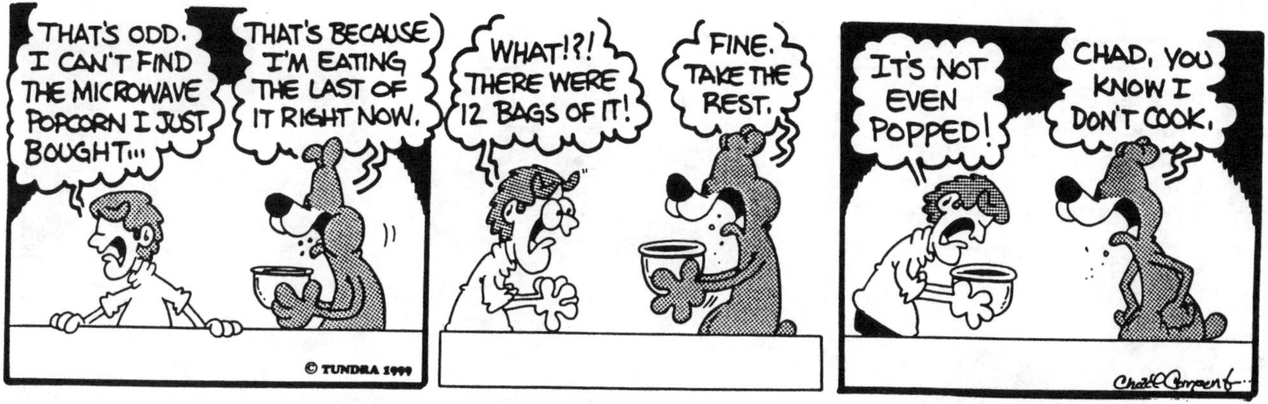
THAT'S ODD. I CAN'T FIND THE MICROWAVE POPCORN I JUST BOUGHT...
THAT'S BECAUSE I'M EATING THE LAST OF IT RIGHT NOW.
© TUNDRA 1999
WHAT!?! THERE WERE 12 BAGS OF IT!
FINE. TAKE THE REST.
IT'S NOT EVEN POPPED!
CHAD, YOU KNOW I DON'T COOK.

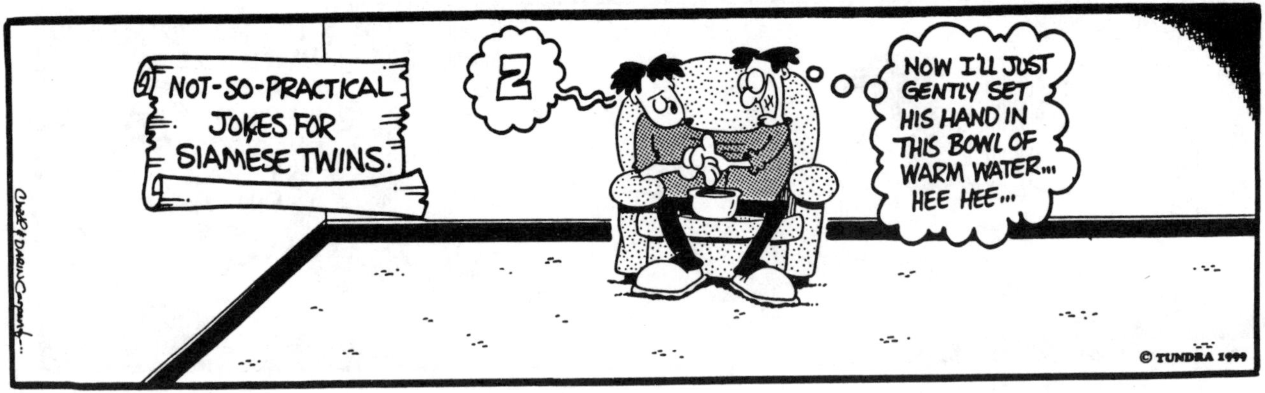
NOT-SO-PRACTICAL JOKES FOR SIAMESE TWINS.
Z
NOW I'LL JUST GENTLY SET HIS HAND IN THIS BOWL OF WARM WATER... HEE HEE...
© TUNDRA 1999

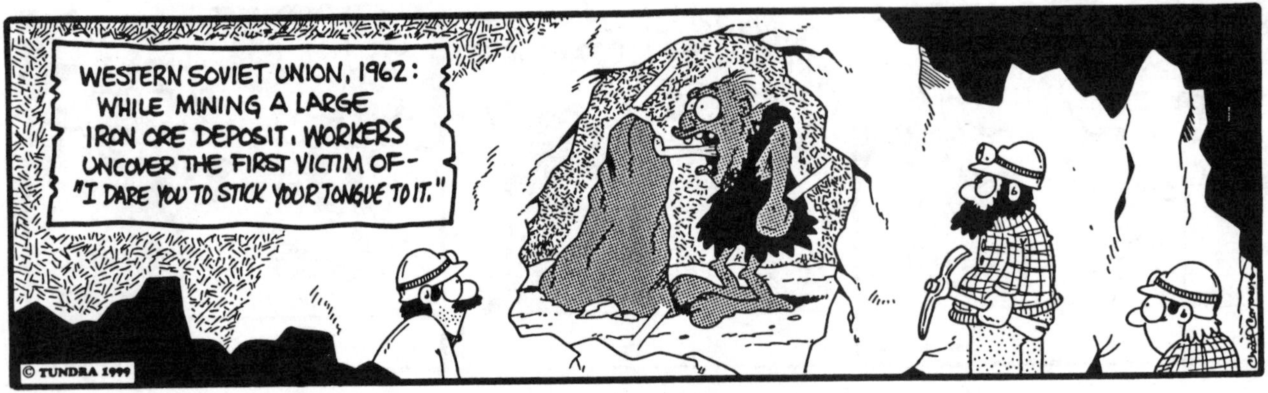
WESTERN SOVIET UNION, 1962: WHILE MINING A LARGE IRON ORE DEPOSIT, WORKERS UNCOVER THE FIRST VICTIM OF- "I DARE YOU TO STICK YOUR TONGUE TO IT."
© TUNDRA 1999

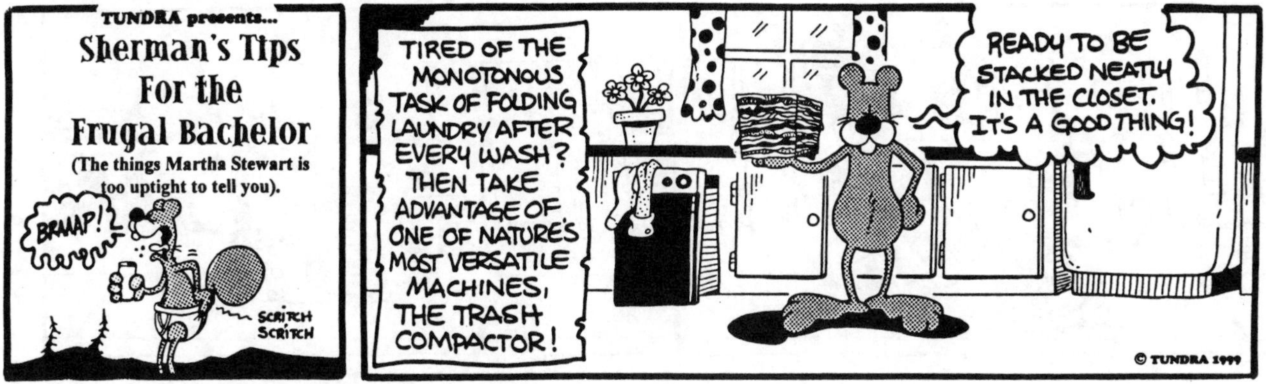
TUNDRA presents...
Sherman's Tips For the Frugal Bachelor
(The things Martha Stewart is too uptight to tell you).
BRAAAP!
SCRITCH SCRITCH
TIRED OF THE MONOTONOUS TASK OF FOLDING LAUNDRY AFTER EVERY WASH? THEN TAKE ADVANTAGE OF ONE OF NATURE'S MOST VERSATILE MACHINES, THE TRASH COMPACTOR!
READY TO BE STACKED NEATLY IN THE CLOSET. IT'S A GOOD THING!
© TUNDRA 1999

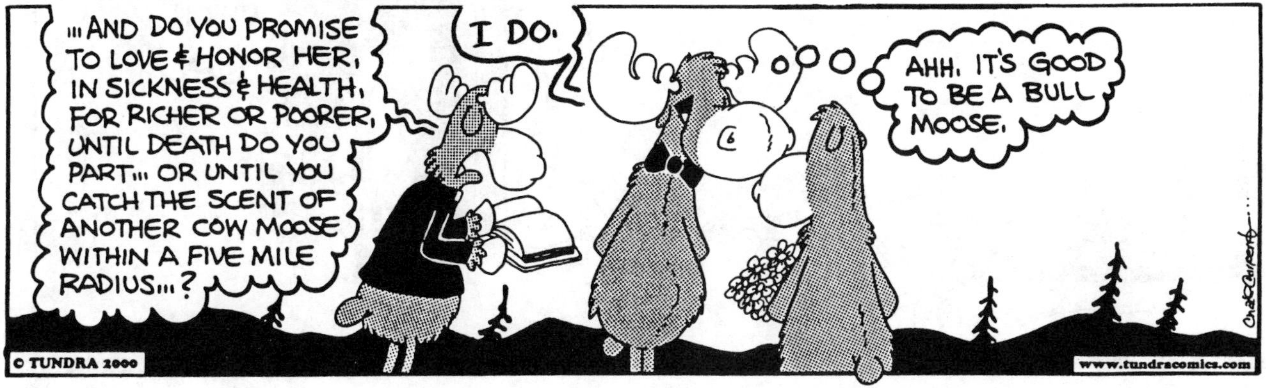
...AND DO YOU PROMISE TO LOVE & HONOR HER, IN SICKNESS & HEALTH, FOR RICHER OR POORER, UNTIL DEATH DO YOU PART... OR UNTIL YOU CATCH THE SCENT OF ANOTHER COW MOOSE WITHIN A FIVE MILE RADIUS...?
I DO.
AHH. IT'S GOOD TO BE A BULL MOOSE.
© TUNDRA 2000
www.tundracomics.com

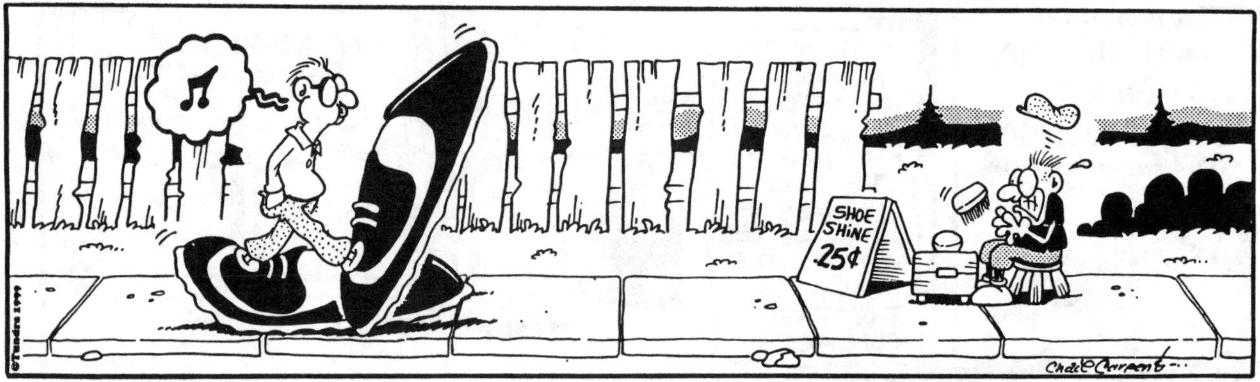
SHOE SHINE .25¢
©Tundra 1999
Chad Carpenter

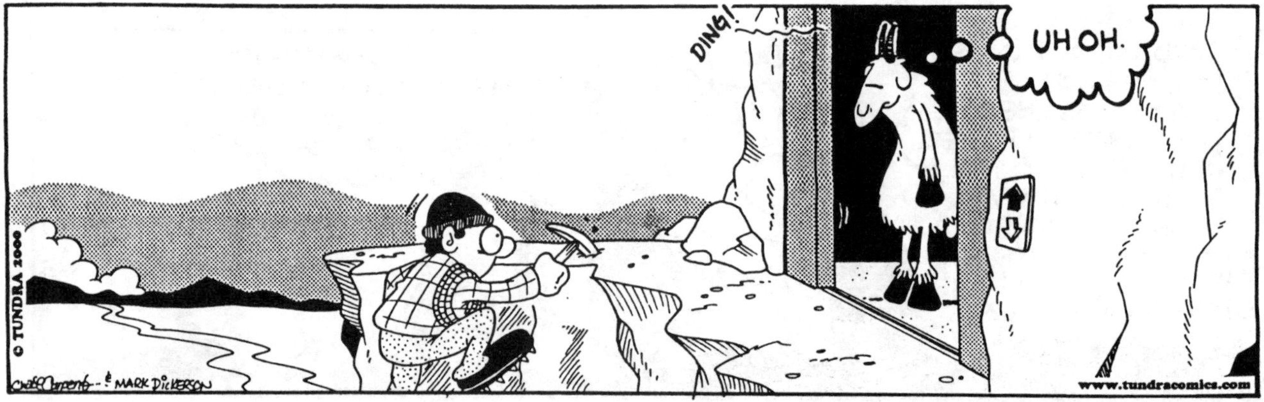
DING!
UH OH.
© TUNDRA 2000
Chad Carpenter & MARK DICKERSON
www.tundracomics.com

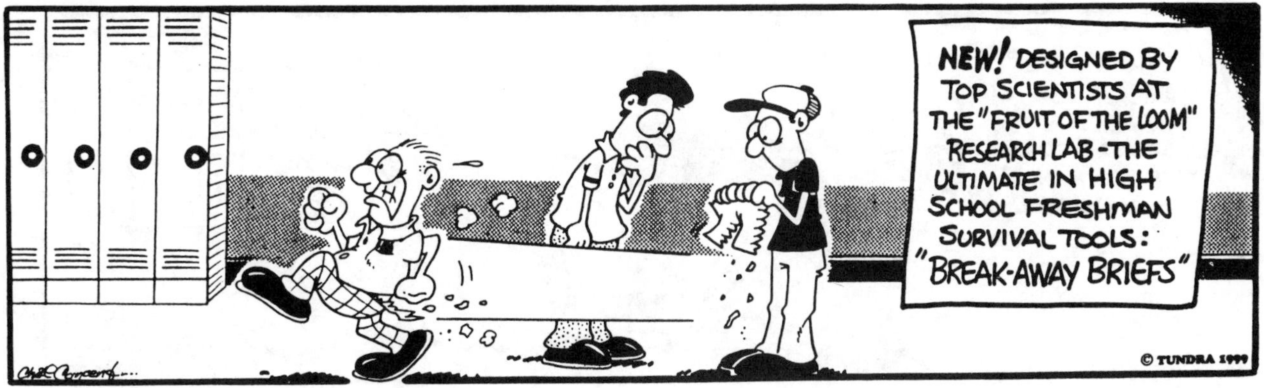
NEW! DESIGNED BY TOP SCIENTISTS AT THE "FRUIT OF THE LOOM" RESEARCH LAB - THE ULTIMATE IN HIGH SCHOOL FRESHMAN SURVIVAL TOOLS: "BREAK-AWAY BRIEFS"
© TUNDRA 1999

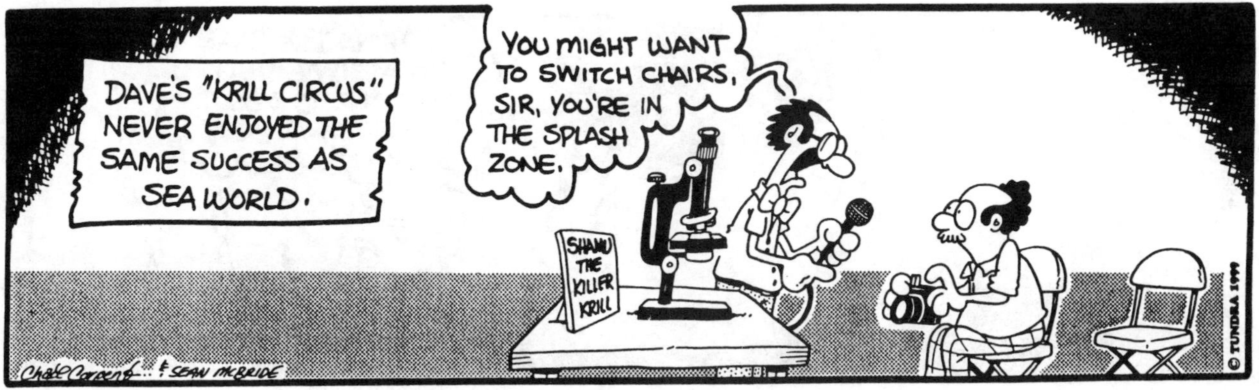
DAVE'S "KRILL CIRCUS" NEVER ENJOYED THE SAME SUCCESS AS SEA WORLD.
YOU MIGHT WANT TO SWITCH CHAIRS, SIR, YOU'RE IN THE SPLASH ZONE.
SHAMU THE KILLER KRILL
© TUNDRA 1999

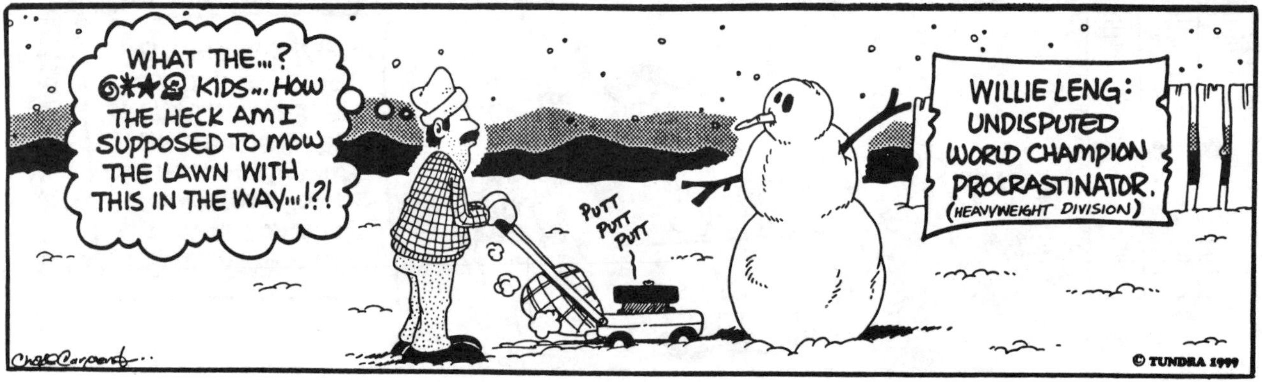
WHAT THE...? @*★& KIDS... HOW THE HECK AM I SUPPOSED TO MOW THE LAWN WITH THIS IN THE WAY...!?!
PUTT PUTT PUTT
WILLIE LENG: UNDISPUTED WORLD CHAMPION PROCRASTINATOR. (HEAVYWEIGHT DIVISION)
© TUNDRA 1999

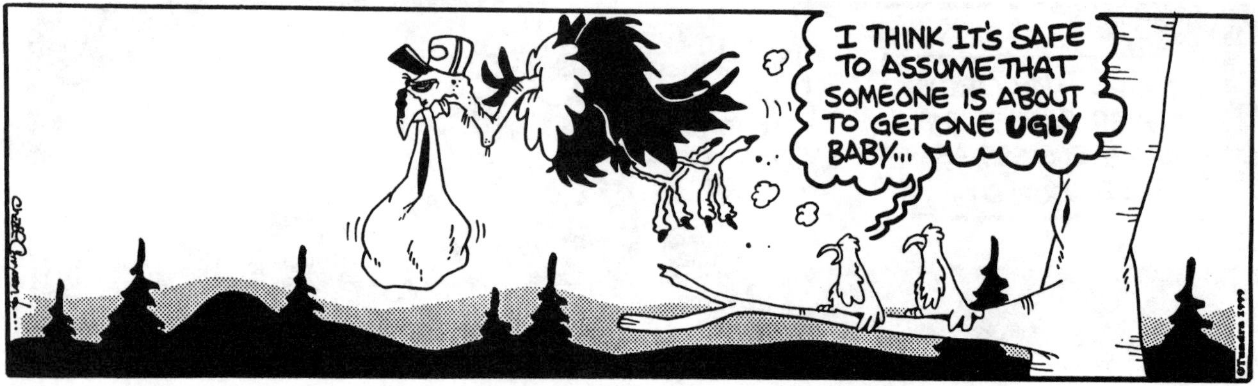
I THINK IT'S SAFE TO ASSUME THAT SOMEONE IS ABOUT TO GET ONE UGLY BABY...
©Tundra 1999

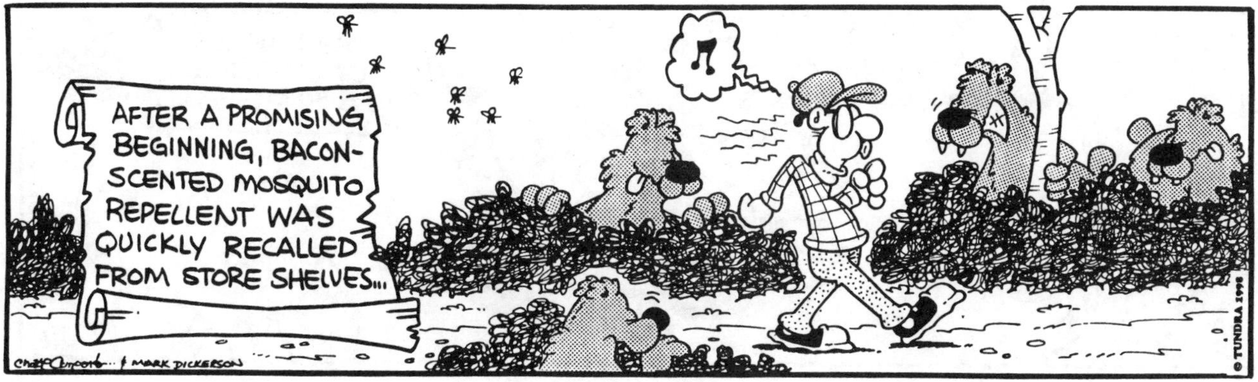
AFTER A PROMISING BEGINNING, BACON-SCENTED MOSQUITO REPELLENT WAS QUICKLY RECALLED FROM STORE SHELVES...
CHAD CARPENTER & MARK DICKERSON
© TUNDRA 1998

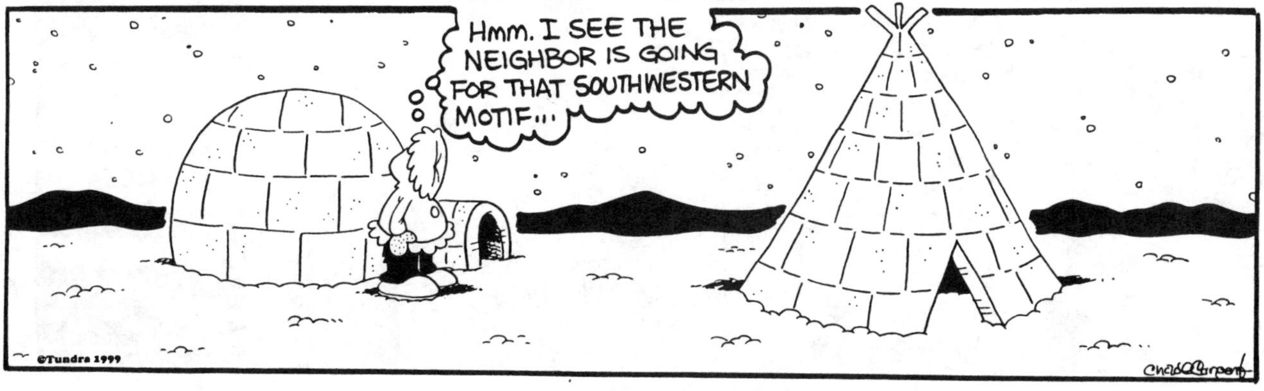
Hmm. I SEE THE NEIGHBOR IS GOING FOR THAT SOUTHWESTERN MOTIF...
©Tundra 1999
Chad Carpenter

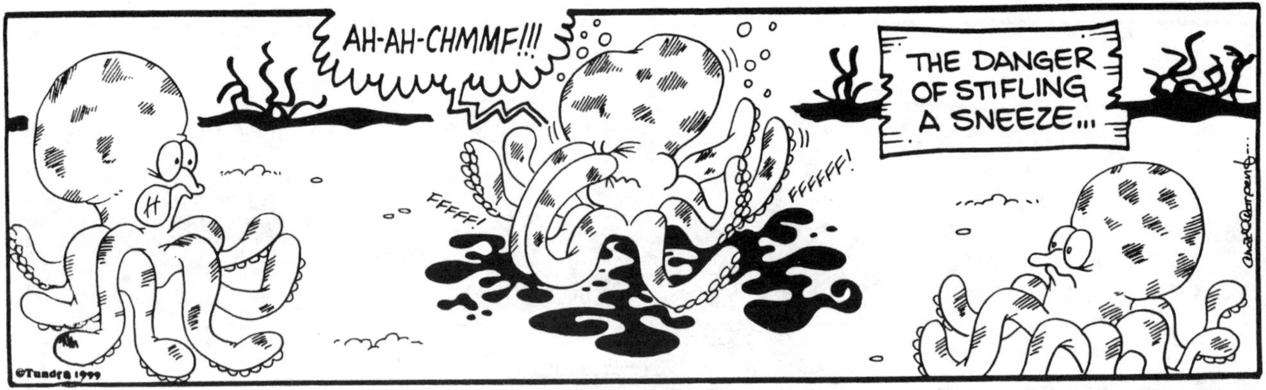
AH-AH-CHMMF!!!
FFFFFF!
FFFFFF!
THE DANGER OF STIFLING A SNEEZE...
©Tundra 1999

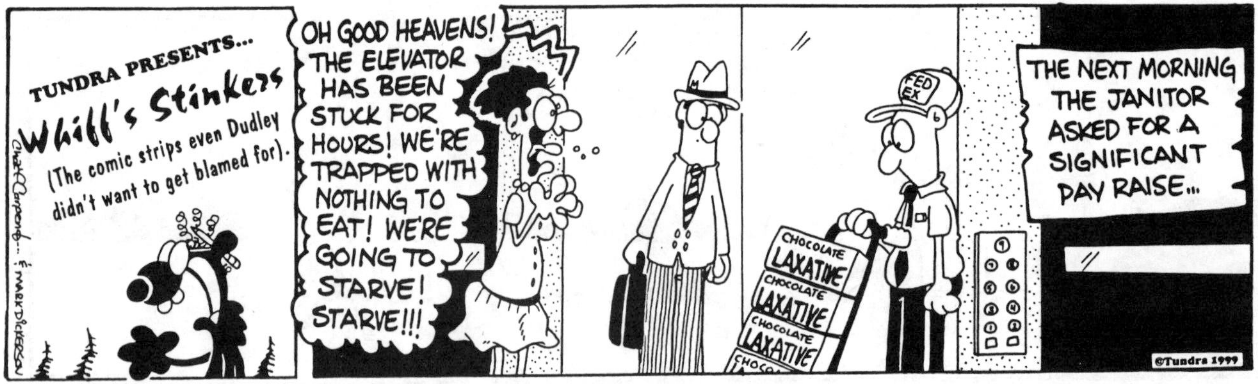
TUNDRA PRESENTS...
Whiff's Stinkers
(The comic strips even Dudley didn't want to get blamed for).
OH GOOD HEAVENS! THE ELEVATOR HAS BEEN STUCK FOR HOURS! WE'RE TRAPPED WITH NOTHING TO EAT! WE'RE GOING TO STARVE! STARVE!!!
FED EX
CHOCOLATE LAXATIVE
CHOCOLATE LAXATIVE
CHOCOLATE LAXATIVE
THE NEXT MORNING THE JANITOR ASKED FOR A SIGNIFICANT PAY RAISE...
©Tundra 1999

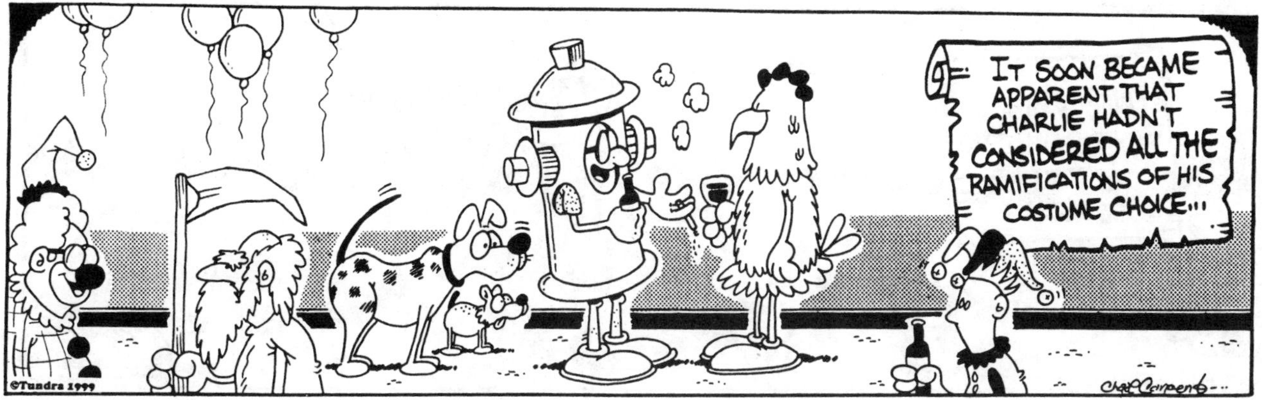
IT SOON BECAME APPARENT THAT CHARLIE HADN'T CONSIDERED ALL THE RAMIFICATIONS OF HIS COSTUME CHOICE...
©Tundra 1999

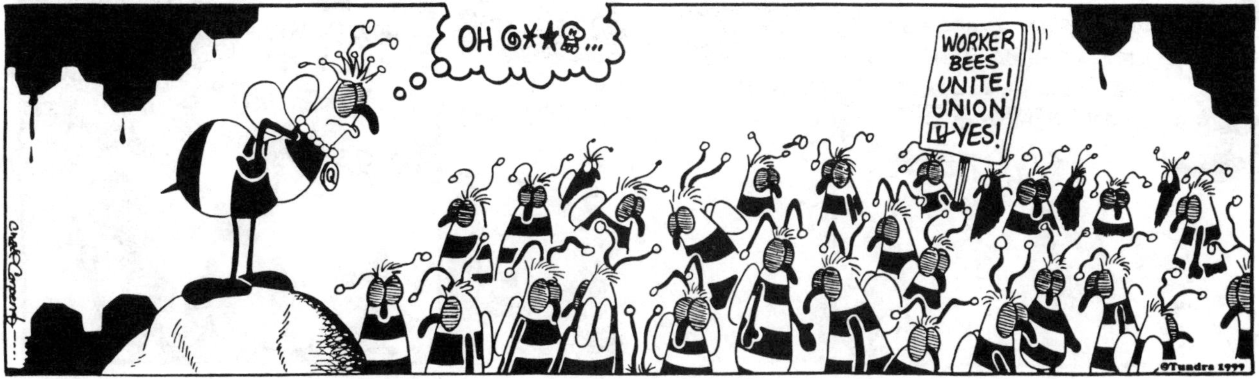
OH @*★...
WORKER BEES UNITE! UNION YES!
©Tundra 1999

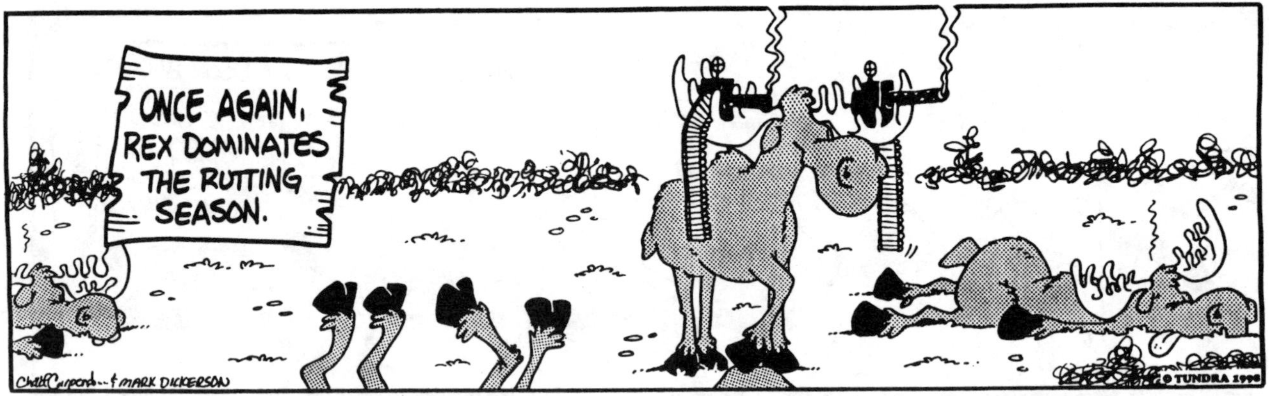
ONCE AGAIN, REX DOMINATES THE RUTTING SEASON.
Chad Carpenter & MARK DICKERSON
© TUNDRA 1998

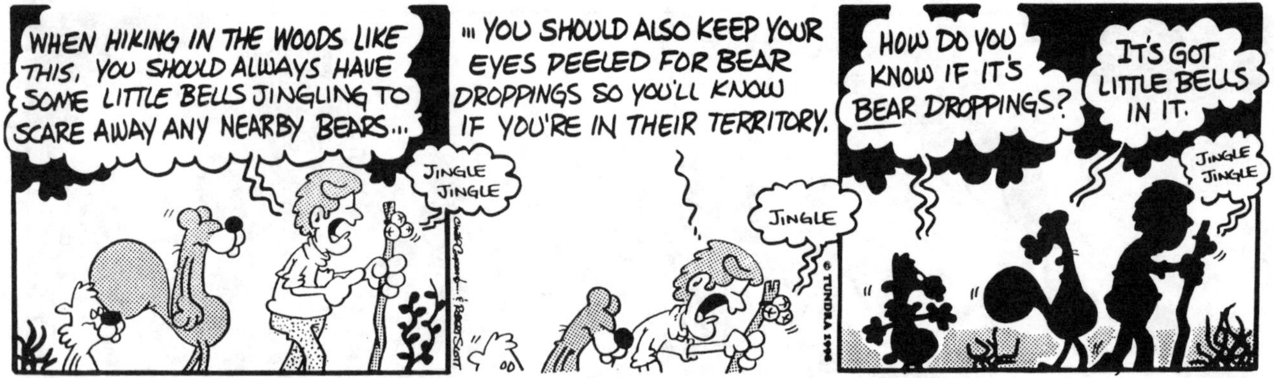
WHEN HIKING IN THE WOODS LIKE THIS, YOU SHOULD ALWAYS HAVE SOME LITTLE BELLS JINGLING TO SCARE AWAY ANY NEARBY BEARS...
JINGLE JINGLE
...YOU SHOULD ALSO KEEP YOUR EYES PEELED FOR BEAR DROPPINGS SO YOU'LL KNOW IF YOU'RE IN THEIR TERRITORY.
JINGLE
© TUNDRA 1998
HOW DO YOU KNOW IF IT'S BEAR DROPPINGS?
IT'S GOT LITTLE BELLS IN IT.
JINGLE JINGLE

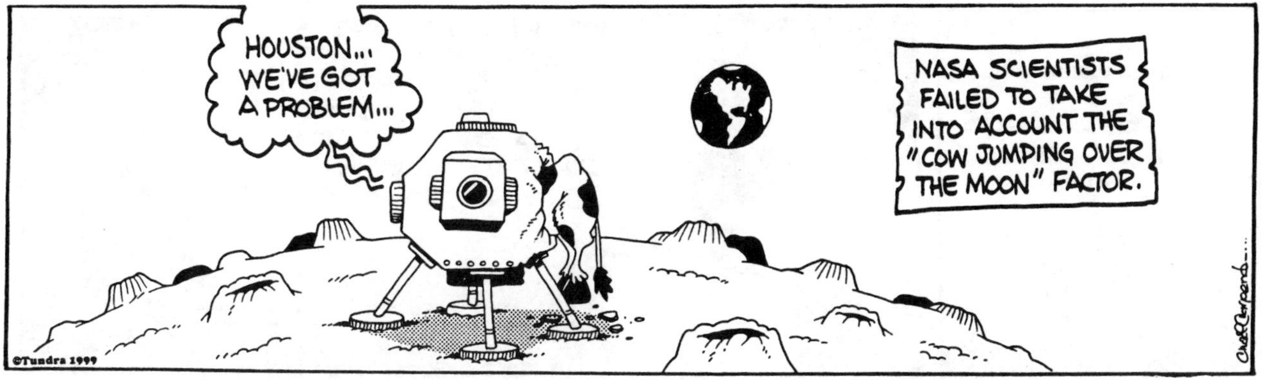
HOUSTON... WE'VE GOT A PROBLEM...
NASA SCIENTISTS FAILED TO TAKE INTO ACCOUNT THE "COW JUMPING OVER THE MOON" FACTOR.
©Tundra 1999

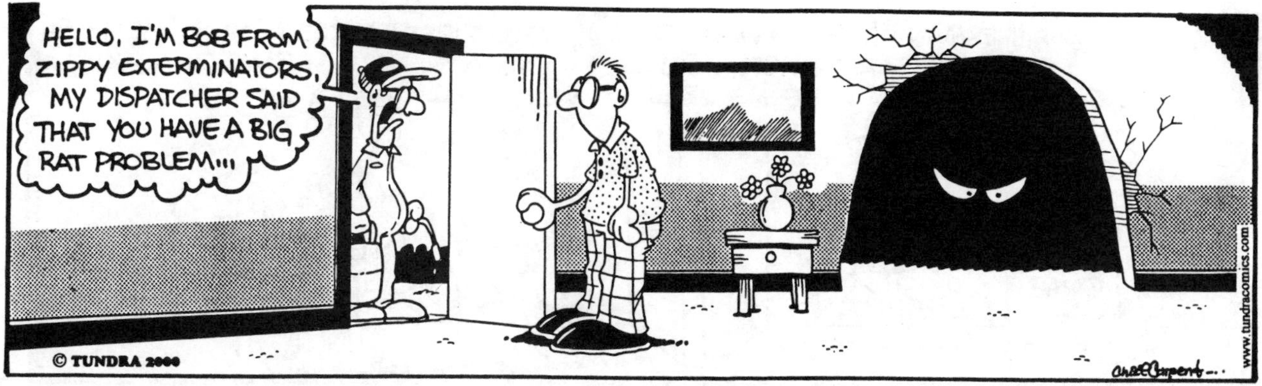
HELLO, I'M BOB FROM ZIPPY EXTERMINATORS, MY DISPATCHER SAID THAT YOU HAVE A BIG RAT PROBLEM...
© TUNDRA 2000
www.tundracomics.com

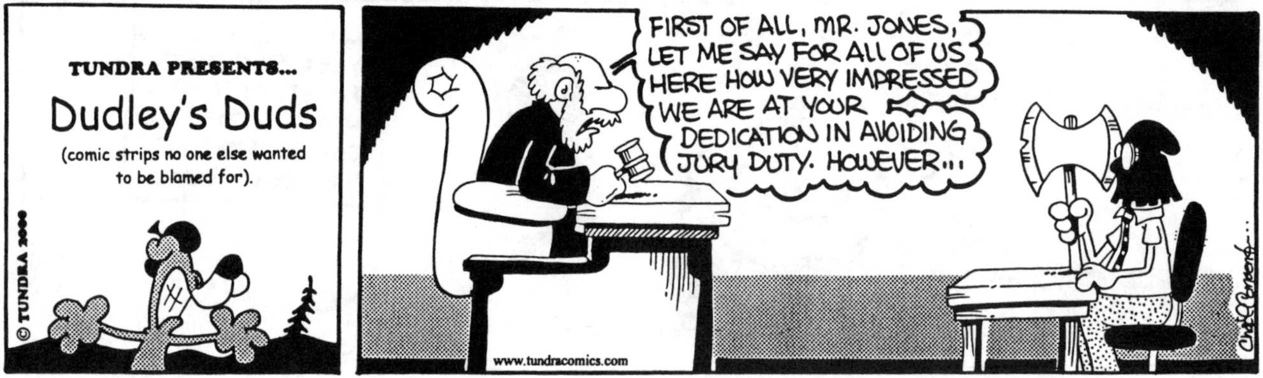
TUNDRA PRESENTS...
Dudley's Duds
(comic strips no one else wanted to be blamed for).
© TUNDRA 2000
FIRST OF ALL, MR. JONES, LET ME SAY FOR ALL OF US HERE HOW VERY IMPRESSED WE ARE AT YOUR DEDICATION IN AVOIDING JURY DUTY. HOWEVER...
www.tundracomics.com

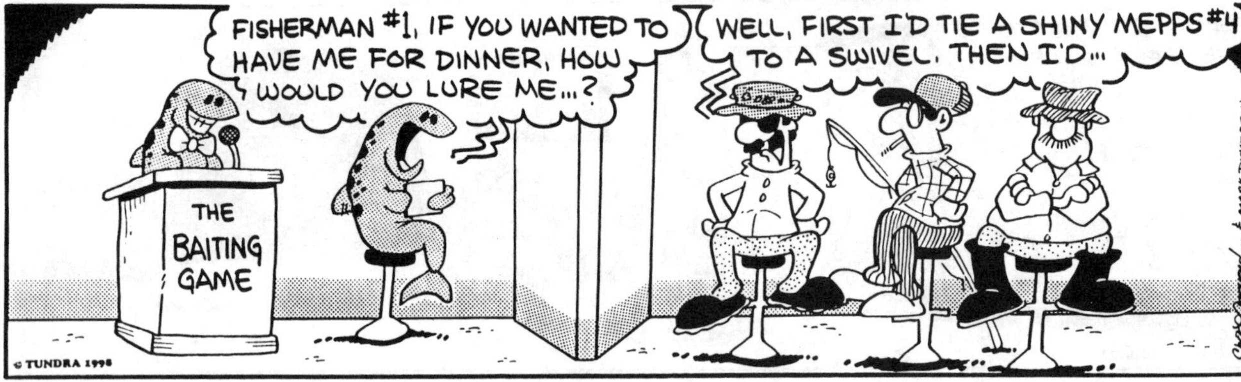
FISHERMAN #1, IF YOU WANTED TO HAVE ME FOR DINNER, HOW WOULD YOU LURE ME...?
WELL, FIRST I'D TIE A SHINY MEPPS #4 TO A SWIVEL. THEN I'D...
THE BAITING GAME
& MARK DICKERSON
© TUNDRA 1998

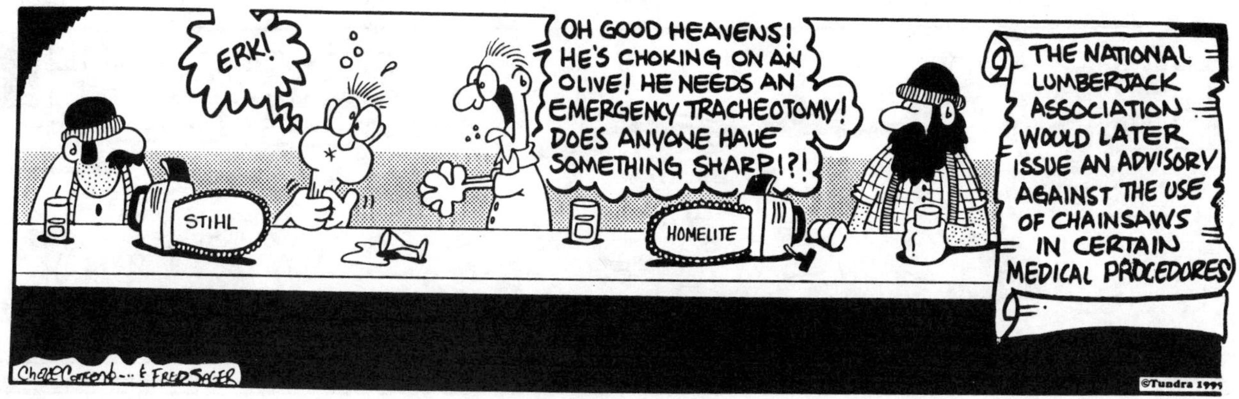
ERK!
OH GOOD HEAVENS! HE'S CHOKING ON AN OLIVE! HE NEEDS AN EMERGENCY TRACHEOTOMY! DOES ANYONE HAVE SOMETHING SHARP!?!
STIHL
HOMELITE
THE NATIONAL LUMBERJACK ASSOCIATION WOULD LATER ISSUE AN ADVISORY AGAINST THE USE OF CHAINSAWS IN CERTAIN MEDICAL PROCEDURES
©Tundra 1999

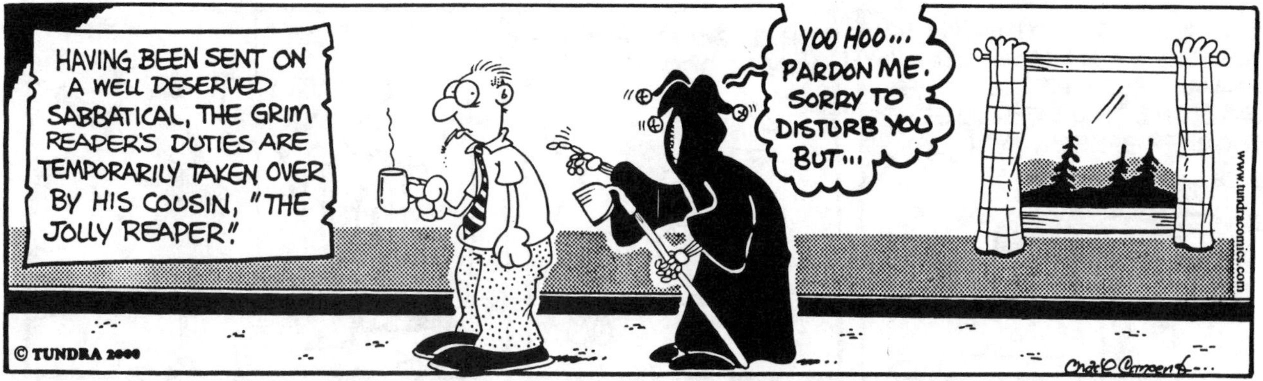
HAVING BEEN SENT ON A WELL DESERVED SABBATICAL, THE GRIM REAPER'S DUTIES ARE TEMPORARILY TAKEN OVER BY HIS COUSIN, "THE JOLLY REAPER".
YOO HOO... PARDON ME. SORRY TO DISTURB YOU BUT...
www.tundracomics.com
© TUNDRA 2000

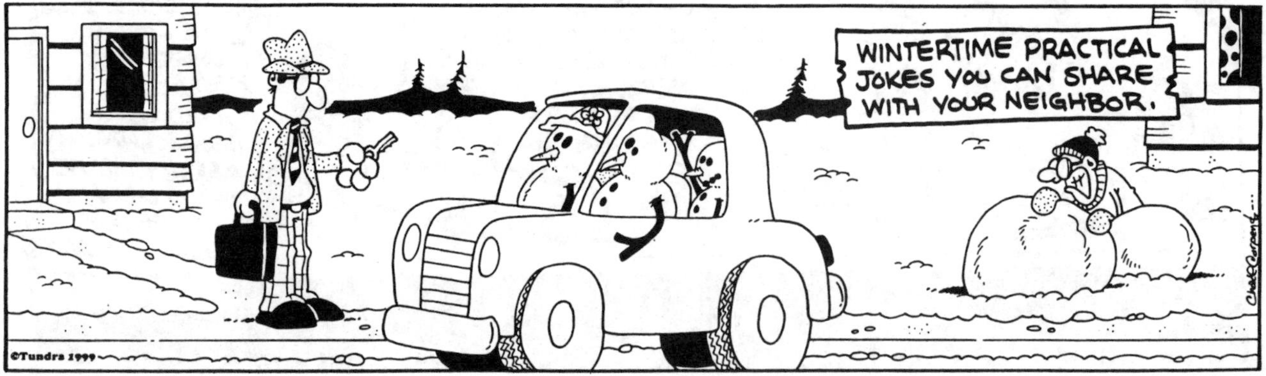
WINTERTIME PRACTICAL JOKES YOU CAN SHARE WITH YOUR NEIGHBOR.
©Tundra 1999

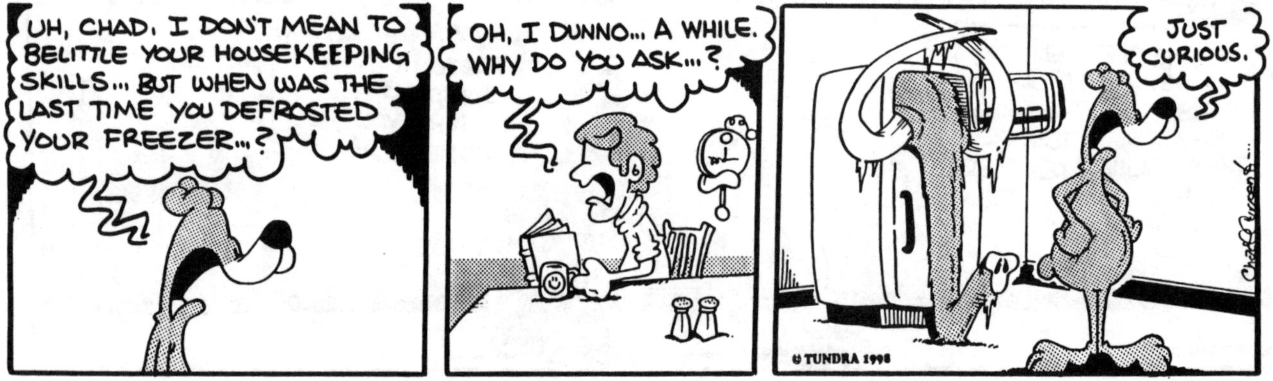
UH, CHAD, I DON'T MEAN TO BELITTLE YOUR HOUSEKEEPING SKILLS... BUT WHEN WAS THE LAST TIME YOU DEFROSTED YOUR FREEZER...?
OH, I DUNNO... A WHILE. WHY DO YOU ASK...?
JUST CURIOUS.
© TUNDRA 1998

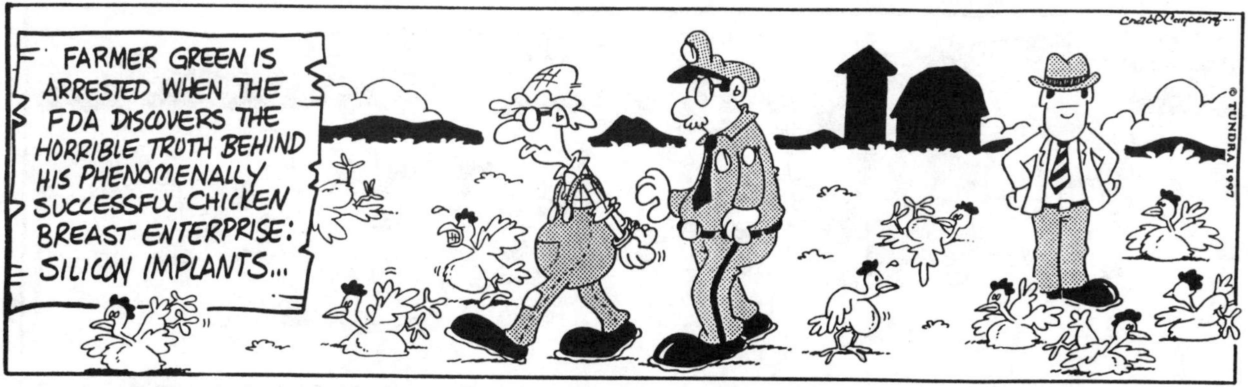
FARMER GREEN IS ARRESTED WHEN THE FDA DISCOVERS THE HORRIBLE TRUTH BEHIND HIS PHENOMENALLY SUCCESSFUL CHICKEN BREAST ENTERPRISE: SILICON IMPLANTS...
© TUNDRA 1997

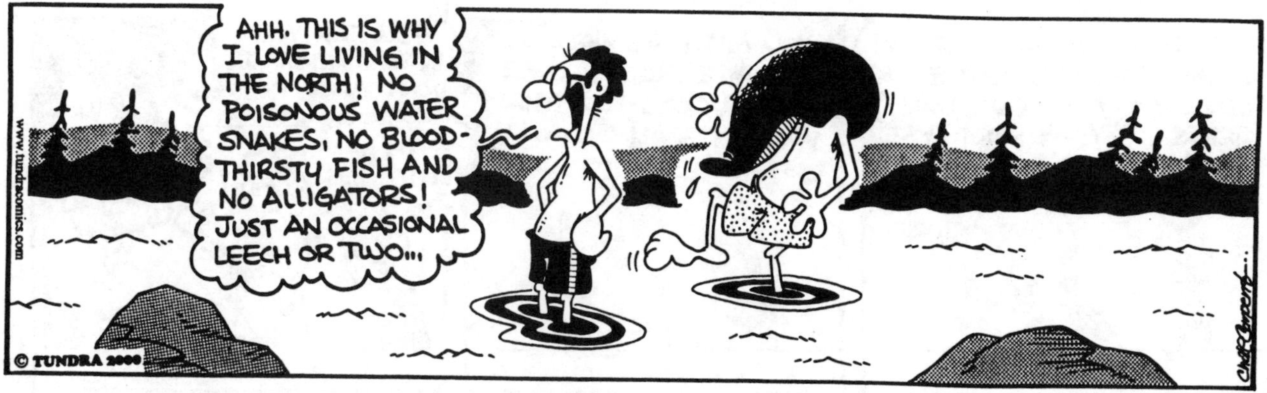
AHH. THIS IS WHY I LOVE LIVING IN THE NORTH! NO POISONOUS WATER SNAKES, NO BLOOD-THIRSTY FISH AND NO ALLIGATORS! JUST AN OCCASIONAL LEECH OR TWO...
www.tundracomics.com
© TUNDRA 2000

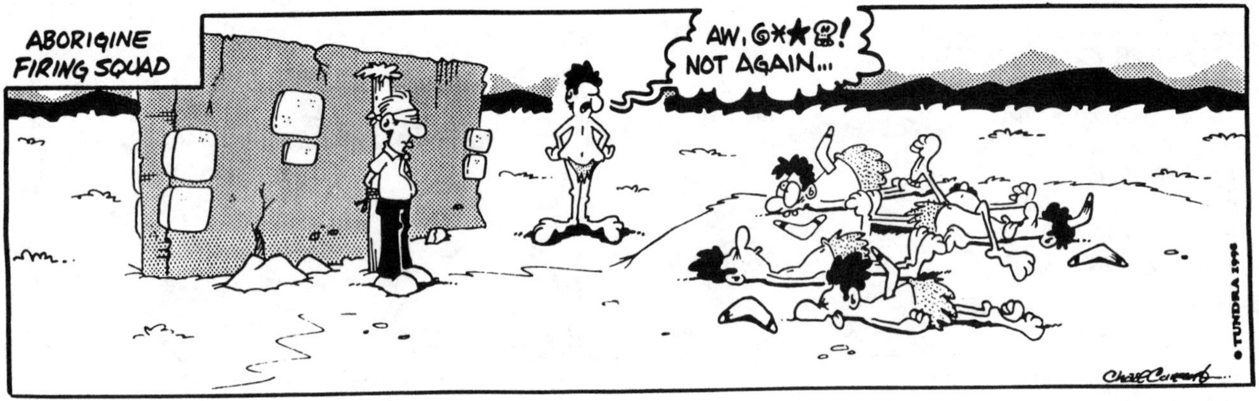
ABORIGINE FIRING SQUAD
AW, @*★☠! NOT AGAIN...
© TUNDRA 1998

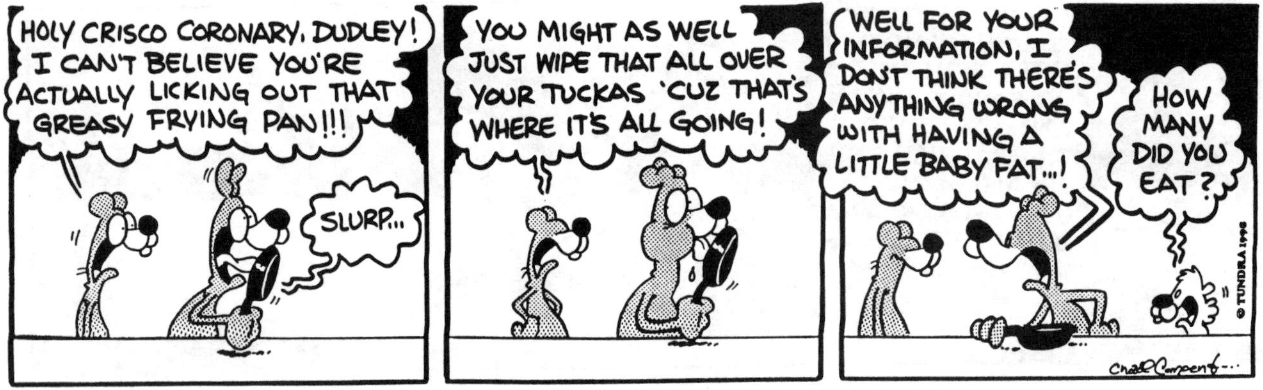
HOLY CRISCO CORONARY, DUDLEY! I CAN'T BELIEVE YOU'RE ACTUALLY LICKING OUT THAT GREASY FRYING PAN!!!
SLURP...
YOU MIGHT AS WELL JUST WIPE THAT ALL OVER YOUR TUCKAS 'CUZ THAT'S WHERE IT'S ALL GOING!
WELL FOR YOUR INFORMATION, I DON'T THINK THERE'S ANYTHING WRONG WITH HAVING A LITTLE BABY FAT...!
HOW MANY DID YOU EAT?
© TUNDRA 1998

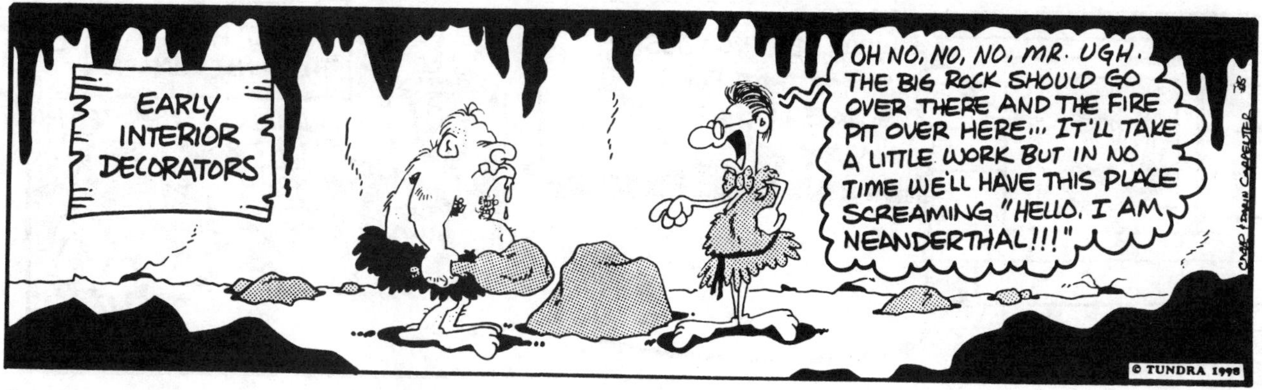
EARLY INTERIOR DECORATORS
OH NO, NO, NO, MR. UGH. THE BIG ROCK SHOULD GO OVER THERE AND THE FIRE PIT OVER HERE... IT'LL TAKE A LITTLE WORK BUT IN NO TIME WE'LL HAVE THIS PLACE SCREAMING "HELLO, I AM NEANDERTHAL!!!"
© TUNDRA 1998

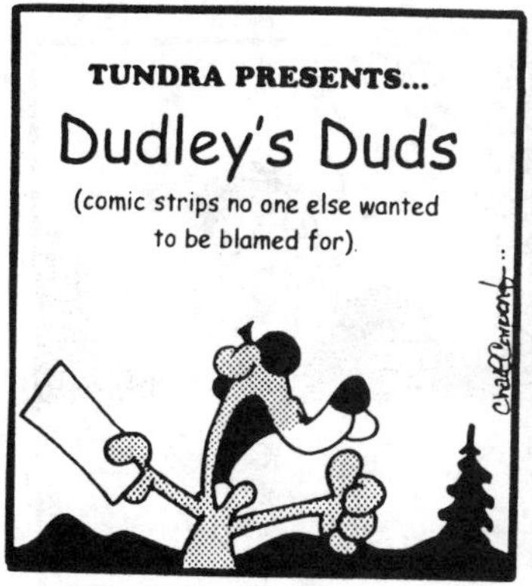
TUNDRA PRESENTS...
Dudley's Duds
(comic strips no one else wanted to be blamed for).

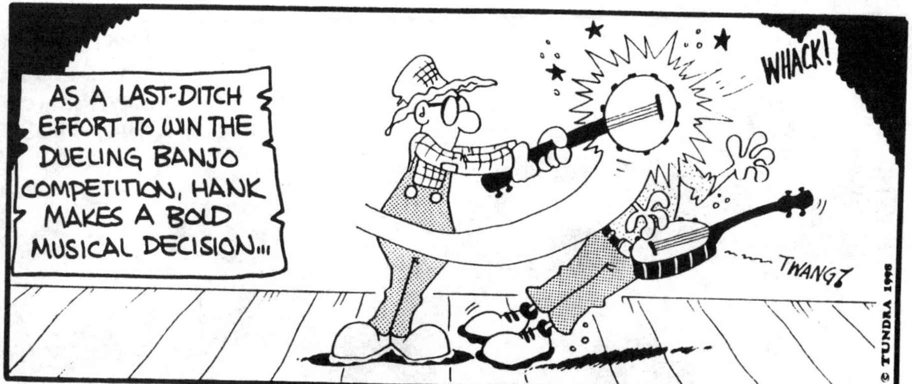
AS A LAST-DITCH EFFORT TO WIN THE DUELING BANJO COMPETITION, HANK MAKES A BOLD MUSICAL DECISION...
WHACK!
TWANG!
© TUNDRA 1998

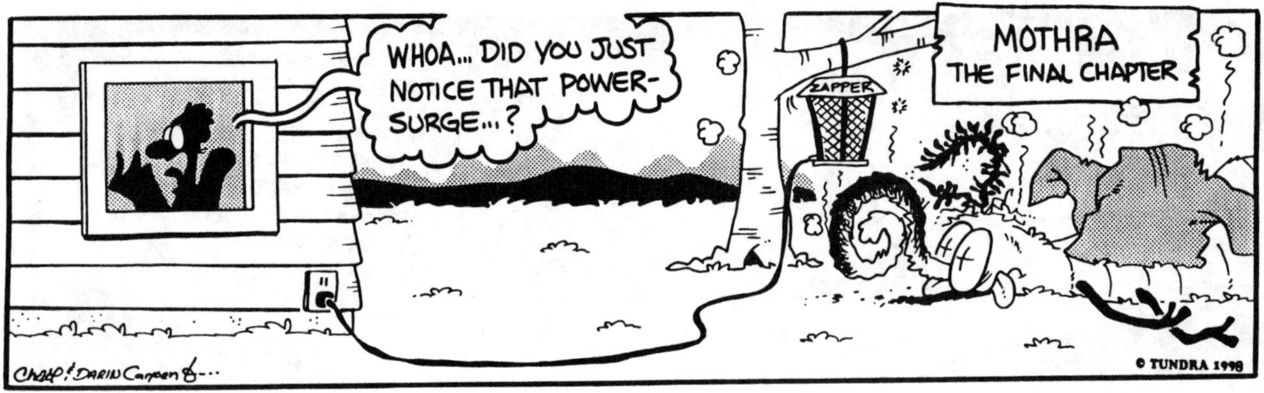
WHOA... DID YOU JUST NOTICE THAT POWER-SURGE...?
MOTHRA
THE FINAL CHAPTER
ZAPPER
© TUNDRA 1998

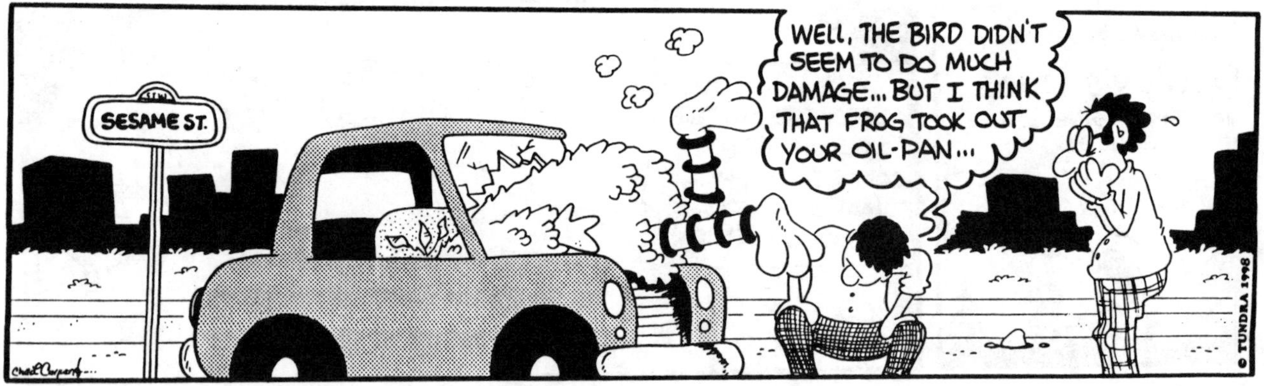
SESAME ST.
WELL, THE BIRD DIDN'T SEEM TO DO MUCH DAMAGE... BUT I THINK THAT FROG TOOK OUT YOUR OIL-PAN...
© TUNDRA 1998

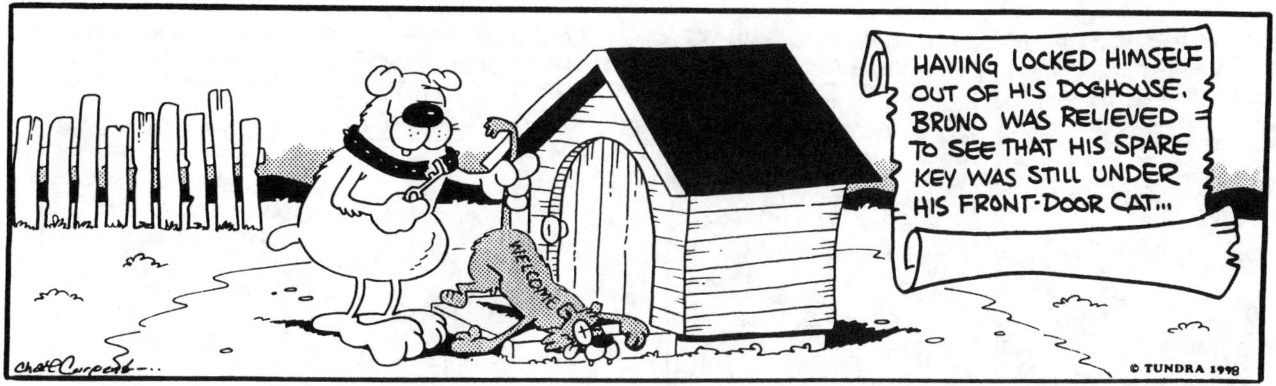
HAVING LOCKED HIMSELF OUT OF HIS DOGHOUSE, BRUNO WAS RELIEVED TO SEE THAT HIS SPARE KEY WAS STILL UNDER HIS FRONT-DOOR CAT...
WELCOME
© TUNDRA 1998

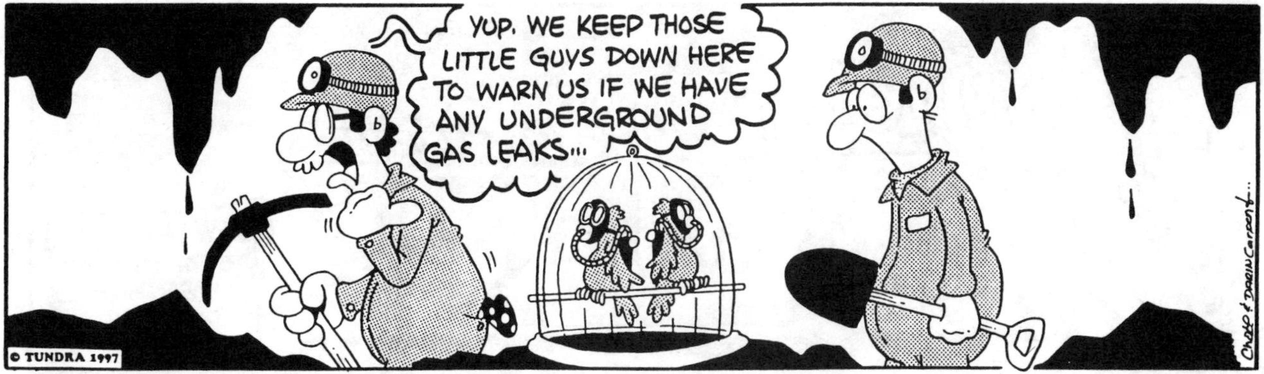
YUP, WE KEEP THOSE LITTLE GUYS DOWN HERE TO WARN US IF WE HAVE ANY UNDERGROUND GAS LEAKS...
© TUNDRA 1997

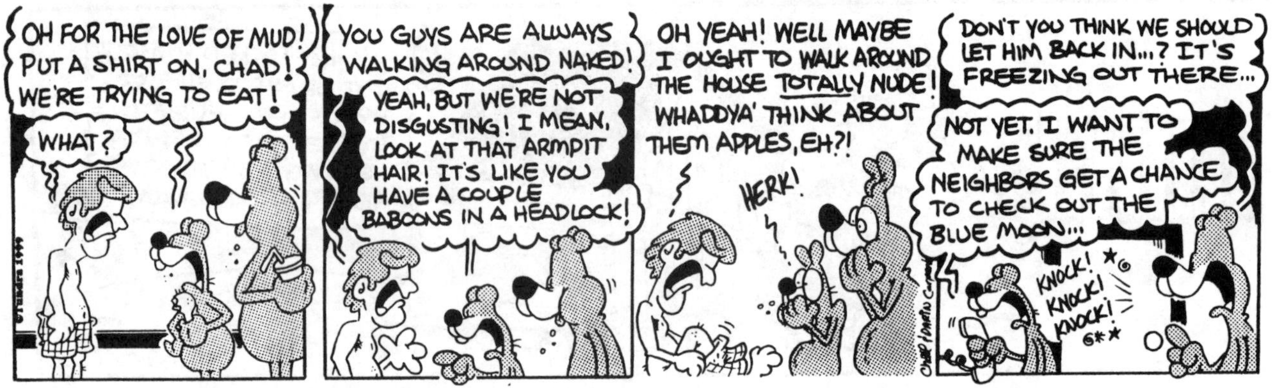

OH FOR THE LOVE OF MUD! PUT A SHIRT ON, CHAD! WE'RE TRYING TO EAT!
WHAT?
YOU GUYS ARE ALWAYS WALKING AROUND NAKED!
YEAH, BUT WE'RE NOT DISGUSTING! I MEAN, LOOK AT THAT ARMPIT HAIR! IT'S LIKE YOU HAVE A COUPLE BABOONS IN A HEADLOCK!
OH YEAH! WELL MAYBE I OUGHT TO WALK AROUND THE HOUSE TOTALLY NUDE! WHADDYA' THINK ABOUT THEM APPLES, EH?!
HERK!
DON'T YOU THINK WE SHOULD LET HIM BACK IN...? IT'S FREEZING OUT THERE...
NOT YET. I WANT TO MAKE SURE THE NEIGHBORS GET A CHANCE TO CHECK OUT THE BLUE MOON...
KNOCK! KNOCK! KNOCK!

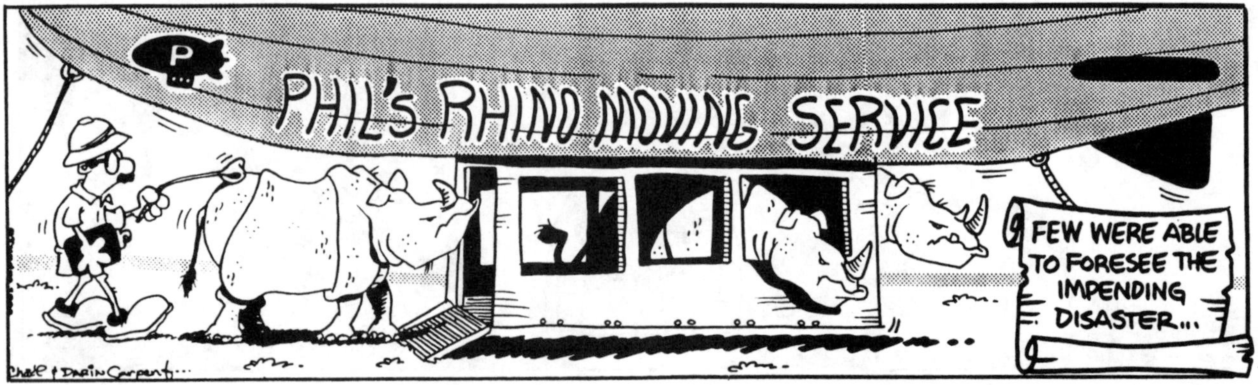

P
PHIL'S RHINO MOVING SERVICE
FEW WERE ABLE TO FORESEE THE IMPENDING DISASTER...

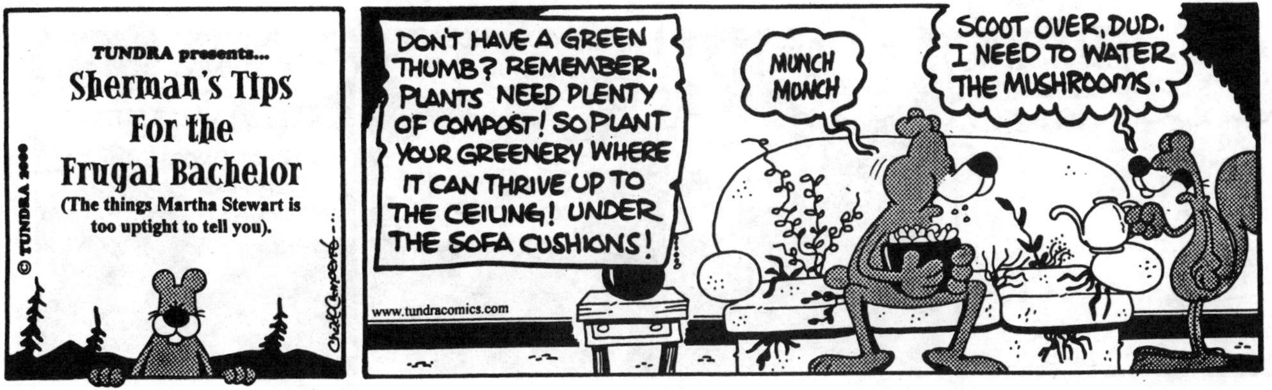
TUNDRA presents...
Sherman's Tips For the Frugal Bachelor
(The things Martha Stewart is too uptight to tell you).
© TUNDRA 2000
DON'T HAVE A GREEN THUMB? REMEMBER, PLANTS NEED PLENTY OF COMPOST! SO PLANT YOUR GREENERY WHERE IT CAN THRIVE UP TO THE CEILING! UNDER THE SOFA CUSHIONS!
MUNCH MUNCH
SCOOT OVER, DUD. I NEED TO WATER THE MUSHROOMS.
www.tundracomics.com

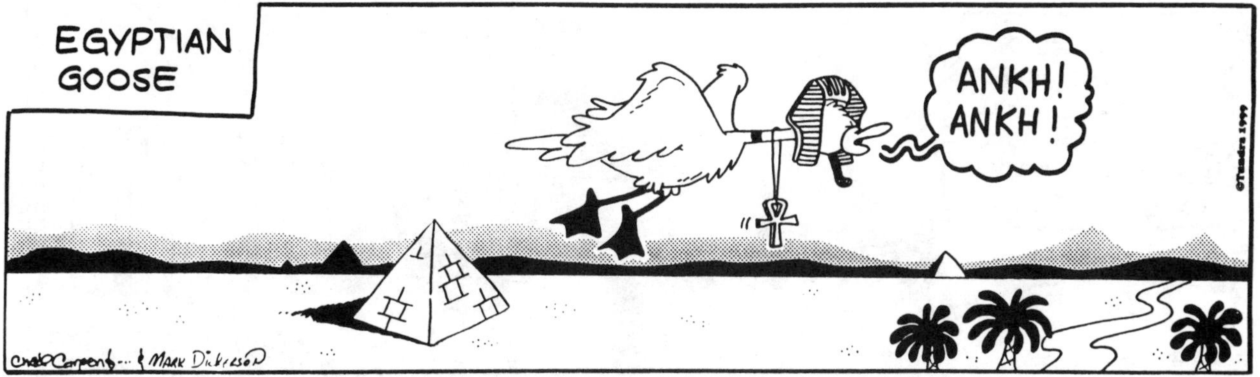
EGYPTIAN GOOSE
ANKH! ANKH!
©Tundra 1999
& MARK DICKERSON

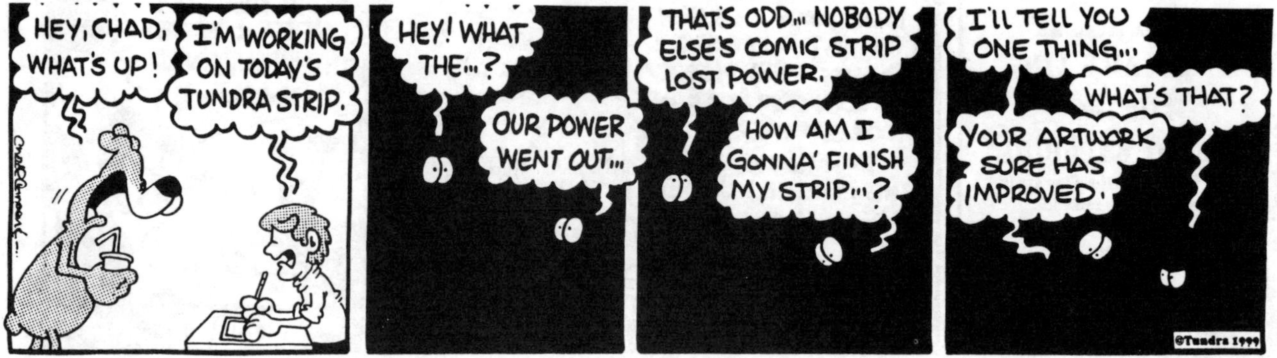
HEY, CHAD, WHAT'S UP!
I'M WORKING ON TODAY'S TUNDRA STRIP.
HEY! WHAT THE...?
OUR POWER WENT OUT...
THAT'S ODD... NOBODY ELSE'S COMIC STRIP LOST POWER.
HOW AM I GONNA' FINISH MY STRIP...?
I'LL TELL YOU ONE THING...
WHAT'S THAT?
YOUR ARTWORK SURE HAS IMPROVED.
©Tundra 1999

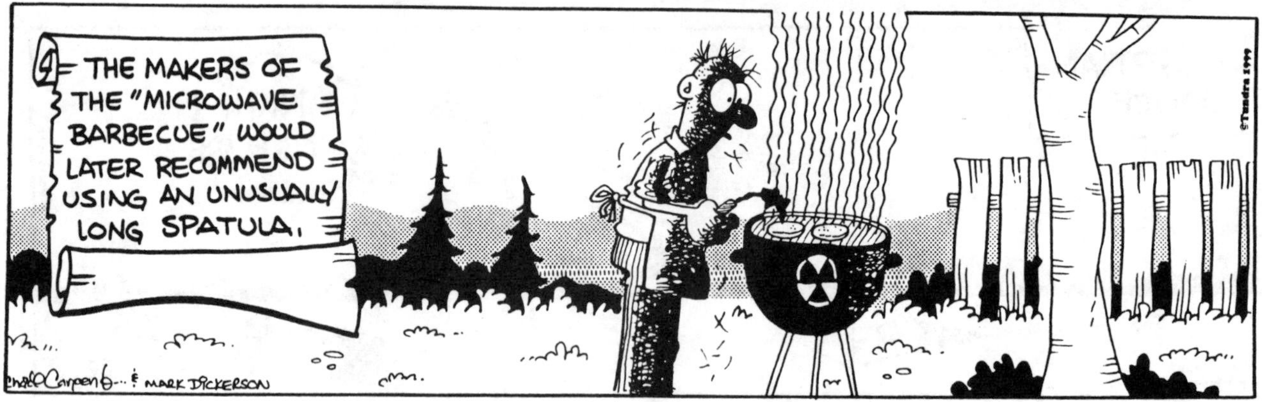
4
THE MAKERS OF THE "MICROWAVE BARBECUE" WOULD LATER RECOMMEND USING AN UNUSUALLY LONG SPATULA.
©Tundra 1999
& MARK DICKERSON

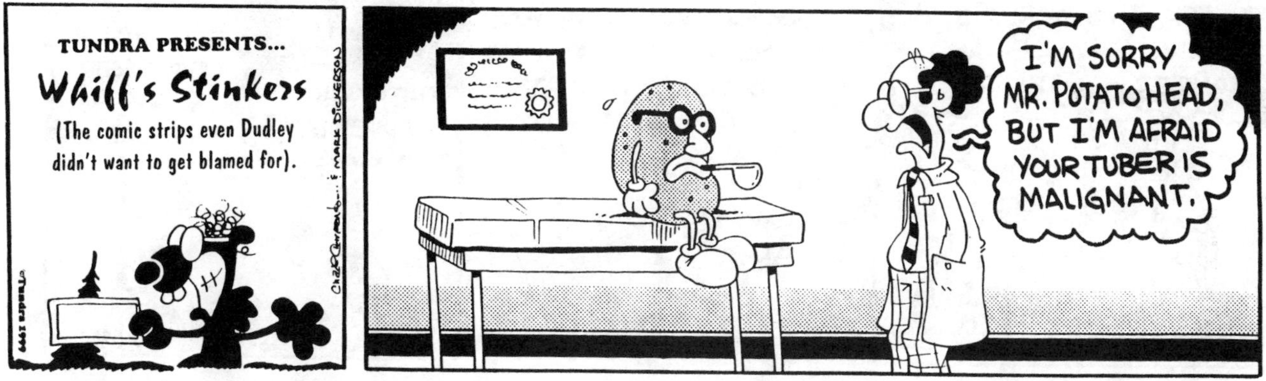
TUNDRA PRESENTS...
Whiff's Stinkers
(The comic strips even Dudley didn't want to get blamed for).
I'M SORRY MR. POTATO HEAD, BUT I'M AFRAID YOUR TUBER IS MALIGNANT.

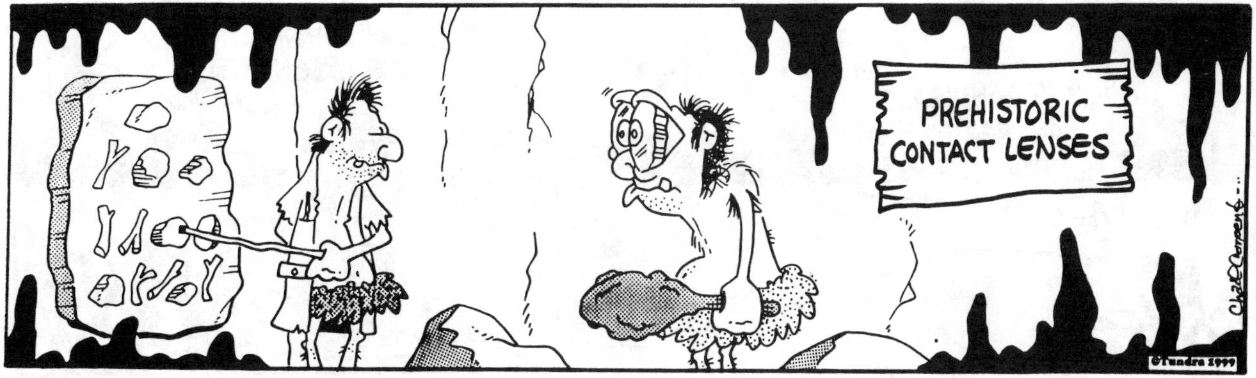
PREHISTORIC CONTACT LENSES
©Tundra 1999

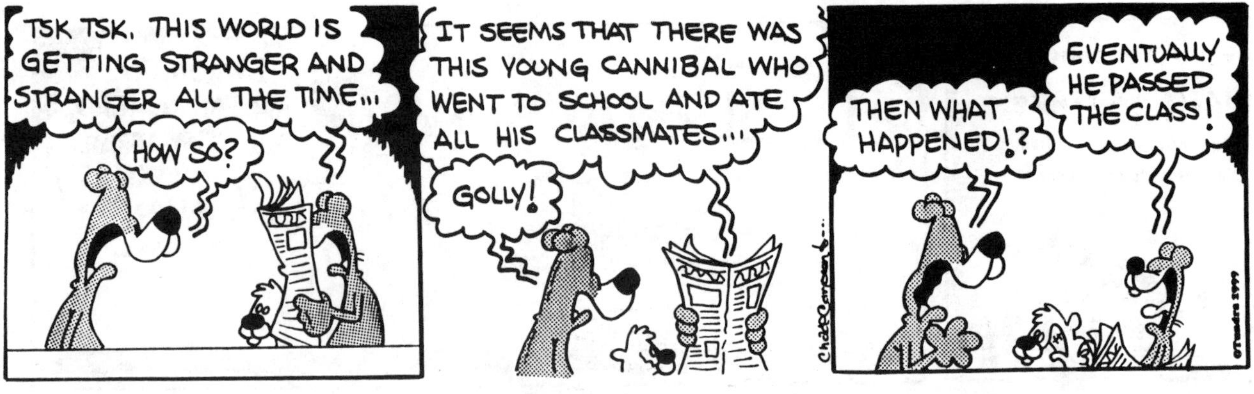
TSK TSK. THIS WORLD IS GETTING STRANGER AND STRANGER ALL THE TIME...
HOW SO?
IT SEEMS THAT THERE WAS THIS YOUNG CANNIBAL WHO WENT TO SCHOOL AND ATE ALL HIS CLASSMATES...
GOLLY!
THEN WHAT HAPPENED!?
EVENTUALLY HE PASSED THE CLASS!

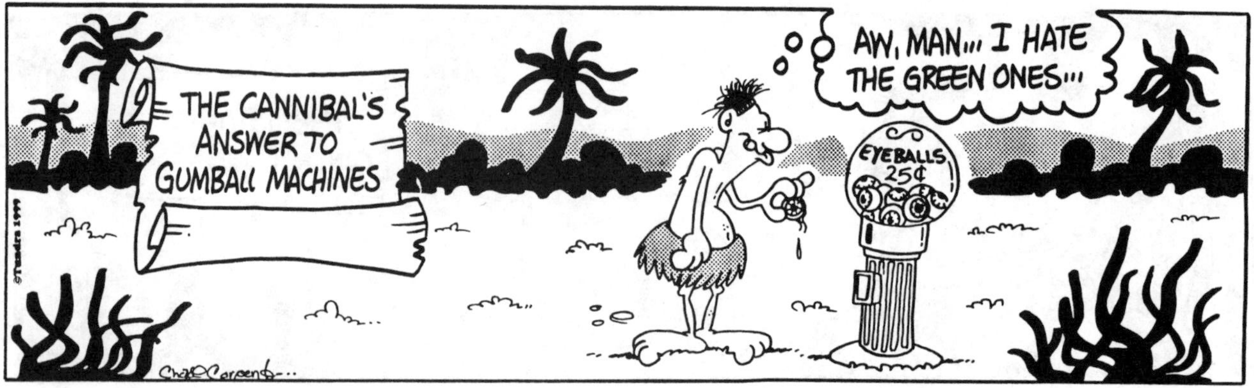
THE CANNIBAL'S ANSWER TO GUMBALL MACHINES
AW, MAN... I HATE THE GREEN ONES...
EYEBALLS 25¢

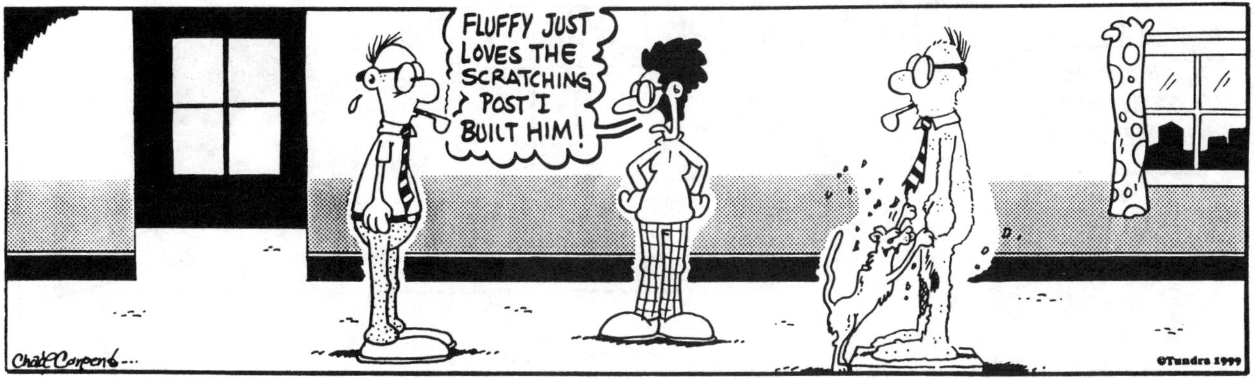
FLUFFY JUST LOVES THE SCRATCHING POST I BUILT HIM!
©Tundra 1999

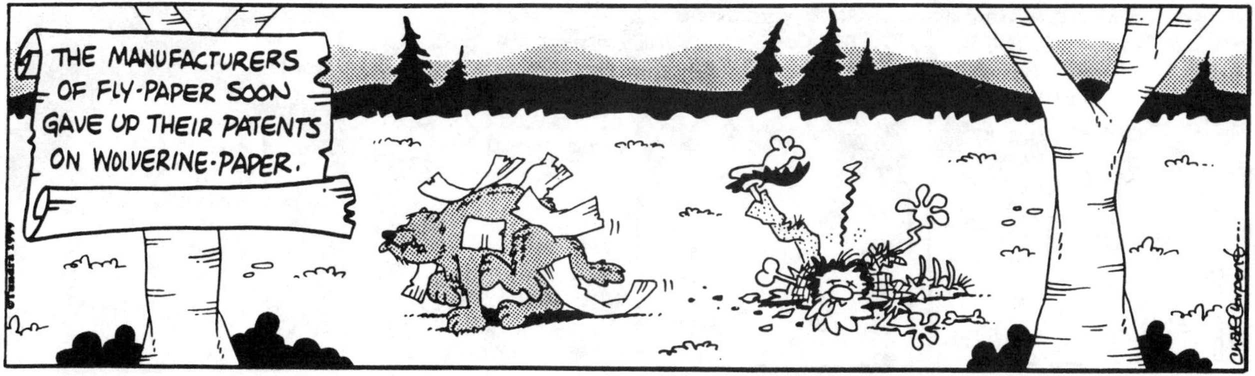
THE MANUFACTURERS OF FLY-PAPER SOON GAVE UP THEIR PATENTS ON WOLVERINE-PAPER.

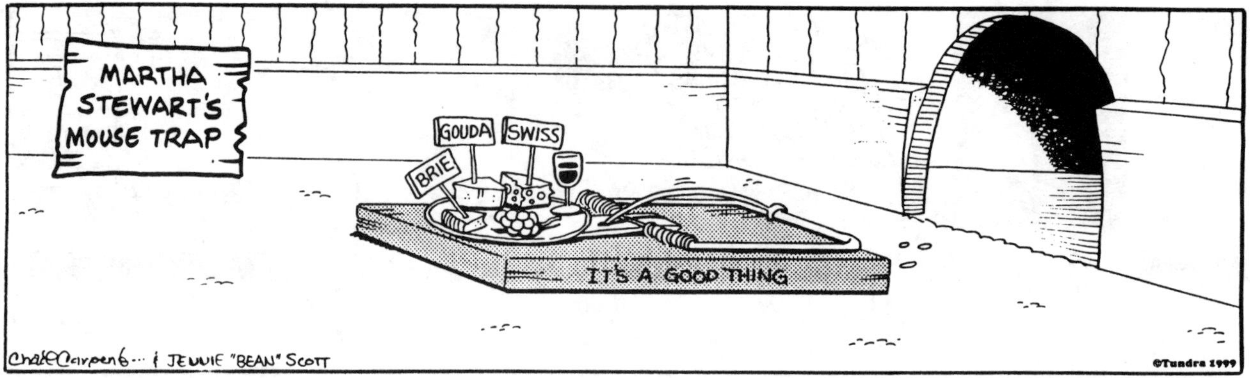
MARTHA STEWART'S MOUSE TRAP
GOUDA
SWISS
BRIE
IT'S A GOOD THING
ChadCarpenter... & JENNIE "BEAN" SCOTT
©Tundra 1999

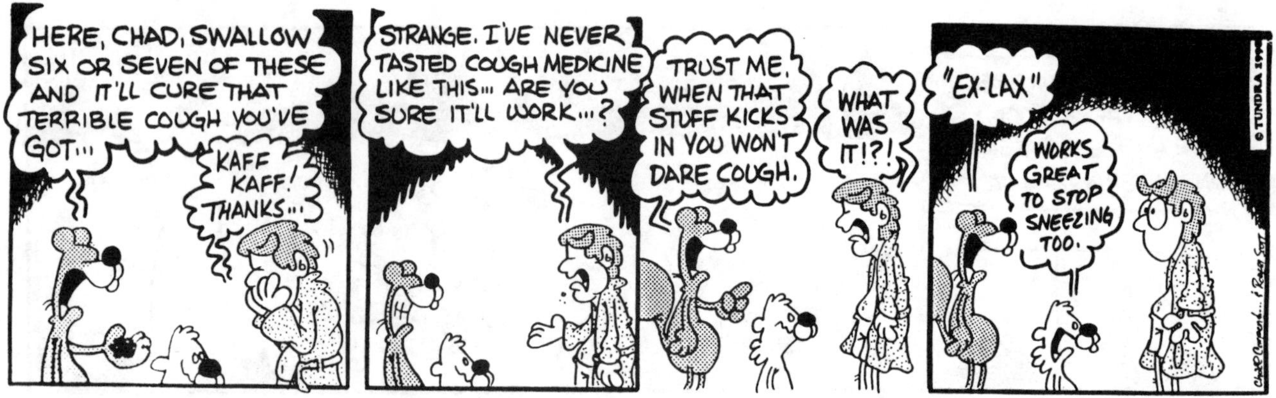
HERE, CHAD, SWALLOW SIX OR SEVEN OF THESE AND IT'LL CURE THAT TERRIBLE COUGH YOU'VE GOT...
KAFF KAFF! THANKS...
STRANGE. I'VE NEVER TASTED COUGH MEDICINE LIKE THIS... ARE YOU SURE IT'LL WORK...?
TRUST ME. WHEN THAT STUFF KICKS IN YOU WON'T DARE COUGH.
WHAT WAS IT!?!
"EX-LAX"
WORKS GREAT TO STOP SNEEZING TOO.
© TUNDRA 1999

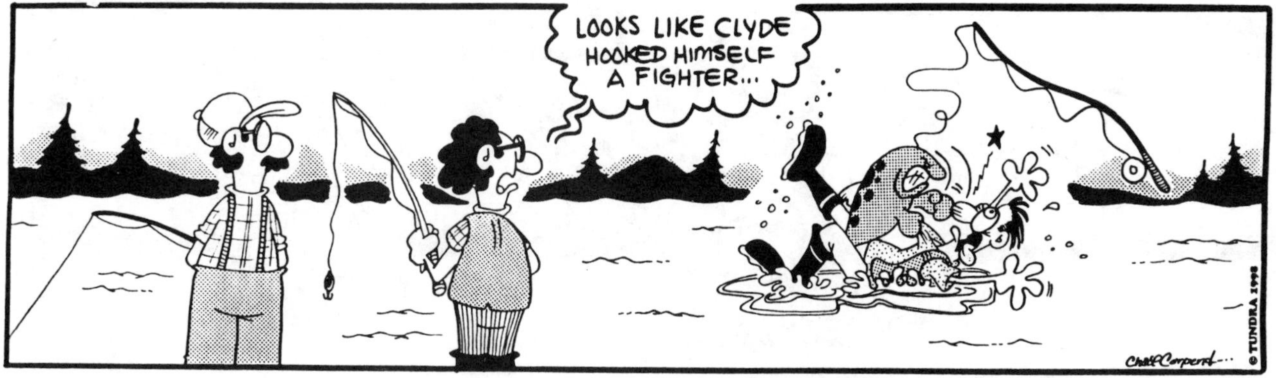
LOOKS LIKE CLYDE HOOKED HIMSELF A FIGHTER...
© TUNDRA 1998

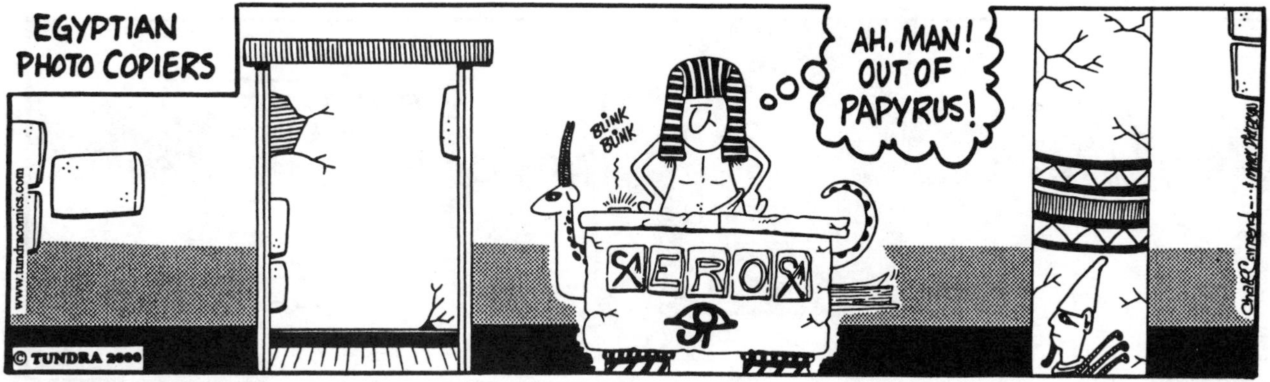
EGYPTIAN PHOTO COPIERS
BLINK BLINK
AH, MAN! OUT OF PAPYRUS!
www.tundracomics.com
© TUNDRA 2000

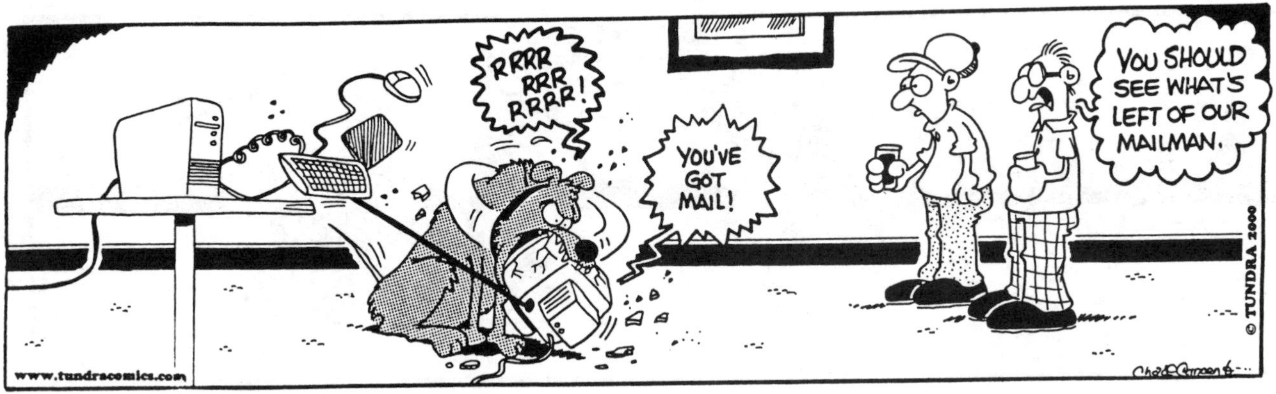
RRRR RRR RRRR!
YOU'VE GOT MAIL!
YOU SHOULD SEE WHAT'S LEFT OF OUR MAILMAN.
www.tundracomics.com
© TUNDRA 2000

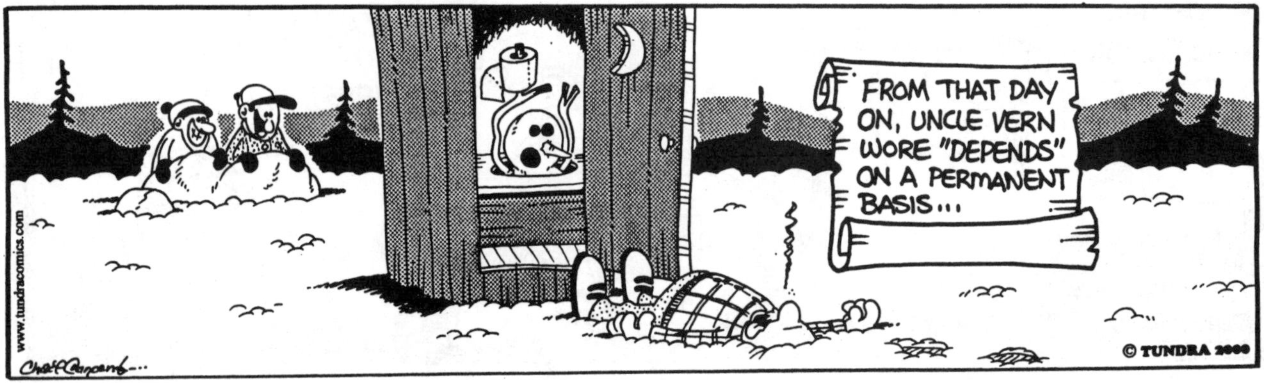
FROM THAT DAY ON, UNCLE VERN WORE "DEPENDS" ON A PERMANENT BASIS...
www.tundracomics.com
© TUNDRA 2000

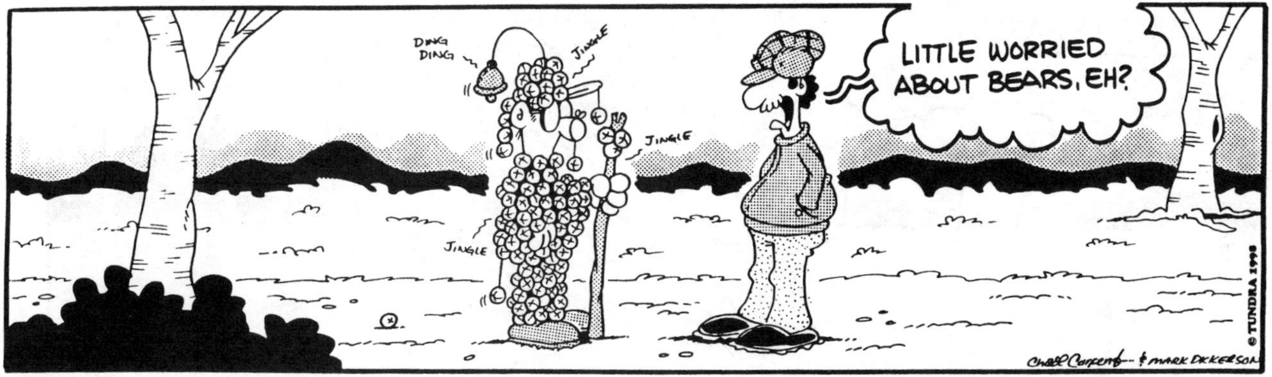
DING DING
JINGLE
JINGLE
JINGLE
LITTLE WORRIED ABOUT BEARS, EH?
© TUNDRA 1998
Chad Carpenter & MARK DICKERSON

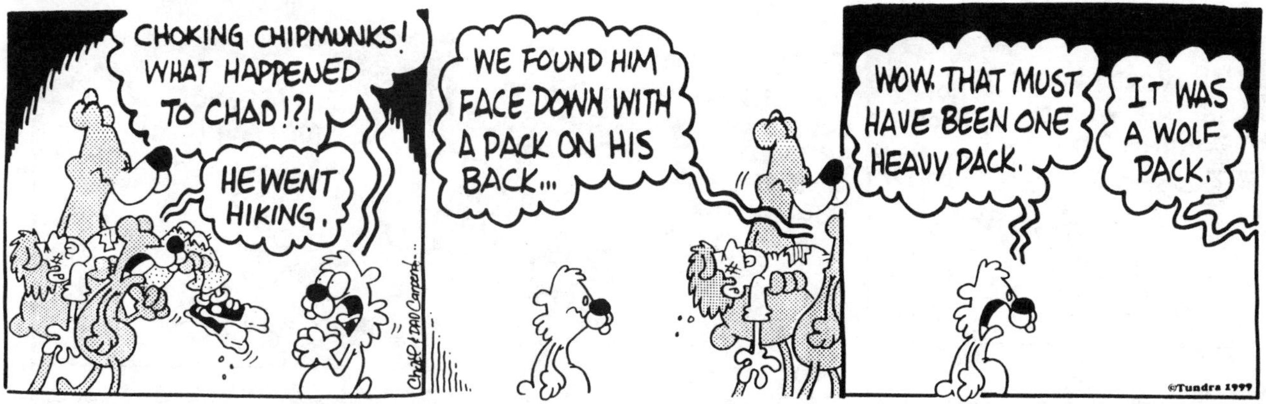
CHOKING CHIPMUNKS! WHAT HAPPENED TO CHAD!?!
HE WENT HIKING.
WE FOUND HIM FACE DOWN WITH A PACK ON HIS BACK...
WOW. THAT MUST HAVE BEEN ONE HEAVY PACK.
IT WAS A WOLF PACK.
©Tundra 1999

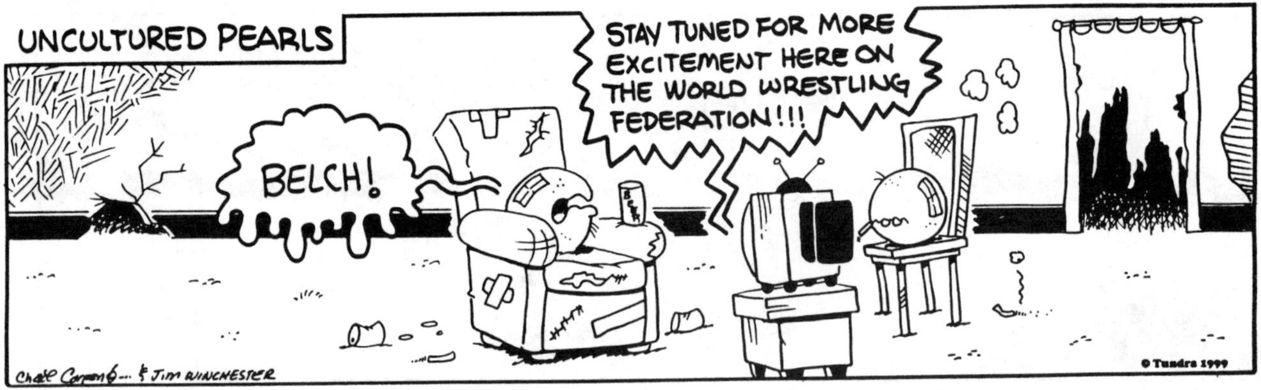
UNCULTURED PEARLS
BELCH!
STAY TUNED FOR MORE EXCITEMENT HERE ON THE WORLD WRESTLING FEDERATION!!!
© Tundra 1999

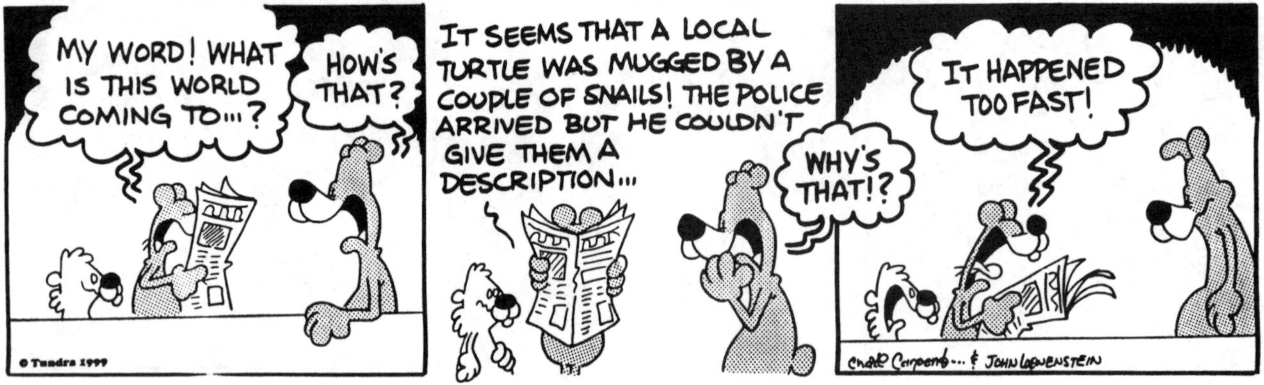
MY WORD! WHAT IS THIS WORLD COMING TO...?
HOW'S THAT?
IT SEEMS THAT A LOCAL TURTLE WAS MUGGED BY A COUPLE OF SNAILS! THE POLICE ARRIVED BUT HE COULDN'T GIVE THEM A DESCRIPTION...
WHY'S THAT!?
IT HAPPENED TOO FAST!
© Tundra 1999

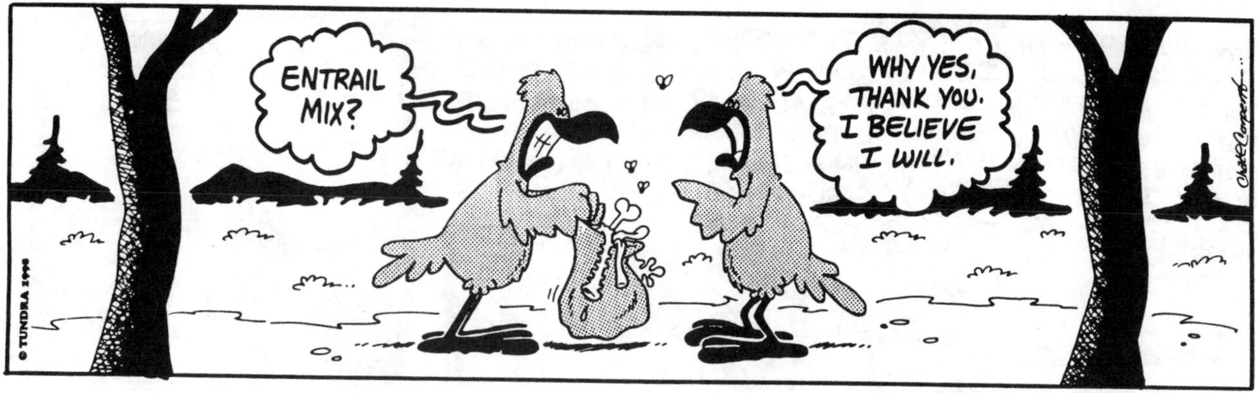
ENTRAIL MIX?
WHY YES, THANK YOU. I BELIEVE I WILL.
© TUNDRA 1998

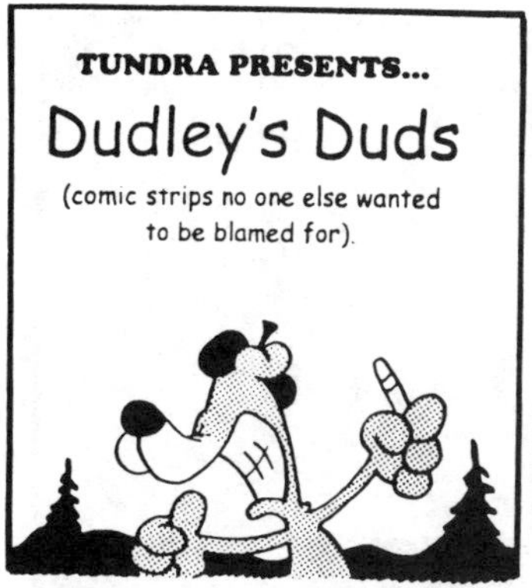
TUNDRA PRESENTS...
Dudley's Duds
(comic strips no one else wanted to be blamed for).

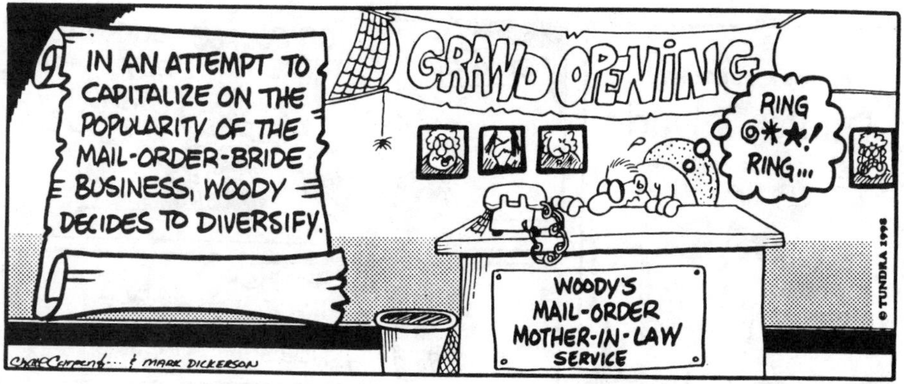
IN AN ATTEMPT TO CAPITALIZE ON THE POPULARITY OF THE MAIL-ORDER-BRIDE BUSINESS, WOODY DECIDES TO DIVERSIFY.
GRAND OPENING
RING @*★! RING...
WOODY'S MAIL-ORDER MOTHER-IN-LAW SERVICE
© TUNDRA 1998
& MARK DICKERSON

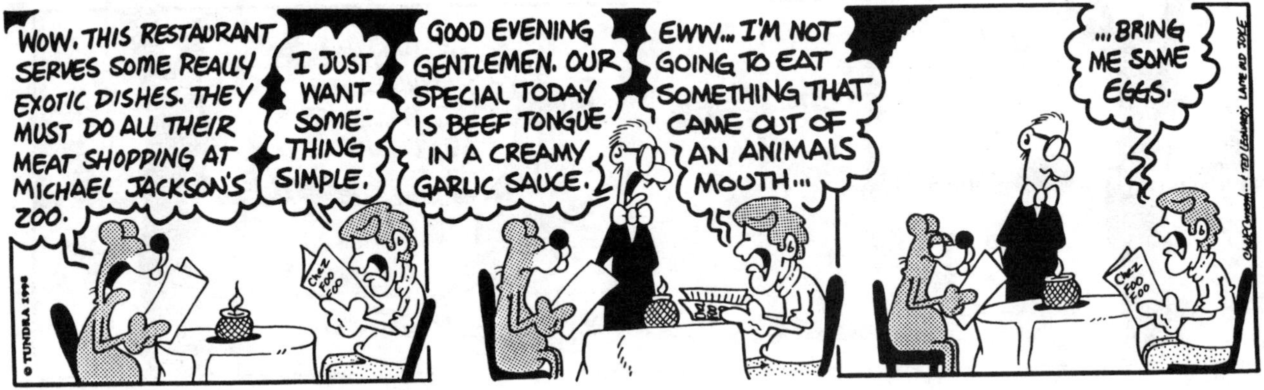
WOW. THIS RESTAURANT SERVES SOME REALLY EXOTIC DISHES. THEY MUST DO ALL THEIR MEAT SHOPPING AT MICHAEL JACKSON'S ZOO.
I JUST WANT SOME-THING SIMPLE.
CHEZ FOO FOO
GOOD EVENING GENTLEMEN. OUR SPECIAL TODAY IS BEEF TONGUE IN A CREAMY GARLIC SAUCE.
EWW... I'M NOT GOING TO EAT SOMETHING THAT CAME OUT OF AN ANIMALS MOUTH...
...BRING ME SOME EGGS.
CHEZ FOO FOO

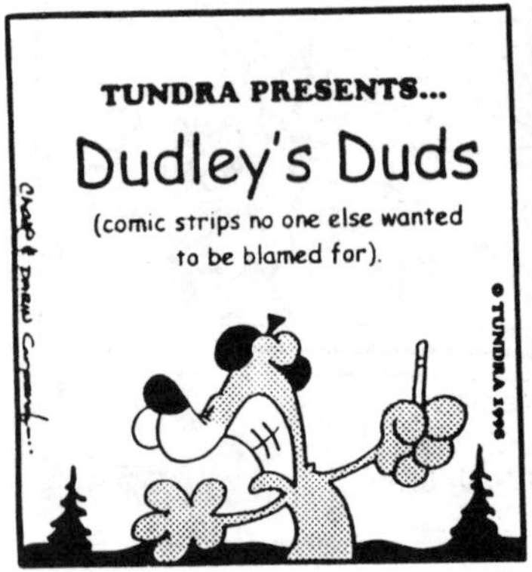
TUNDRA PRESENTS...
Dudley's Duds
(comic strips no one else wanted to be blamed for).

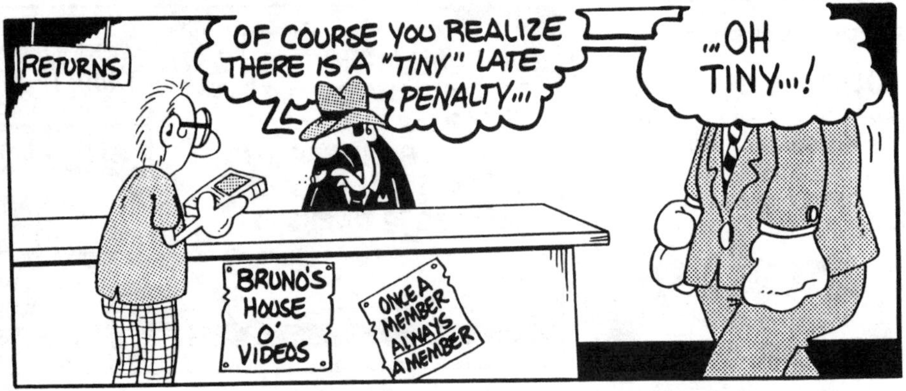
RETURNS
OF COURSE YOU REALIZE THERE IS A "TINY" LATE PENALTY...
...OH TINY...!
BRUNO'S HOUSE O' VIDEOS
ONCE A MEMBER ALWAYS A MEMBER

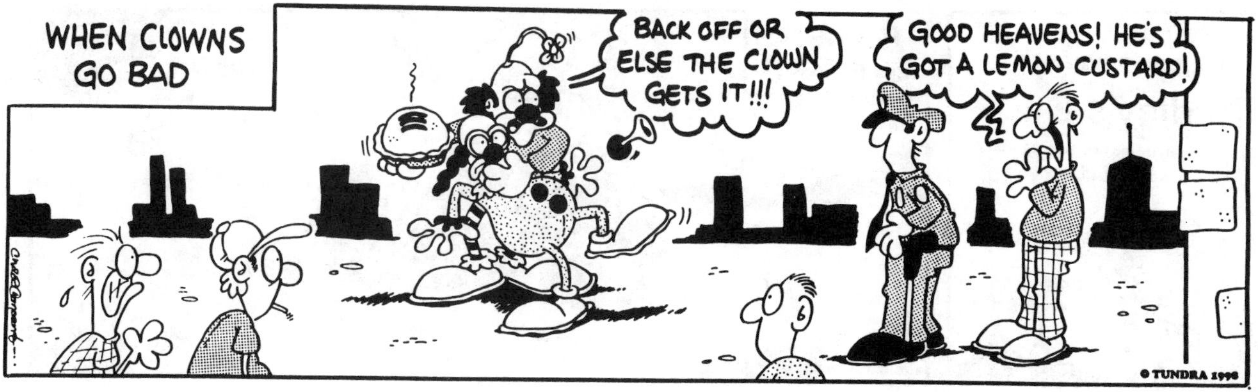
WHEN CLOWNS GO BAD
BACK OFF OR ELSE THE CLOWN GETS IT!!!
GOOD HEAVENS! HE'S GOT A LEMON CUSTARD!
© TUNDRA 1998

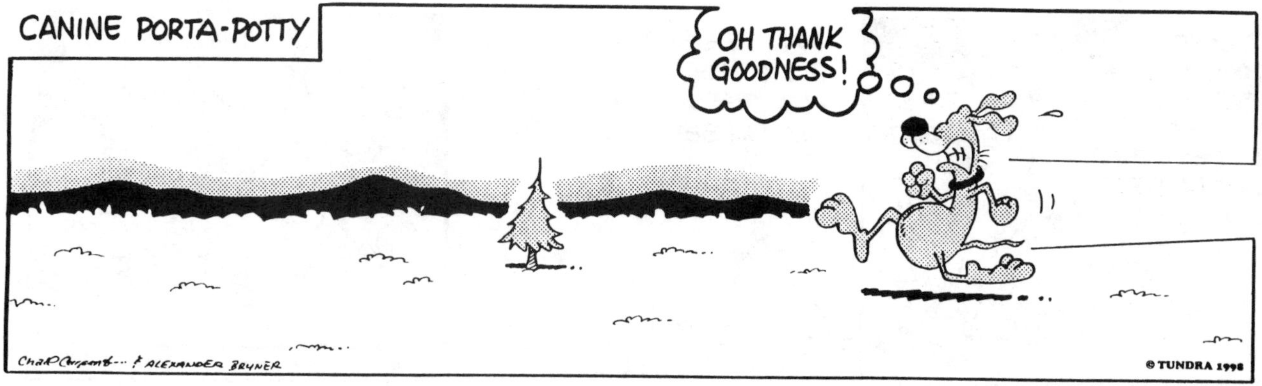
CANINE PORTA-POTTY
OH THANK GOODNESS!
© TUNDRA 1998

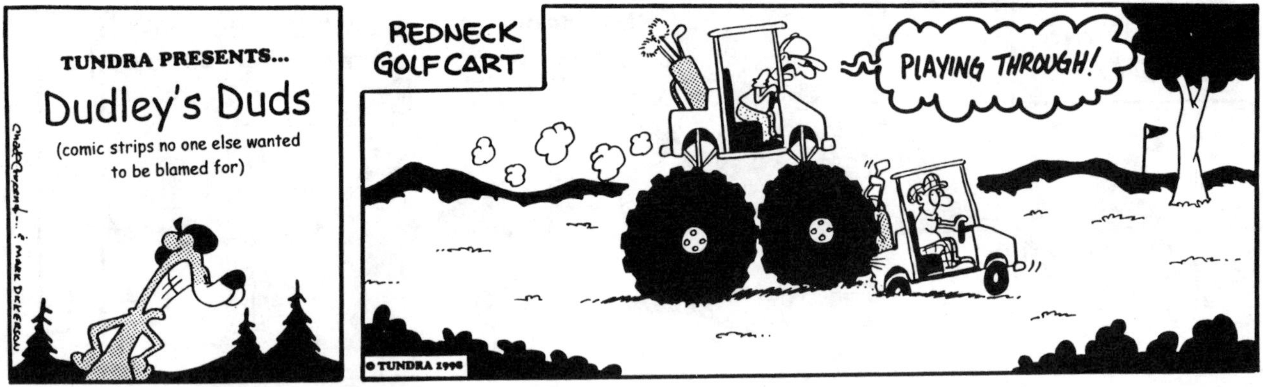
TUNDRA PRESENTS...
Dudley's Duds
(comic strips no one else wanted to be blamed for)
REDNECK GOLF CART
PLAYING THROUGH!
© TUNDRA 1998

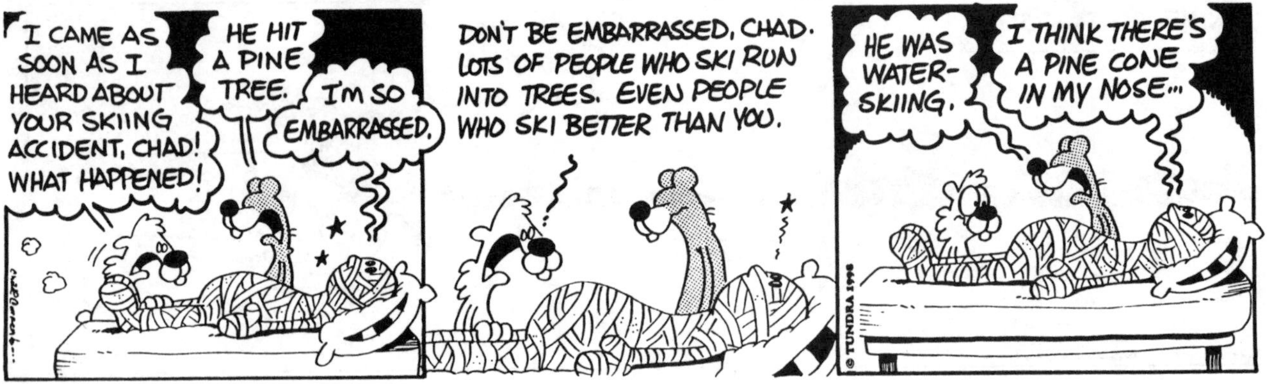
I CAME AS SOON AS I HEARD ABOUT YOUR SKIING ACCIDENT, CHAD! WHAT HAPPENED!
HE HIT A PINE TREE.
I'M SO EMBARRASSED.
DON'T BE EMBARRASSED, CHAD. LOTS OF PEOPLE WHO SKI RUN INTO TREES. EVEN PEOPLE WHO SKI BETTER THAN YOU.
HE WAS WATER-SKIING.
I THINK THERE'S A PINE CONE IN MY NOSE...
© TUNDRA 1998

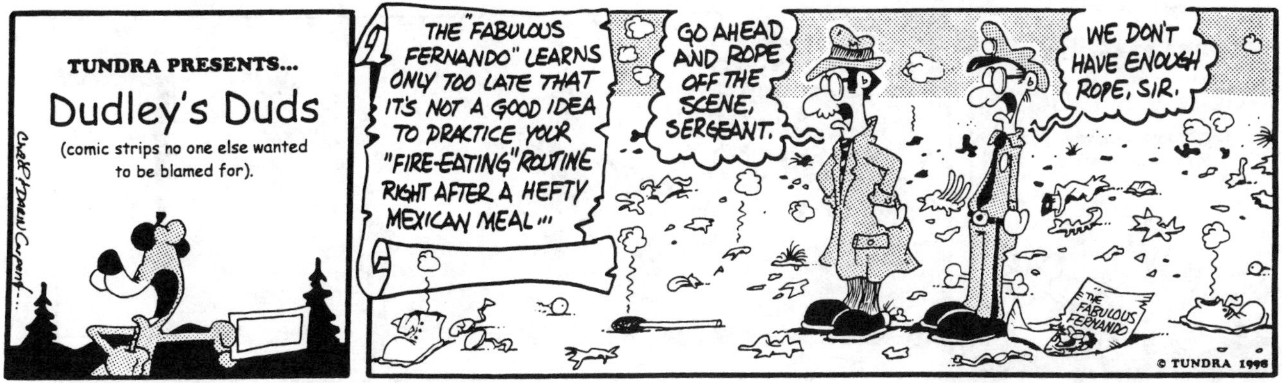
TUNDRA PRESENTS...
Dudley's Duds
(comic strips no one else wanted to be blamed for).
THE "FABULOUS FERNANDO" LEARNS ONLY TOO LATE THAT IT'S NOT A GOOD IDEA TO PRACTICE YOUR "FIRE-EATING" ROUTINE RIGHT AFTER A HEFTY MEXICAN MEAL...
GO AHEAD AND ROPE OFF THE SCENE, SERGEANT.
WE DON'T HAVE ENOUGH ROPE, SIR.
THE FABULOUS FERNANDO
© TUNDRA 1998

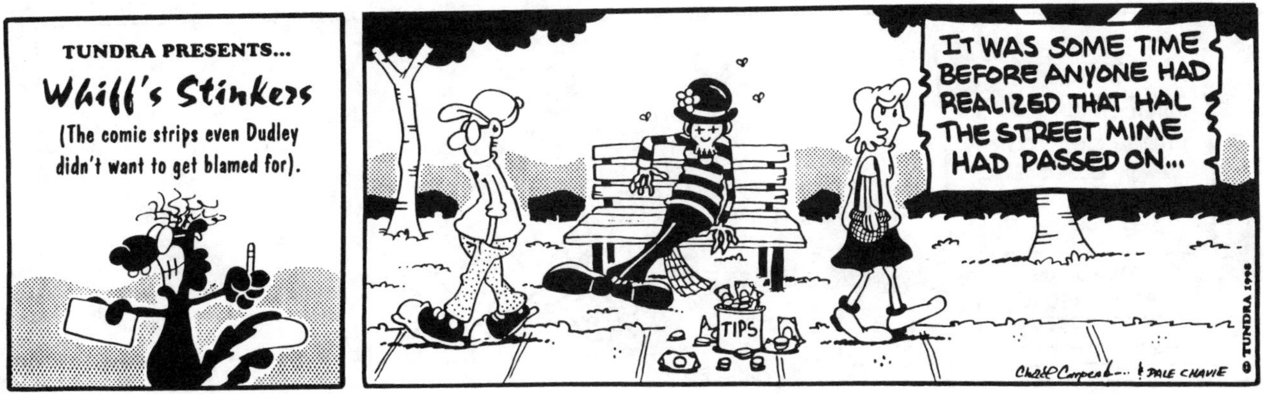
TUNDRA PRESENTS...
Whiff's Stinkers
(The comic strips even Dudley didn't want to get blamed for).
IT WAS SOME TIME BEFORE ANYONE HAD REALIZED THAT HAL THE STREET MIME HAD PASSED ON...
TIPS
© TUNDRA 1998

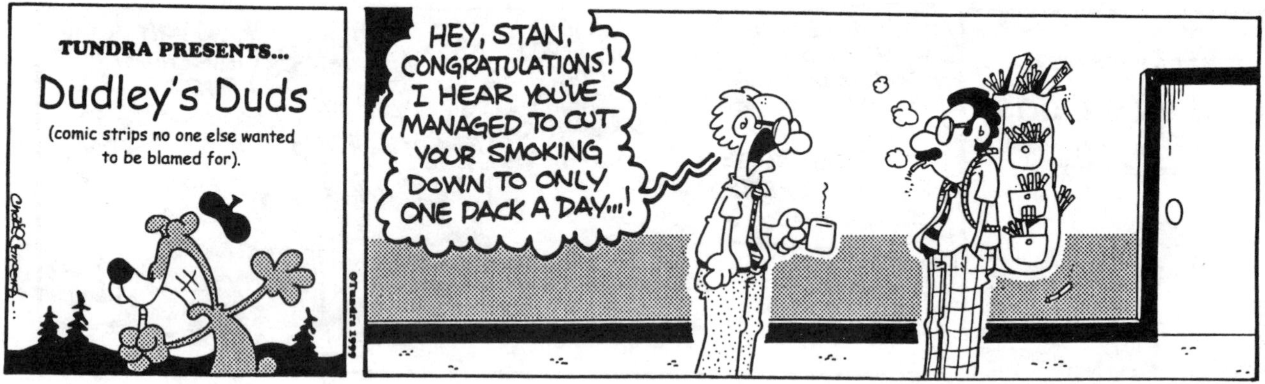
TUNDRA PRESENTS...
Dudley's Duds
(comic strips no one else wanted to be blamed for).
©Tundra 1999
HEY, STAN, CONGRATULATIONS! I HEAR YOU'VE MANAGED TO CUT YOUR SMOKING DOWN TO ONLY ONE PACK A DAY...!

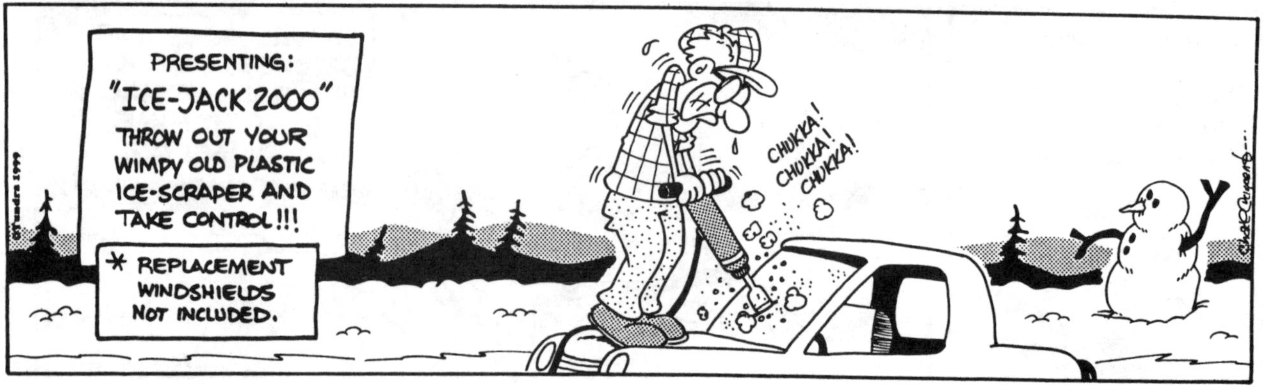
©Tundra 1999
PRESENTING:
"ICE-JACK 2000"
THROW OUT YOUR WIMPY OLD PLASTIC ICE-SCRAPER AND TAKE CONTROL!!!
* REPLACEMENT WINDSHIELDS NOT INCLUDED.
CHUKKA! CHUKKA! CHUKKA!

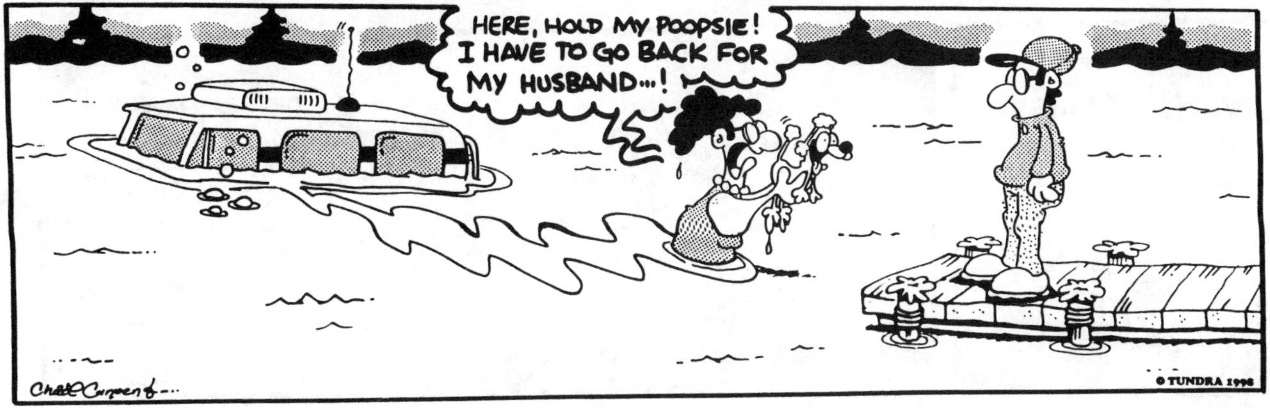
HERE, HOLD MY POOPSIE! I HAVE TO GO BACK FOR MY HUSBAND...!
© TUNDRA 1998

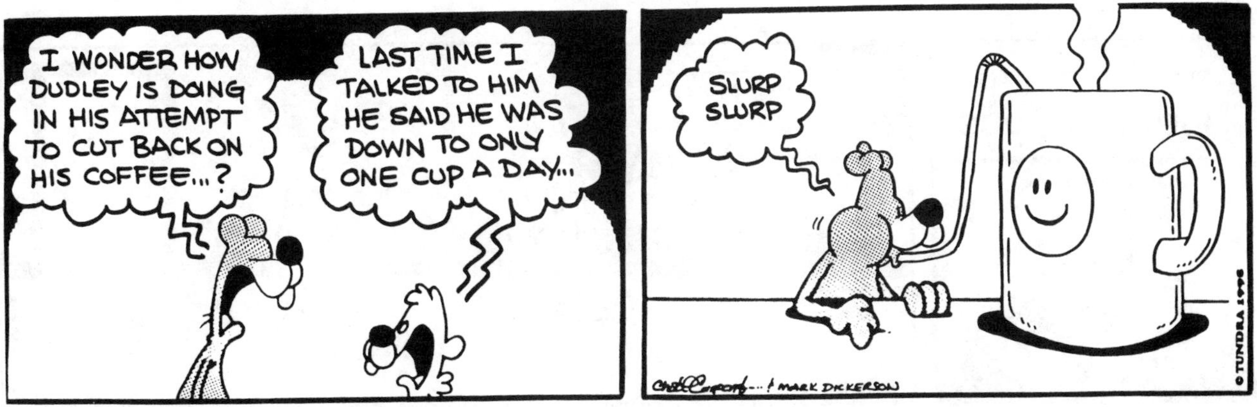
I WONDER HOW DUDLEY IS DOING IN HIS ATTEMPT TO CUT BACK ON HIS COFFEE...?
LAST TIME I TALKED TO HIM HE SAID HE WAS DOWN TO ONLY ONE CUP A DAY...
SLURP SLURP
© TUNDRA 1998
MARK DICKERSON

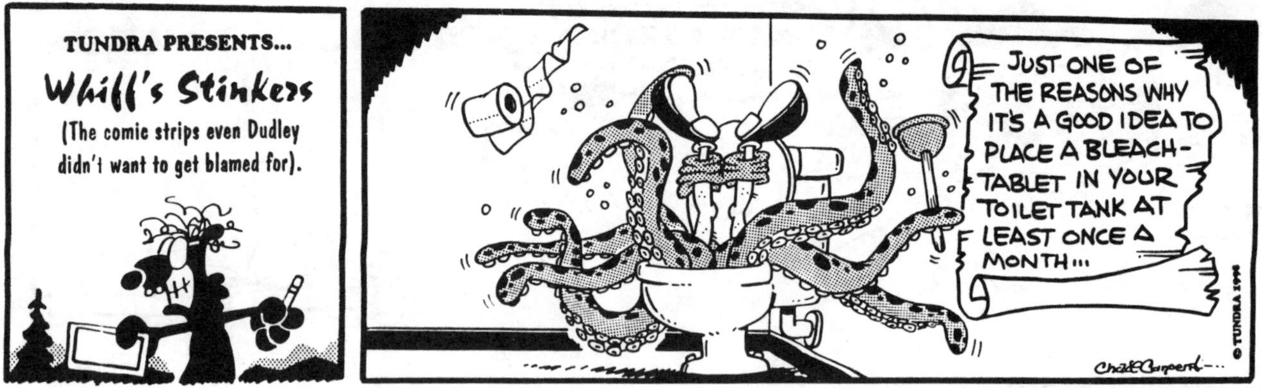
TUNDRA PRESENTS...
Whiff's Stinkers
(The comic strips even Dudley didn't want to get blamed for).
JUST ONE OF THE REASONS WHY IT'S A GOOD IDEA TO PLACE A BLEACH-TABLET IN YOUR TOILET TANK AT LEAST ONCE A MONTH...
© TUNDRA 1998
Chad Carpenter

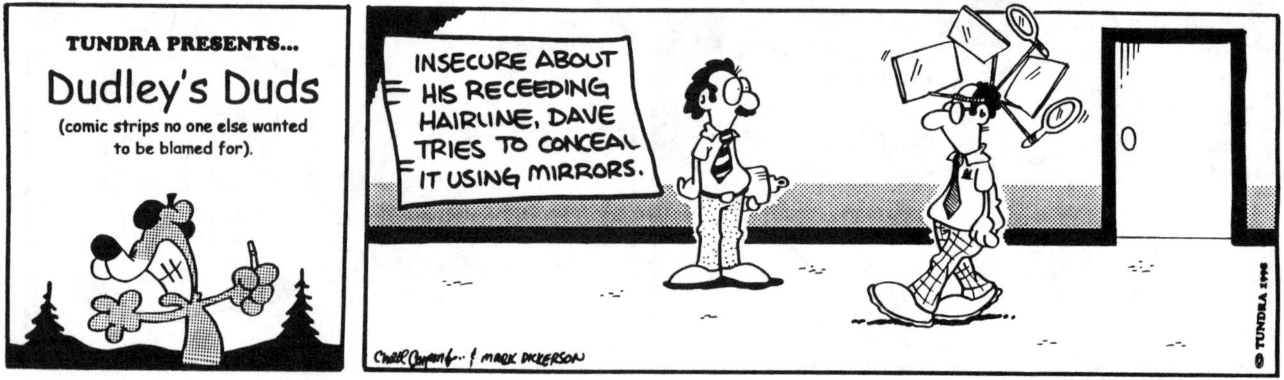
TUNDRA PRESENTS...
Dudley's Duds
(comic strips no one else wanted to be blamed for).
INSECURE ABOUT HIS RECEEDING HAIRLINE, DAVE TRIES TO CONCEAL IT USING MIRRORS.
Chad Carpenter & MARK DICKERSON
© TUNDRA 1998

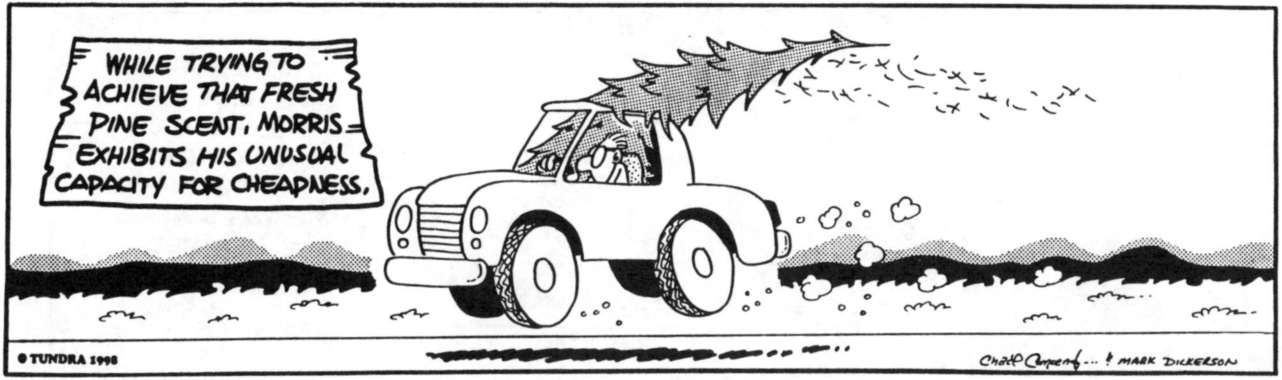
WHILE TRYING TO ACHIEVE THAT FRESH PINE SCENT, MORRIS EXHIBITS HIS UNUSUAL CAPACITY FOR CHEAPNESS.
© TUNDRA 1998
Chad Carpenter... & MARK DICKERSON

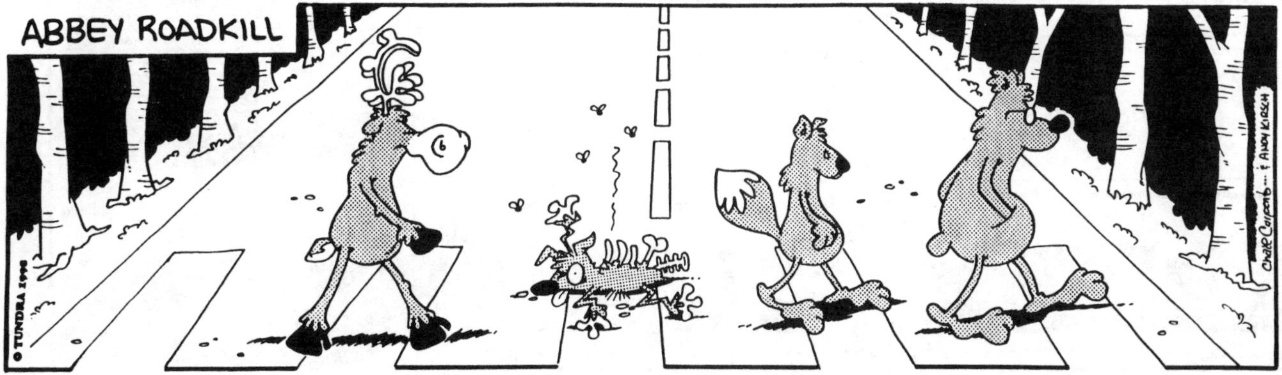
ABBEY ROADKILL
© TUNDRA 1998
Chad Carpenter... & ANDY KIRSCH

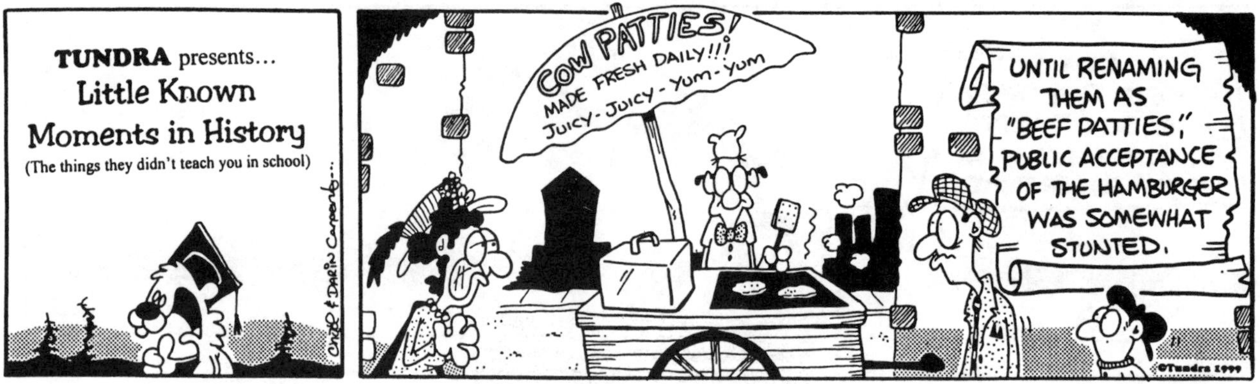
TUNDRA presents…
Little Known
Moments in History
(The things they didn't teach you in school)
COW PATTIES!
MADE FRESH DAILY!!!
Juicy - Juicy - Yum - Yum
UNTIL RENAMING THEM AS "BEEF PATTIES," PUBLIC ACCEPTANCE OF THE HAMBURGER WAS SOMEWHAT STUNTED.
©Tundra 1999

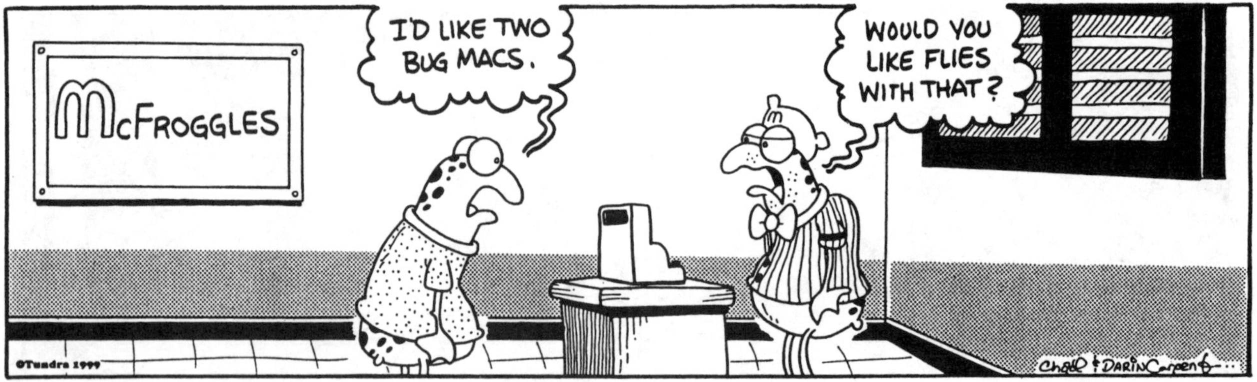
McFROGGLES
I'D LIKE TWO BUG MACS.
WOULD YOU LIKE FLIES WITH THAT?
©Tundra 1999

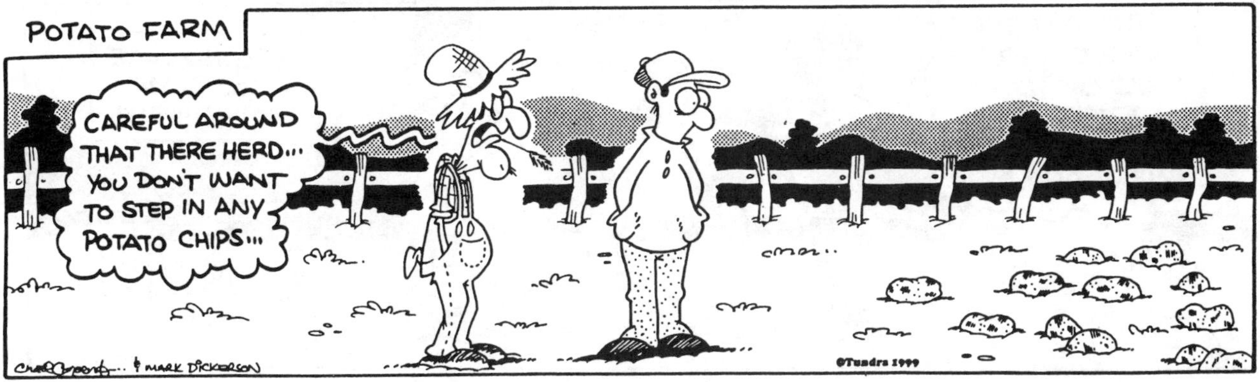
POTATO FARM
CAREFUL AROUND THAT THERE HERD... YOU DON'T WANT TO STEP IN ANY POTATO CHIPS...
©Tundra 1999

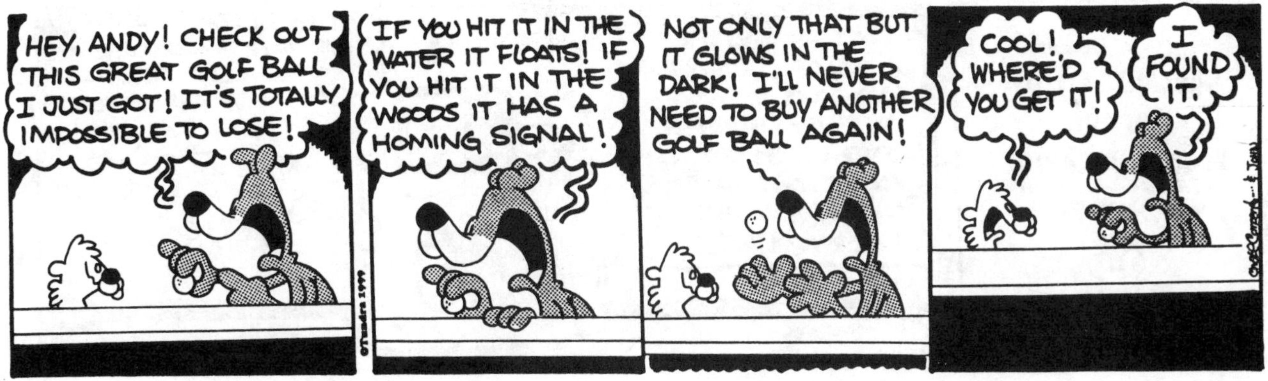
HEY, ANDY! CHECK OUT THIS GREAT GOLF BALL I JUST GOT! IT'S TOTALLY IMPOSSIBLE TO LOSE!
IF YOU HIT IT IN THE WATER IT FLOATS! IF YOU HIT IT IN THE WOODS IT HAS A HOMING SIGNAL!
NOT ONLY THAT BUT IT GLOWS IN THE DARK! I'LL NEVER NEED TO BUY ANOTHER GOLF BALL AGAIN!
COOL! WHERE'D YOU GET IT!
I FOUND IT.
©Tundra 1999

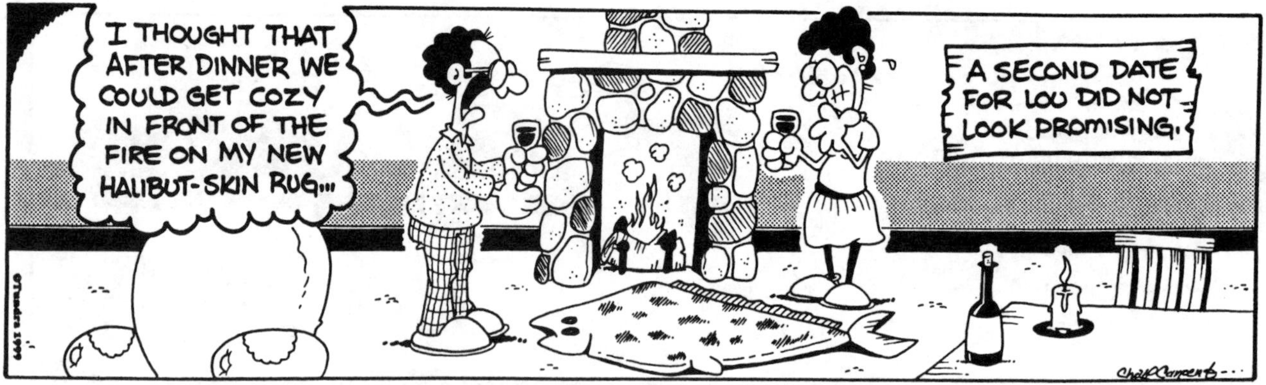

I THOUGHT THAT AFTER DINNER WE COULD GET COZY IN FRONT OF THE FIRE ON MY NEW HALIBUT-SKIN RUG...
A SECOND DATE FOR LOU DID NOT LOOK PROMISING.
©Tundra 1999

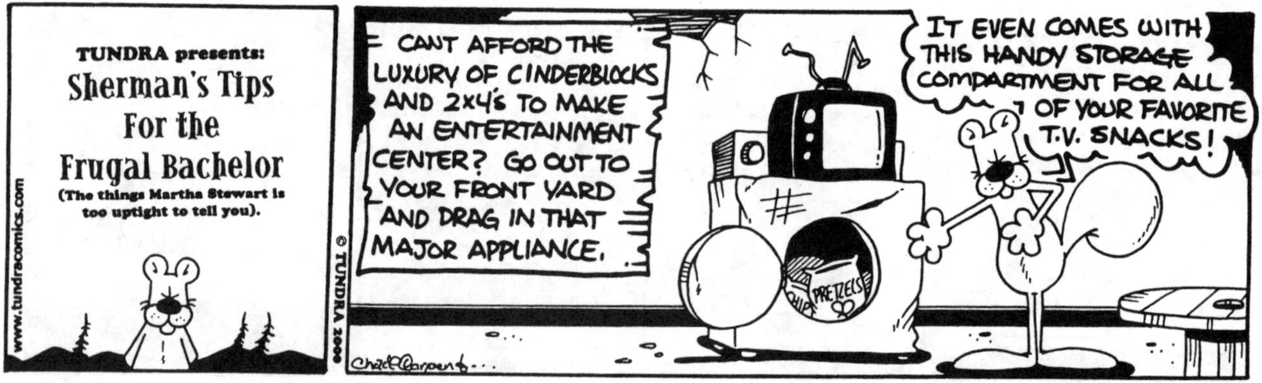

TUNDRA presents:
Sherman's Tips For the Frugal Bachelor
(The things Martha Stewart is too uptight to tell you).
www.tundracomics.com
© TUNDRA 2000
CANT AFFORD THE LUXURY OF CINDERBLOCKS AND 2x4's TO MAKE AN ENTERTAINMENT CENTER? GO OUT TO YOUR FRONT YARD AND DRAG IN THAT MAJOR APPLIANCE.
IT EVEN COMES WITH THIS HANDY STORAGE COMPARTMENT FOR ALL OF YOUR FAVORITE T.V. SNACKS!
PRETZELS

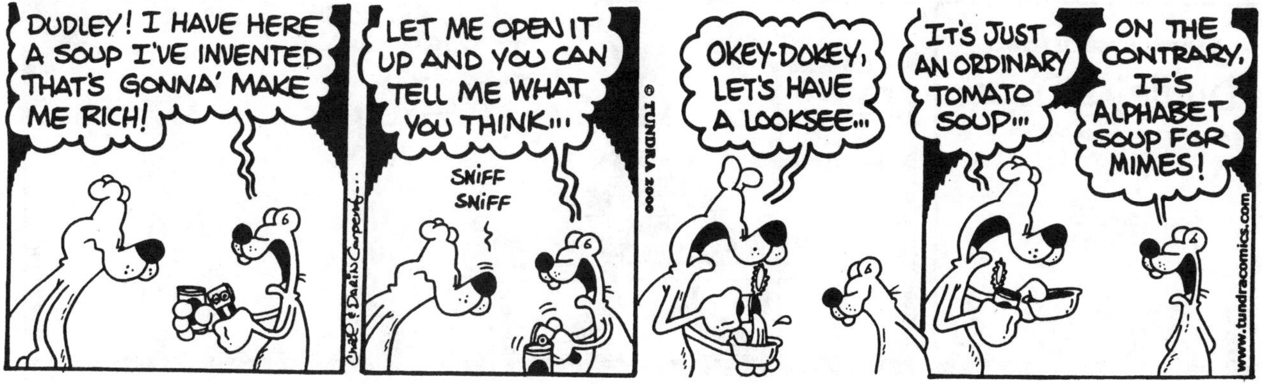
DUDLEY! I HAVE HERE A SOUP I'VE INVENTED THAT'S GONNA' MAKE ME RICH!
LET ME OPEN IT UP AND YOU CAN TELL ME WHAT YOU THINK...
SNIFF SNIFF
OKEY-DOKEY, LET'S HAVE A LOOKSEE...
IT'S JUST AN ORDINARY TOMATO SOUP...
ON THE CONTRARY. IT'S ALPHABET SOUP FOR MIMES!
© TUNDRA 2000
www.tundracomics.com

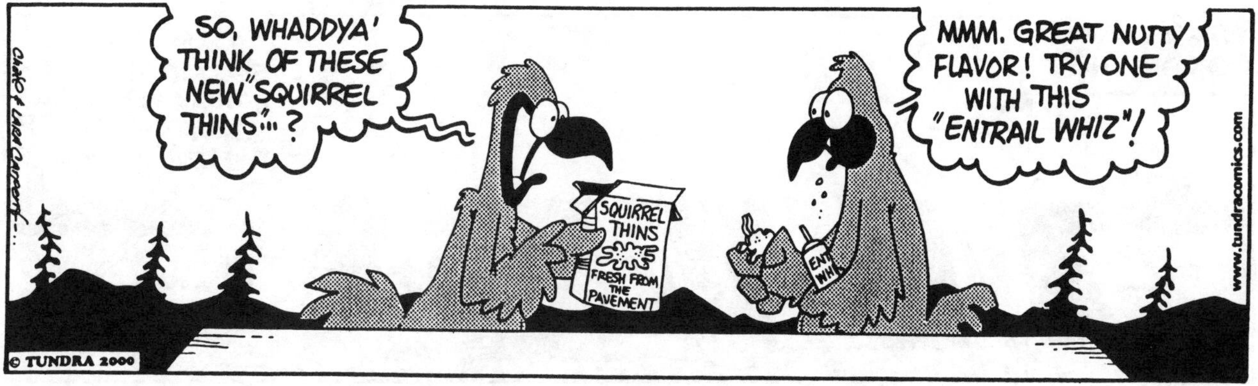
SO, WHADDYA' THINK OF THESE NEW "SQUIRREL THINS"... ?
MMM. GREAT NUTTY FLAVOR! TRY ONE WITH THIS "ENTRAIL WHIZ"!
SQUIRREL THINS
FRESH FROM THE PAVEMENT
© TUNDRA 2000
www.tundracomics.com

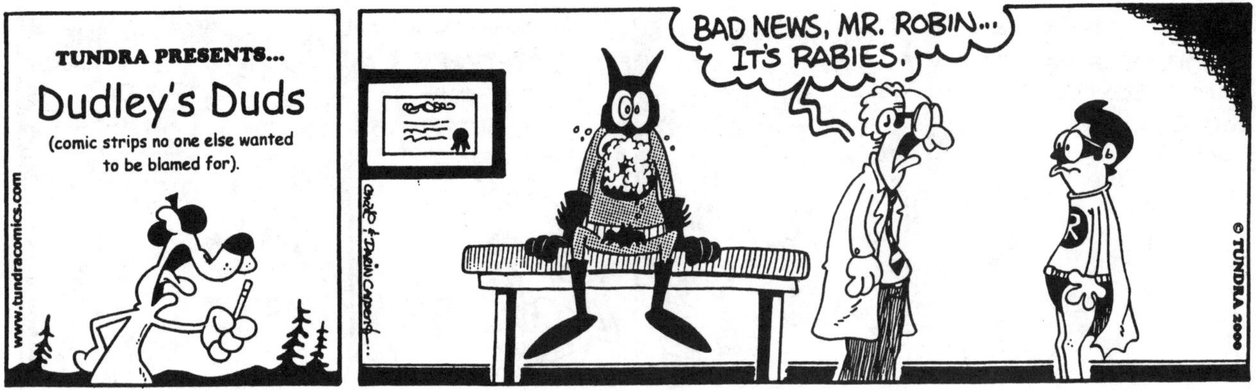
TUNDRA PRESENTS...
Dudley's Duds
(comic strips no one else wanted to be blamed for).
www.tundracomics.com
BAD NEWS, MR. ROBIN... IT'S RABIES.
© TUNDRA 2000

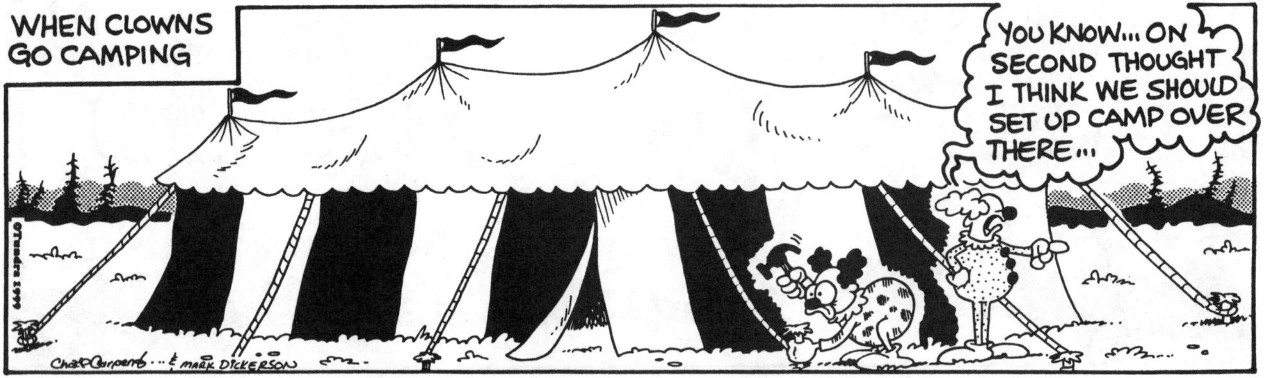
WHEN CLOWNS GO CAMPING
YOU KNOW... ON SECOND THOUGHT I THINK WE SHOULD SET UP CAMP OVER THERE...
©Tundra 1999

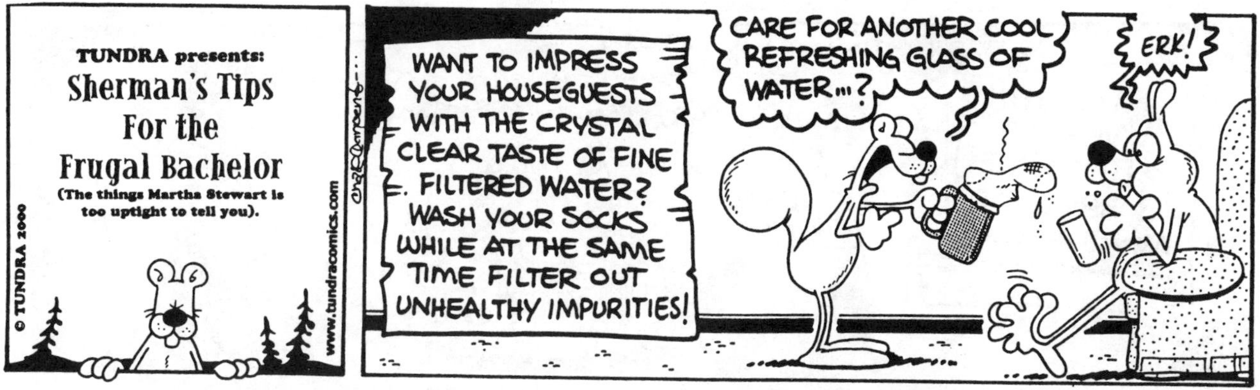
TUNDRA presents:
Sherman's Tips For the Frugal Bachelor
(The things Martha Stewart is too uptight to tell you).
© TUNDRA 2000
www.tundracomics.com
WANT TO IMPRESS YOUR HOUSEGUESTS WITH THE CRYSTAL CLEAR TASTE OF FINE FILTERED WATER? WASH YOUR SOCKS WHILE AT THE SAME TIME FILTER OUT UNHEALTHY IMPURITIES!
CARE FOR ANOTHER COOL REFRESHING GLASS OF WATER...?
ERK!

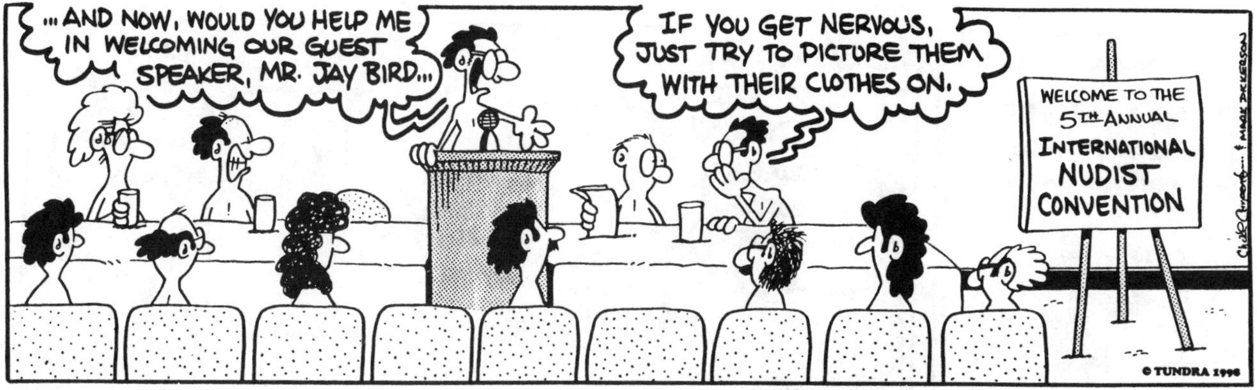
...AND NOW, WOULD YOU HELP ME IN WELCOMING OUR GUEST SPEAKER, MR. JAY BIRD...
IF YOU GET NERVOUS, JUST TRY TO PICTURE THEM WITH THEIR CLOTHES ON.
WELCOME TO THE 5TH ANNUAL INTERNATIONAL NUDIST CONVENTION
© TUNDRA 1998

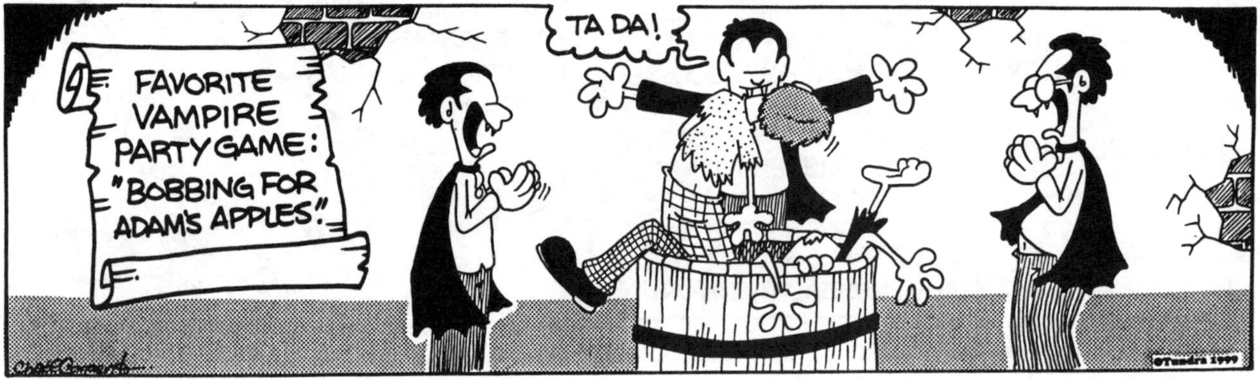
FAVORITE VAMPIRE PARTY GAME: "BOBBING FOR ADAM'S APPLES."
TA DA!
©Tundra 1999

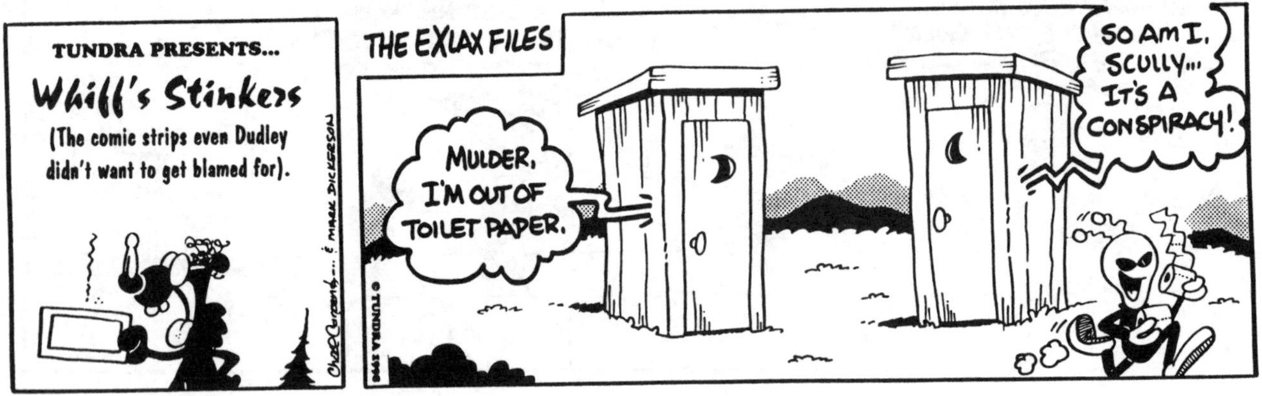
TUNDRA PRESENTS...
Whiff's Stinkers
(The comic strips even Dudley didn't want to get blamed for).
& MARK DICKERSON
© TUNDRA 1998
THE EXLAX FILES
MULDER, I'M OUT OF TOILET PAPER.
SO AM I, SCULLY... IT'S A CONSPIRACY!

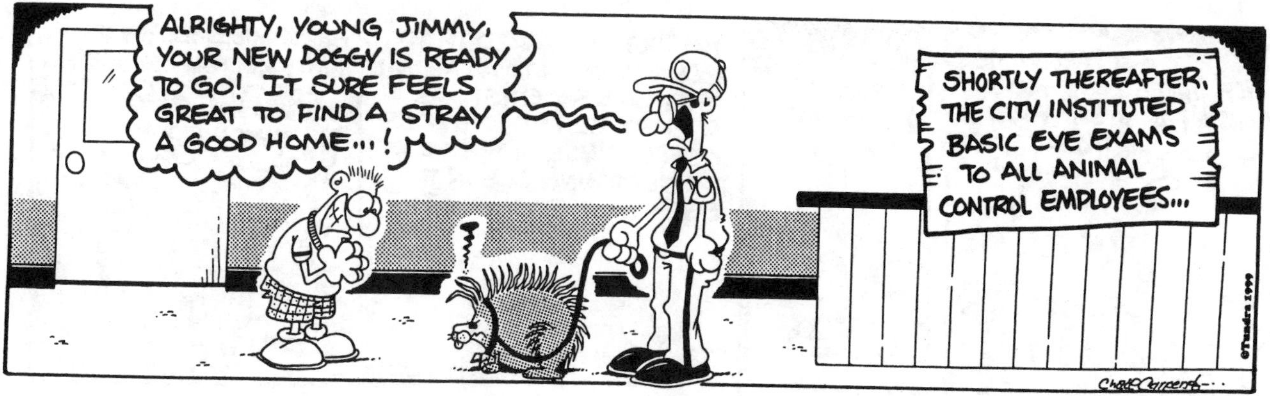
ALRIGHTY, YOUNG JIMMY, YOUR NEW DOGGY IS READY TO GO! IT SURE FEELS GREAT TO FIND A STRAY A GOOD HOME...!
SHORTLY THEREAFTER, THE CITY INSTITUTED BASIC EYE EXAMS TO ALL ANIMAL CONTROL EMPLOYEES...
©Tundra 1999

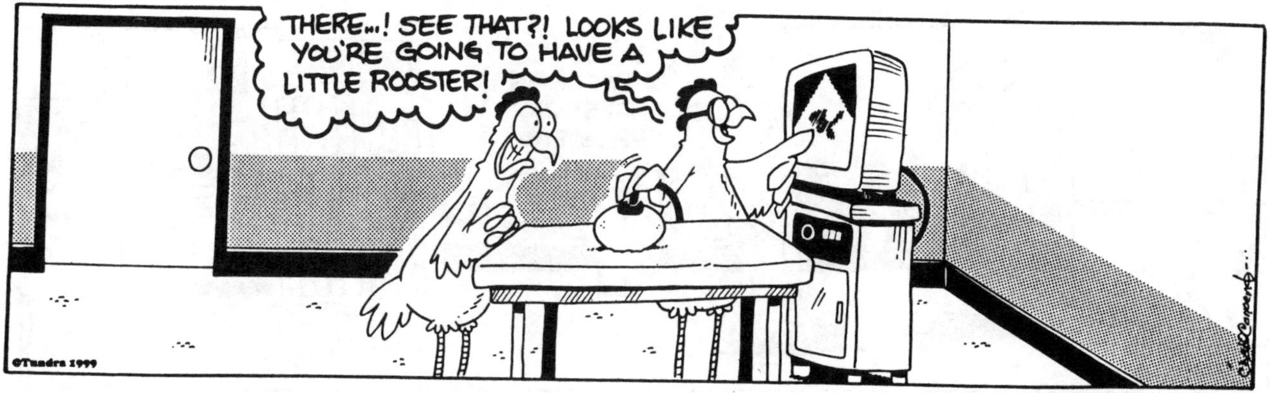
THERE...! SEE THAT?! LOOKS LIKE YOU'RE GOING TO HAVE A LITTLE ROOSTER!
©Tundra 1999

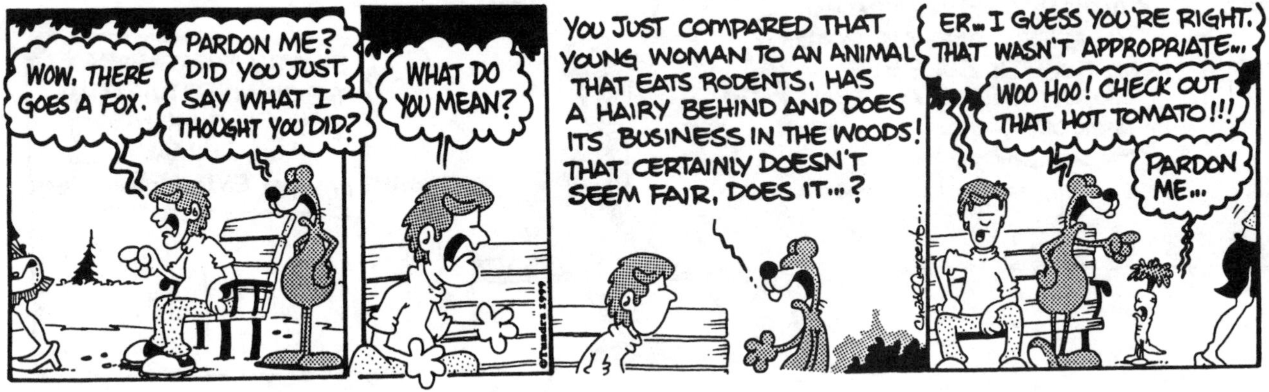
WOW. THERE GOES A FOX.
PARDON ME? DID YOU JUST SAY WHAT I THOUGHT YOU DID?
WHAT DO YOU MEAN?
YOU JUST COMPARED THAT YOUNG WOMAN TO AN ANIMAL THAT EATS RODENTS, HAS A HAIRY BEHIND AND DOES ITS BUSINESS IN THE WOODS! THAT CERTAINLY DOESN'T SEEM FAIR, DOES IT...?
ER... I GUESS YOU'RE RIGHT. THAT WASN'T APPROPRIATE...
WOO HOO! CHECK OUT THAT HOT TOMATO!!!
PARDON ME...
©Tundra 1999

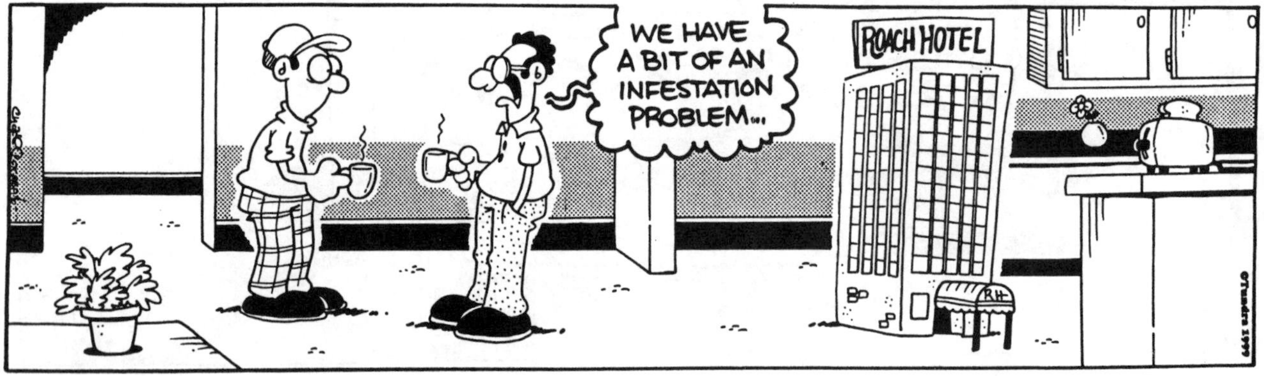
WE HAVE A BIT OF AN INFESTATION PROBLEM...
ROACH HOTEL
RH
©Tundra 1999

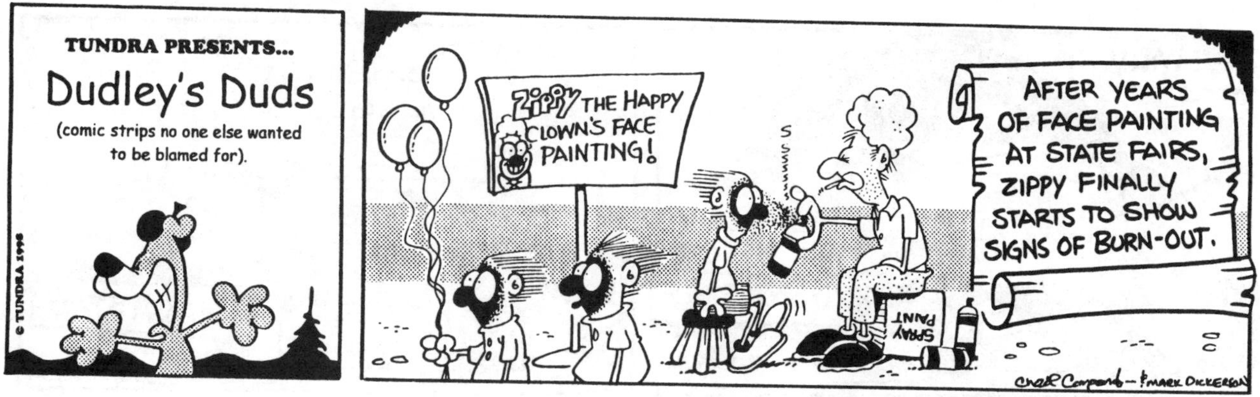
TUNDRA PRESENTS...
Dudley's Duds
(comic strips no one else wanted to be blamed for).
© TUNDRA 1998
ZIPPY THE HAPPY CLOWN'S FACE PAINTING!
SPRAY PAINT
AFTER YEARS OF FACE PAINTING AT STATE FAIRS, ZIPPY FINALLY STARTS TO SHOW SIGNS OF BURN-OUT.
MARK DICKERSON

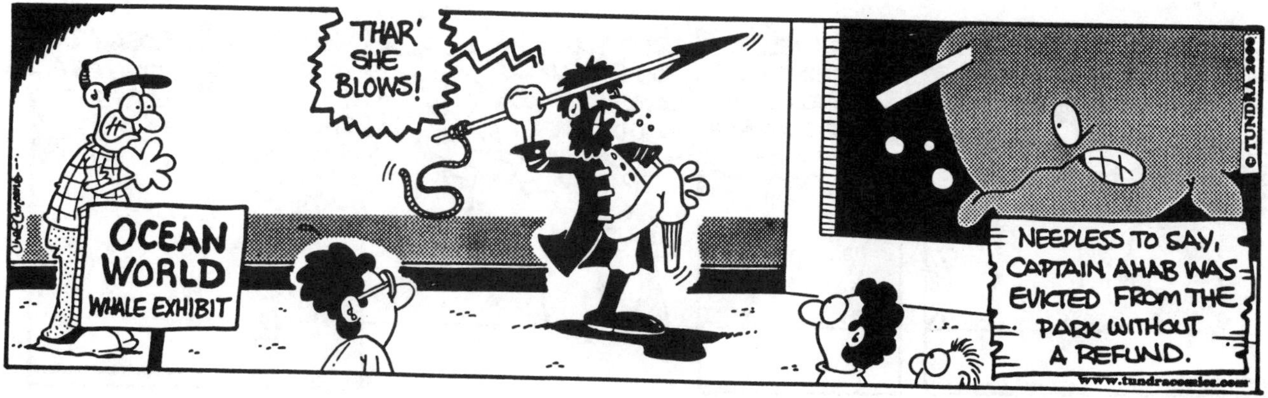
THAR' SHE BLOWS!
OCEAN WORLD
WHALE EXHIBIT
© TUNDRA 2000
NEEDLESS TO SAY, CAPTAIN AHAB WAS EVICTED FROM THE PARK WITHOUT A REFUND.
www.tundracomics.com

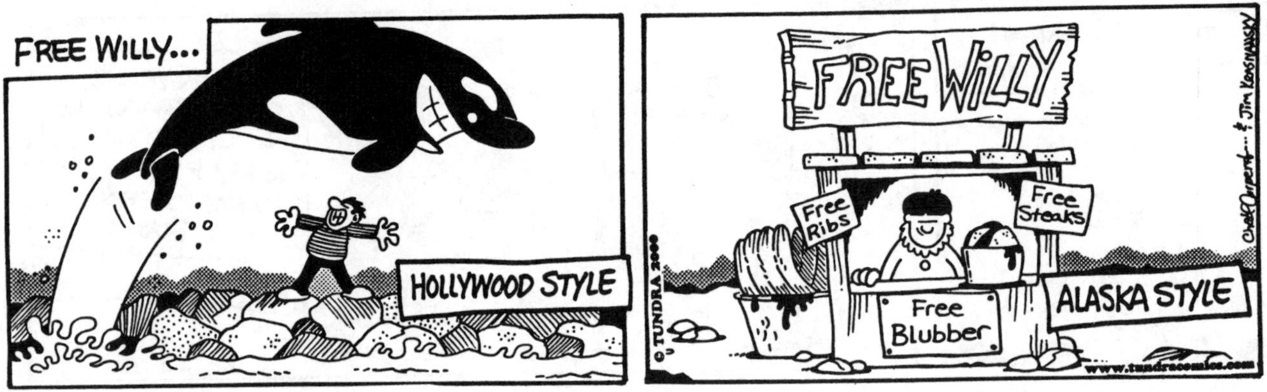

FREE WILLY...
HOLLYWOOD STYLE
FREE WILLY
Free Ribs
Free Steaks
Free Blubber
ALASKA STYLE
© TUNDRA 2000
www.tundracomics.com

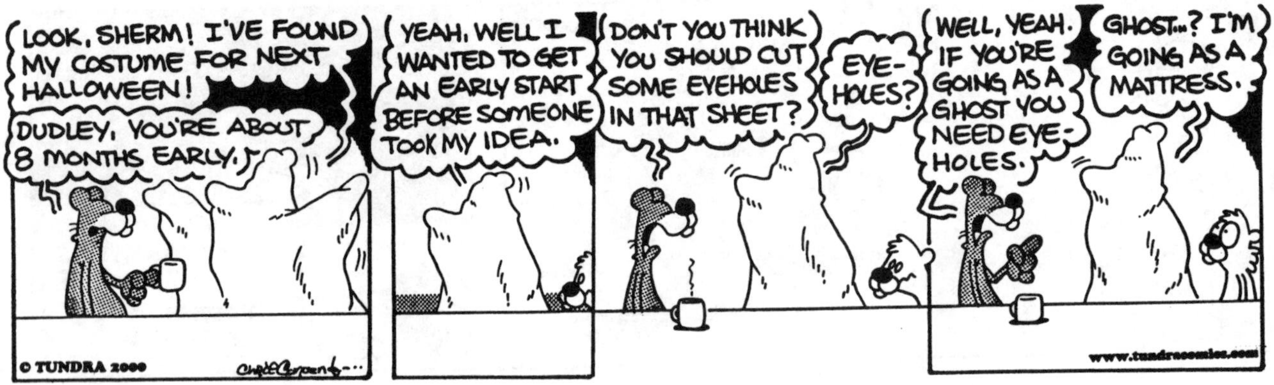

LOOK, SHERM! I'VE FOUND MY COSTUME FOR NEXT HALLOWEEN!
DUDLEY, YOU'RE ABOUT 8 MONTHS EARLY.
YEAH, WELL I WANTED TO GET AN EARLY START BEFORE SOMEONE TOOK MY IDEA.
DON'T YOU THINK YOU SHOULD CUT SOME EYEHOLES IN THAT SHEET?
EYE-HOLES?
WELL, YEAH. IF YOU'RE GOING AS A GHOST YOU NEED EYE-HOLES.
GHOST...? I'M GOING AS A MATTRESS.
© TUNDRA 2000
www.tundracomics.com

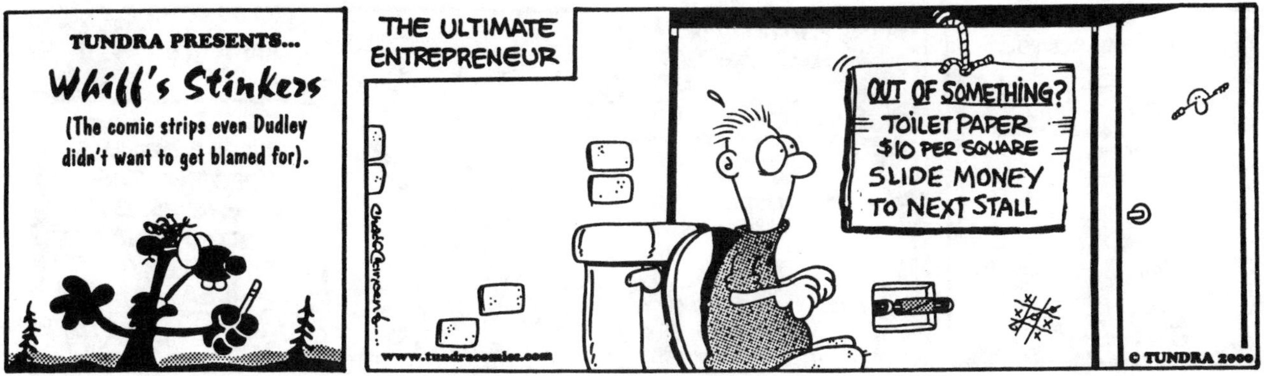
TUNDRA PRESENTS...
Whiff's Stinkers
(The comic strips even Dudley didn't want to get blamed for).
THE ULTIMATE ENTREPRENEUR
OUT OF SOMETHING?
TOILET PAPER
$10 PER SQUARE
SLIDE MONEY
TO NEXT STALL
www.tundracomics.com
© TUNDRA 2000

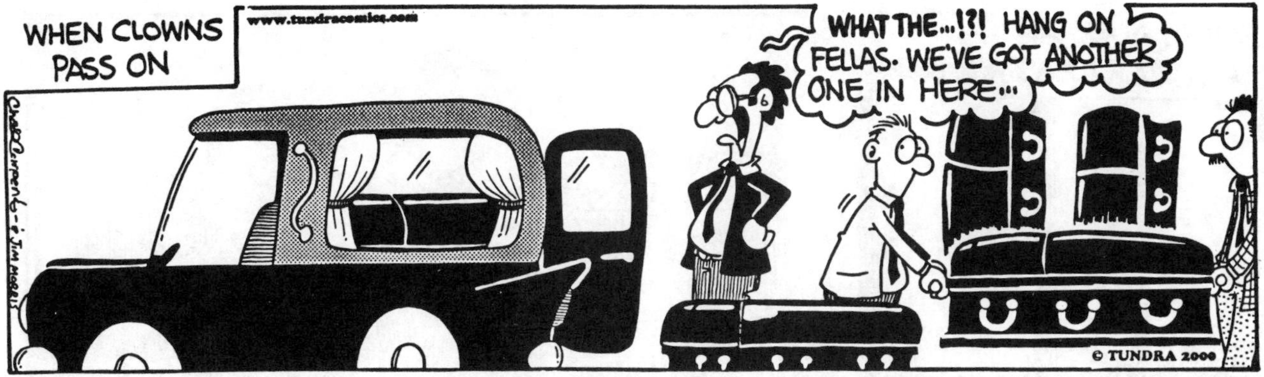
WHEN CLOWNS PASS ON
www.tundracomics.com
WHAT THE...!?! HANG ON FELLAS. WE'VE GOT ANOTHER ONE IN HERE...
© TUNDRA 2000

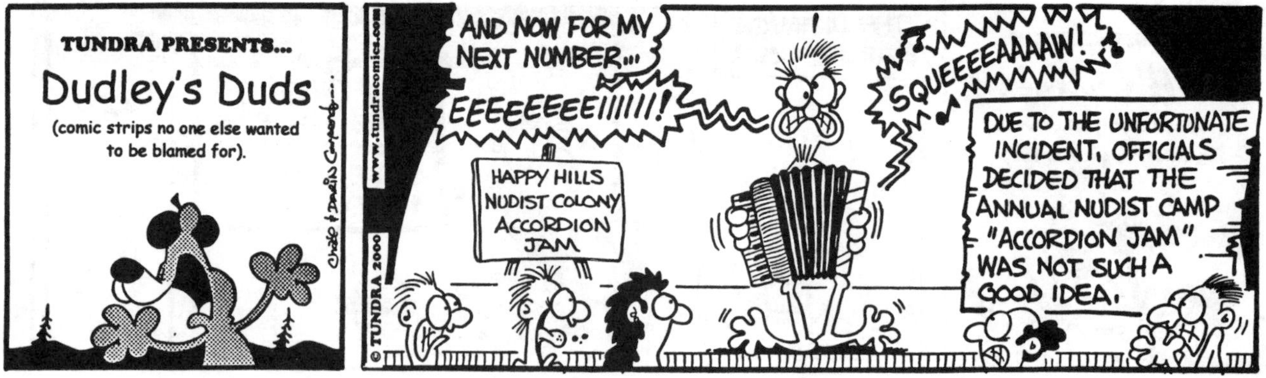
TUNDRA PRESENTS...
Dudley's Duds
(comic strips no one else wanted to be blamed for).
www.tundracomics.com
© TUNDRA 2000
AND NOW FOR MY NEXT NUMBER...
EEEEEEEEIIIIII!
HAPPY HILLS NUDIST COLONY ACCORDION JAM
SQUEEEEAAAAAW!
DUE TO THE UNFORTUNATE INCIDENT, OFFICIALS DECIDED THAT THE ANNUAL NUDIST CAMP "ACCORDION JAM" WAS NOT SUCH A GOOD IDEA.

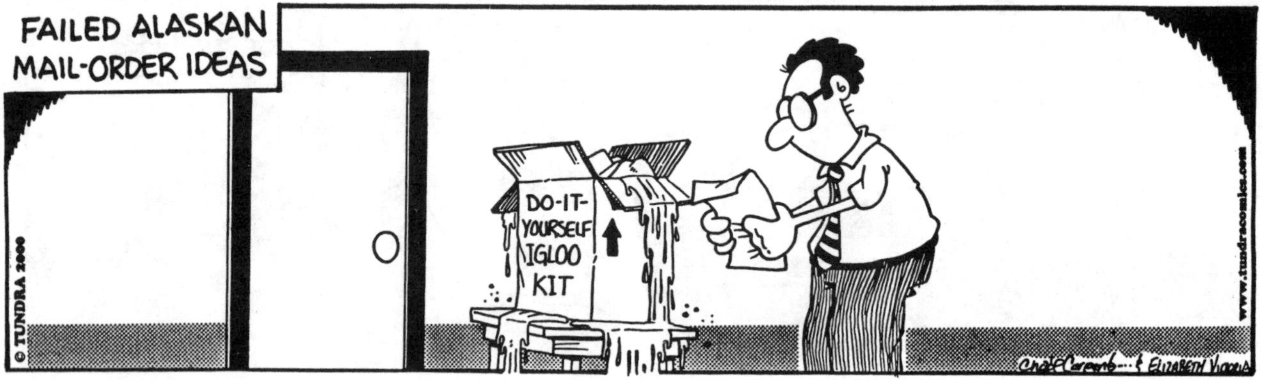
FAILED ALASKAN MAIL-ORDER IDEAS
DO-IT-YOURSELF IGLOO KIT
© TUNDRA 2000
www.tundracomics.com

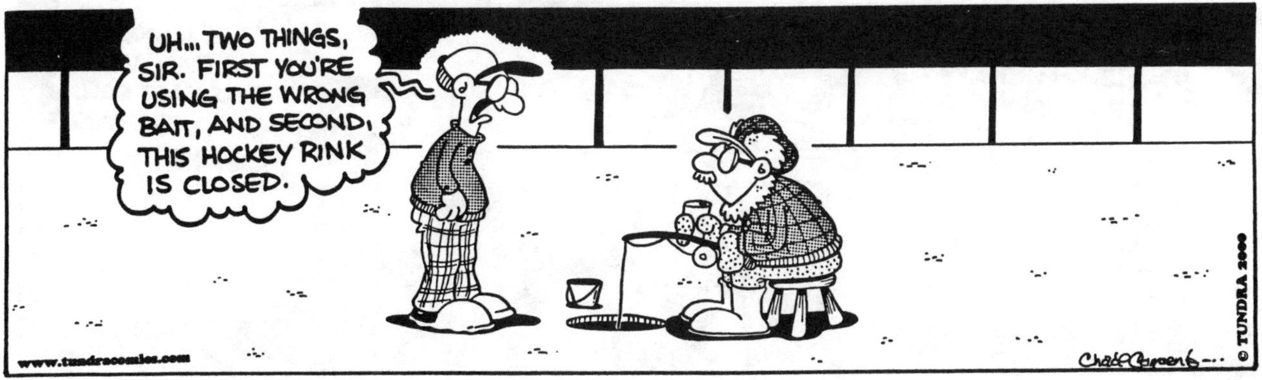
UH... TWO THINGS, SIR. FIRST YOU'RE USING THE WRONG BAIT, AND SECOND, THIS HOCKEY RINK IS CLOSED.
www.tundracomics.com
© TUNDRA 2000

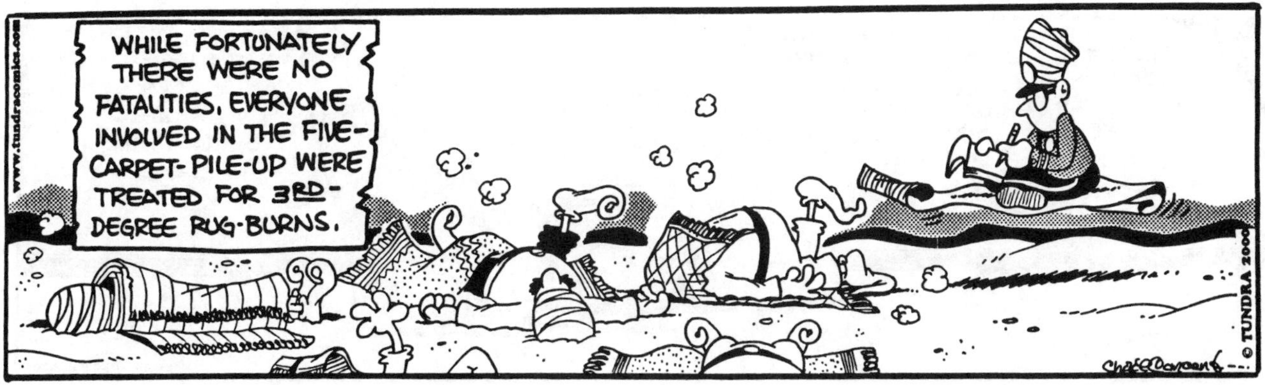
WHILE FORTUNATELY THERE WERE NO FATALITIES, EVERYONE INVOLVED IN THE FIVE-CARPET-PILE-UP WERE TREATED FOR 3RD-DEGREE RUG-BURNS.
www.tundracomics.com
© TUNDRA 2000

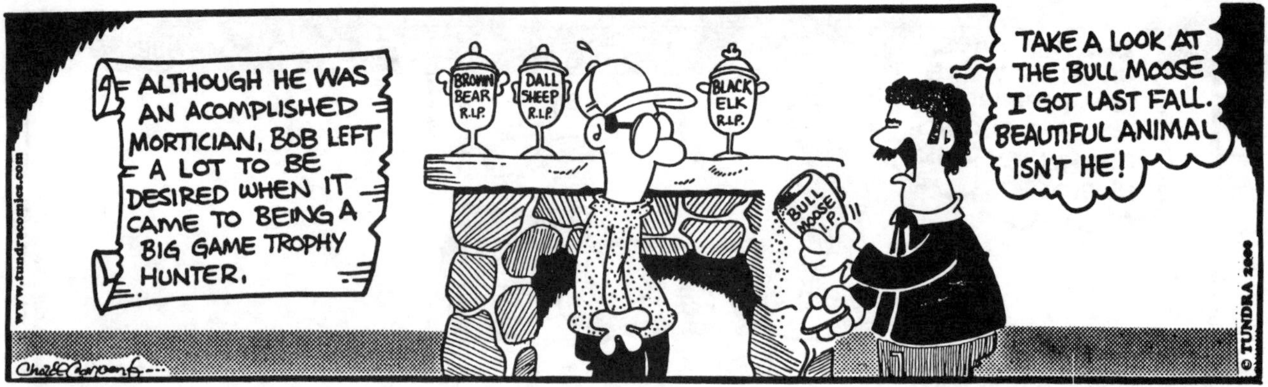
ALTHOUGH HE WAS AN ACOMPLISHED MORTICIAN, BOB LEFT A LOT TO BE DESIRED WHEN IT CAME TO BEING A BIG GAME TROPHY HUNTER.
BROWN BEAR R.I.P.
DALL SHEEP R.I.P.
BLACK ELK R.I.P.
BULL MOOSE R.I.P.
TAKE A LOOK AT THE BULL MOOSE I GOT LAST FALL. BEAUTIFUL ANIMAL ISN'T HE!
www.tundracomics.com
© TUNDRA 2000

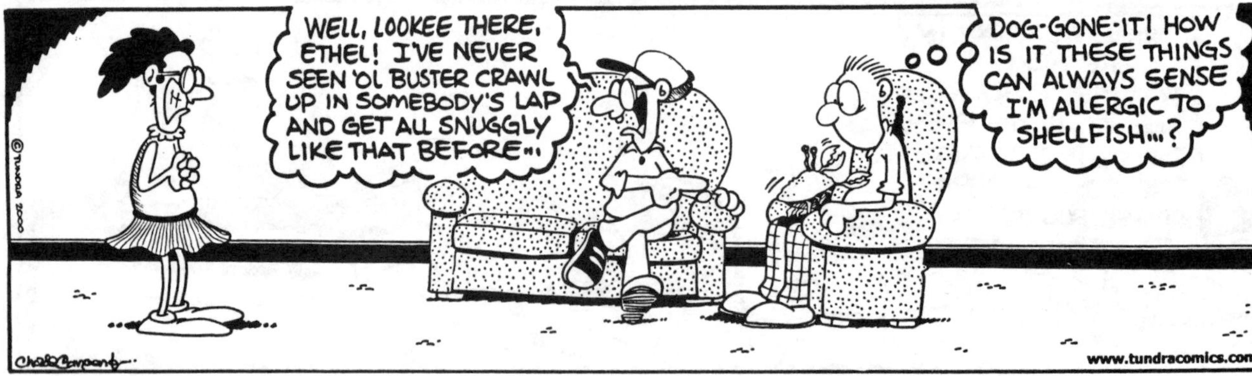
WELL, LOOKEE THERE, ETHEL! I'VE NEVER SEEN 'OL BUSTER CRAWL UP IN SOMEBODY'S LAP AND GET ALL SNUGGLY LIKE THAT BEFORE...
DOG-GONE-IT! HOW IS IT THESE THINGS CAN ALWAYS SENSE I'M ALLERGIC TO SHELLFISH...?
www.tundracomics.com

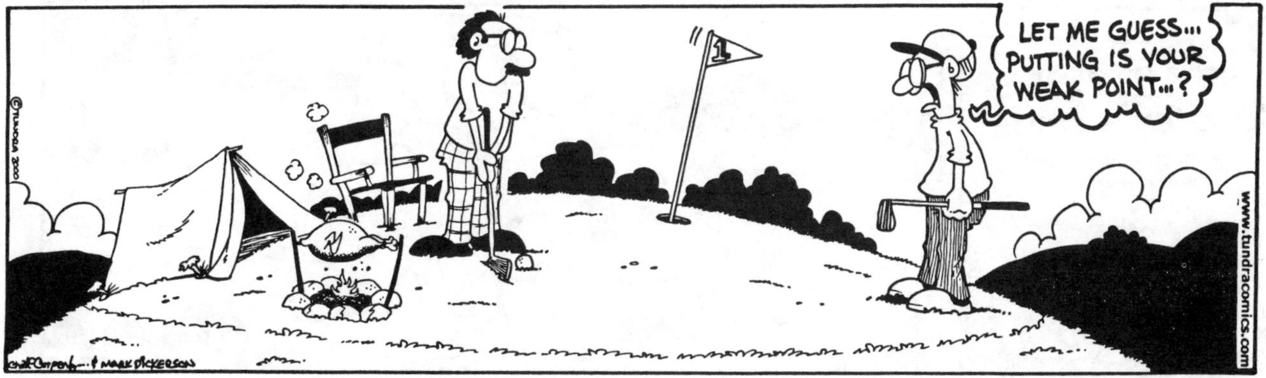
LET ME GUESS... PUTTING IS YOUR WEAK POINT...?
1
www.tundracomics.com

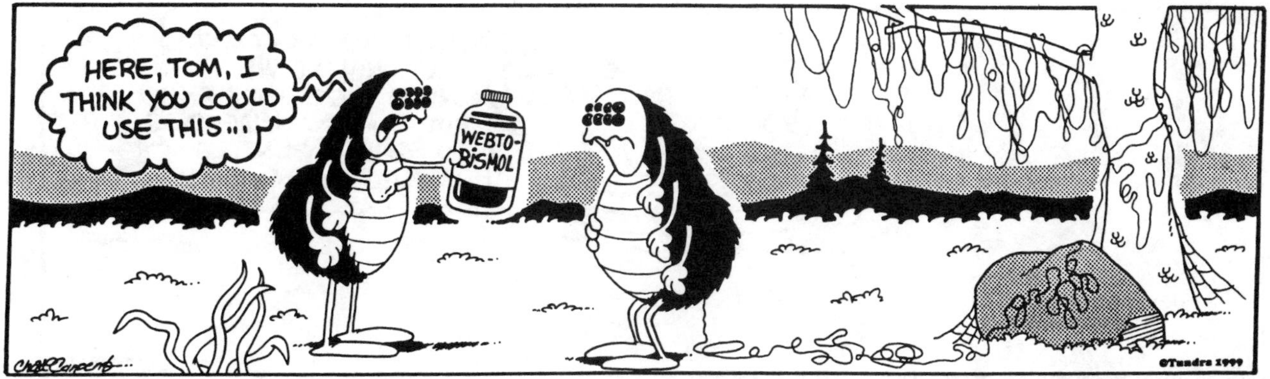
HERE, TOM, I THINK YOU COULD USE THIS...
WEBTO-BISMOL
©Tundra 1999

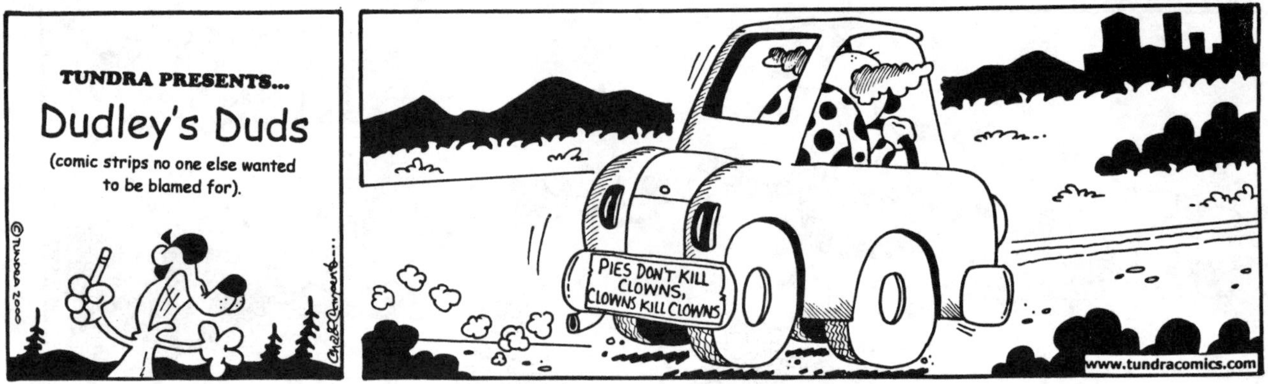
TUNDRA PRESENTS...
Dudley's Duds
(comic strips no one else wanted to be blamed for).
© TUNDRA 2000
Chad Carpenter...
PIES DON'T KILL CLOWNS, CLOWNS KILL CLOWNS
www.tundracomics.com

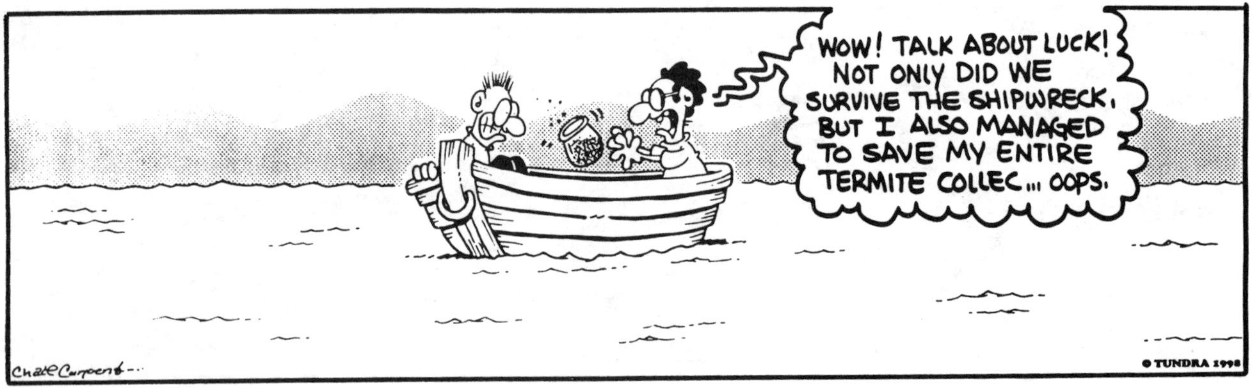
WOW! TALK ABOUT LUCK! NOT ONLY DID WE SURVIVE THE SHIPWRECK, BUT I ALSO MANAGED TO SAVE MY ENTIRE TERMITE COLLEC... OOPS.
Chad Carpenter...
© TUNDRA 1998

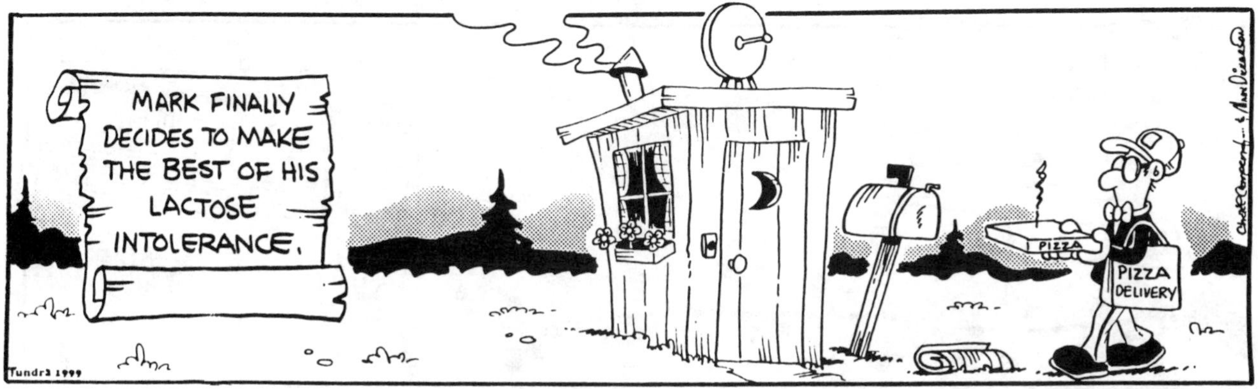
MARK FINALLY DECIDES TO MAKE THE BEST OF HIS LACTOSE INTOLERANCE.
PIZZA
PIZZA DELIVERY
Tundra 1999

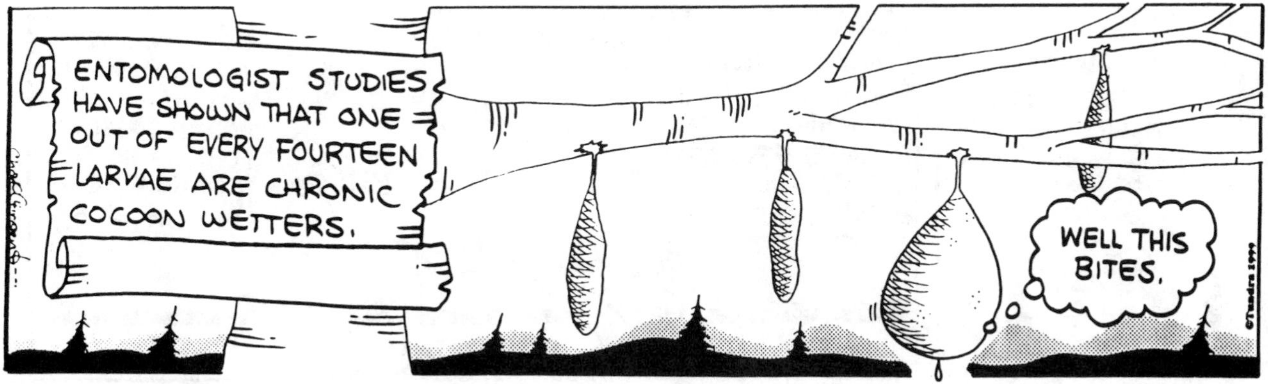
ENTOMOLOGIST STUDIES HAVE SHOWN THAT ONE OUT OF EVERY FOURTEEN LARVAE ARE CHRONIC COCOON WETTERS.
WELL THIS BITES.
©Tundra 1999

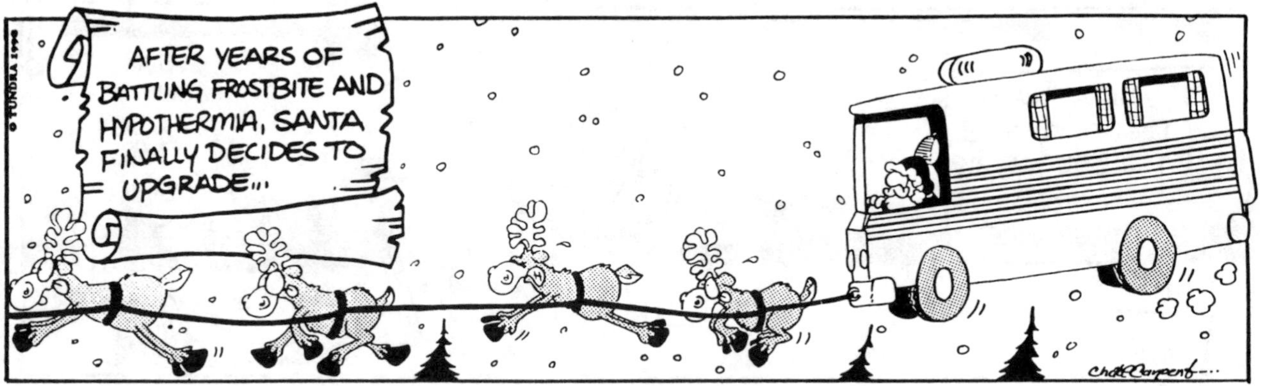
AFTER YEARS OF BATTLING FROSTBITE AND HYPOTHERMIA, SANTA FINALLY DECIDES TO UPGRADE...

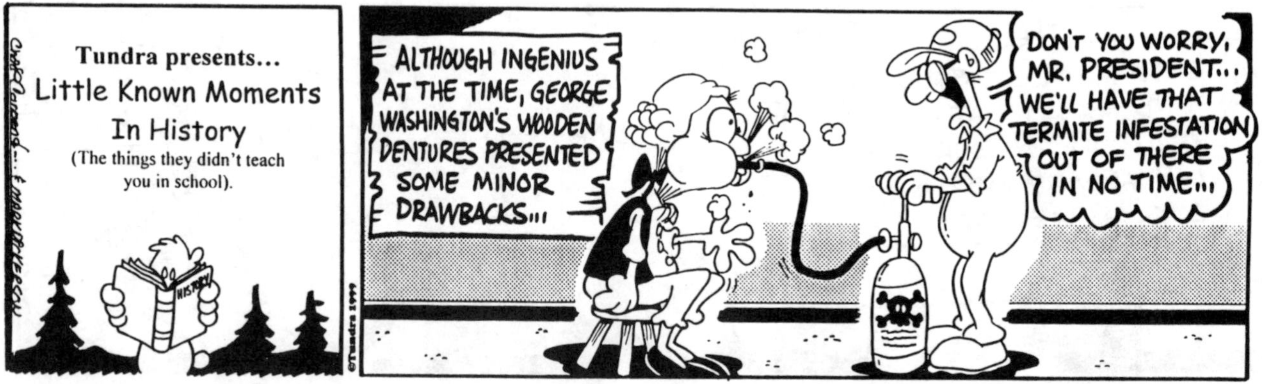
Tundra presents...
Little Known Moments In History
(The things they didn't teach you in school).
HISTORY
ALTHOUGH INGENIUS AT THE TIME, GEORGE WASHINGTON'S WOODEN DENTURES PRESENTED SOME MINOR DRAWBACKS...
DON'T YOU WORRY, MR. PRESIDENT... WE'LL HAVE THAT TERMITE INFESTATION OUT OF THERE IN NO TIME...

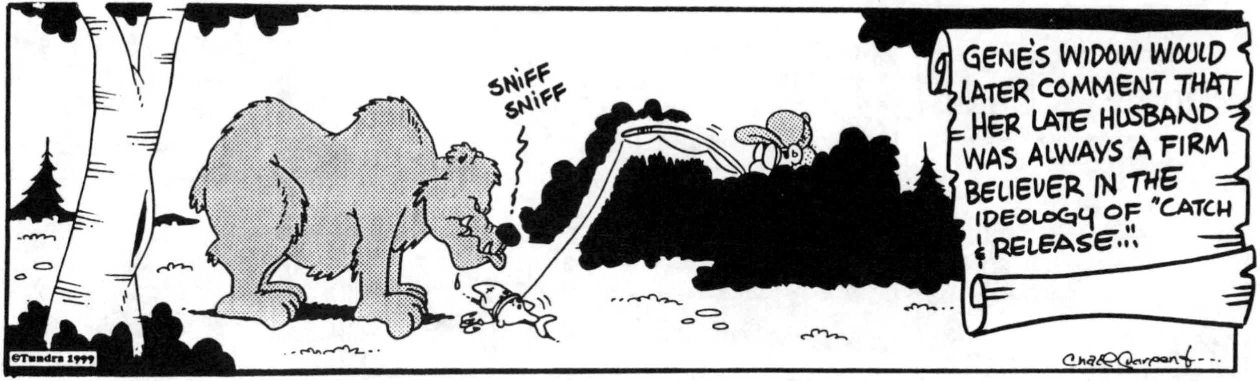
SNIFF
SNIFF
GENE'S WIDOW WOULD LATER COMMENT THAT HER LATE HUSBAND WAS ALWAYS A FIRM BELIEVER IN THE IDEOLOGY OF "CATCH & RELEASE..."
©Tundra 1999

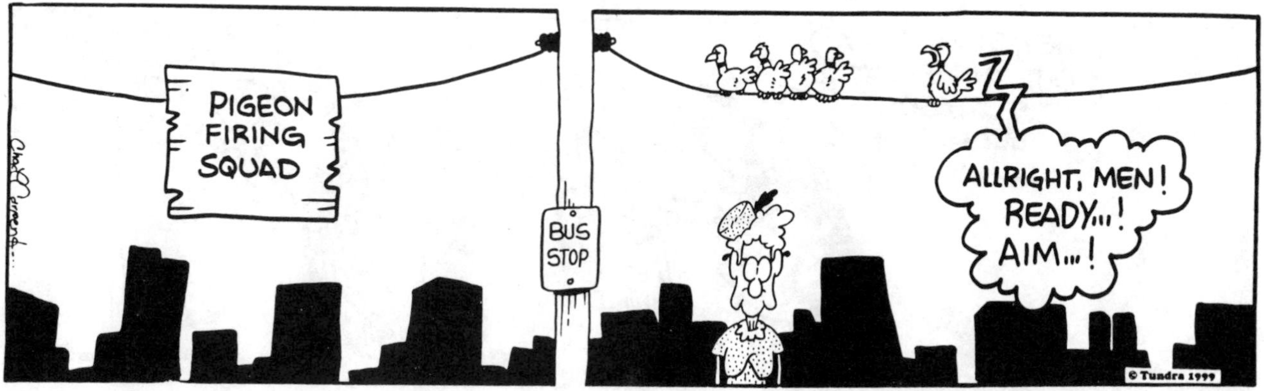
PIGEON
FIRING
SQUAD
BUS
STOP
ALLRIGHT, MEN! READY...! AIM...!
© Tundra 1999

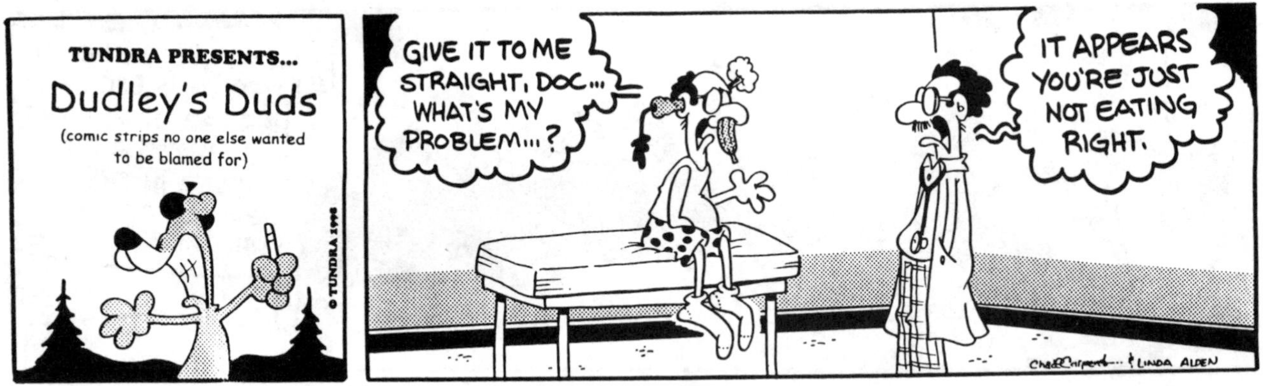
TUNDRA PRESENTS...
Dudley's Duds
(comic strips no one else wanted to be blamed for)
© TUNDRA 1998
GIVE IT TO ME STRAIGHT, DOC... WHAT'S MY PROBLEM...?
IT APPEARS YOU'RE JUST NOT EATING RIGHT.
LINDA ALDEN

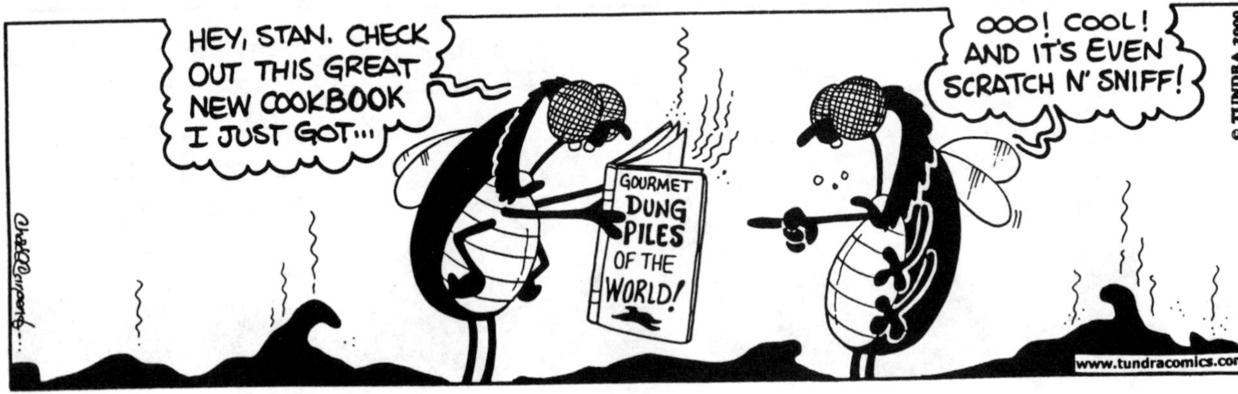
HEY, STAN. CHECK OUT THIS GREAT NEW COOKBOOK I JUST GOT...
GOURMET DUNG PILES OF THE WORLD!
OOO! COOL! AND IT'S EVEN SCRATCH N' SNIFF!
© TUNDRA 2000
www.tundracomics.com

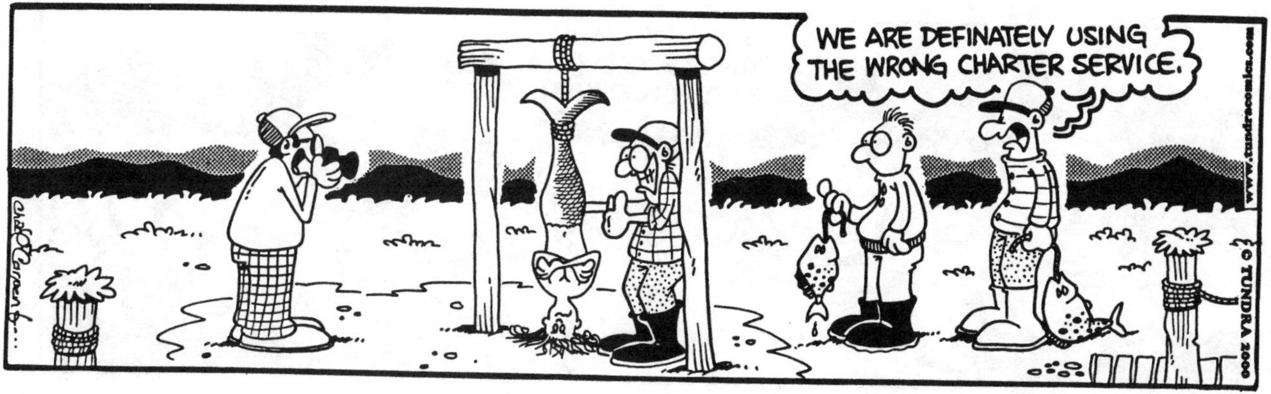
WE ARE DEFINATELY USING THE WRONG CHARTER SERVICE.
www.tundracomics.com
© TUNDRA 2000

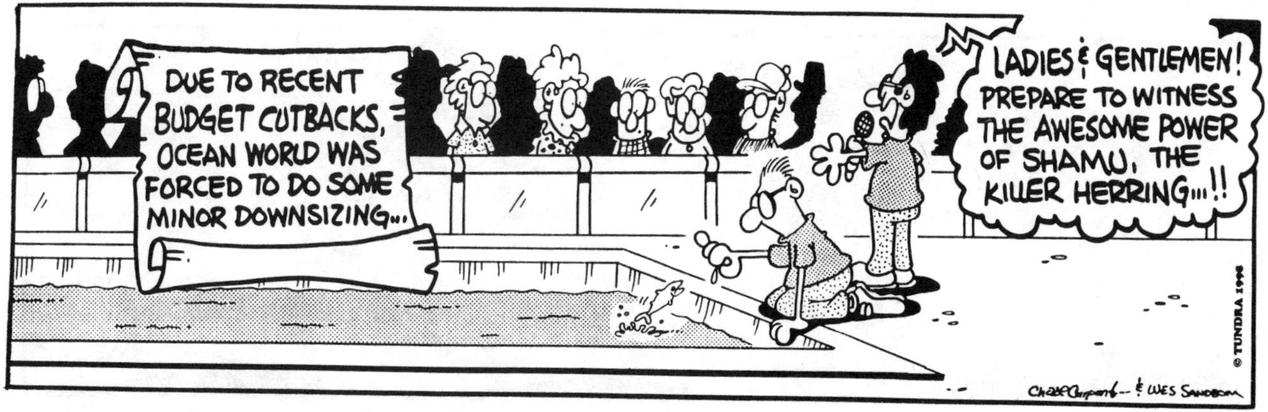
DUE TO RECENT BUDGET CUTBACKS, OCEAN WORLD WAS FORCED TO DO SOME MINOR DOWNSIZING...
LADIES & GENTLEMEN! PREPARE TO WITNESS THE AWESOME POWER OF SHAMU, THE KILLER HERRING...!!
© TUNDRA 1998

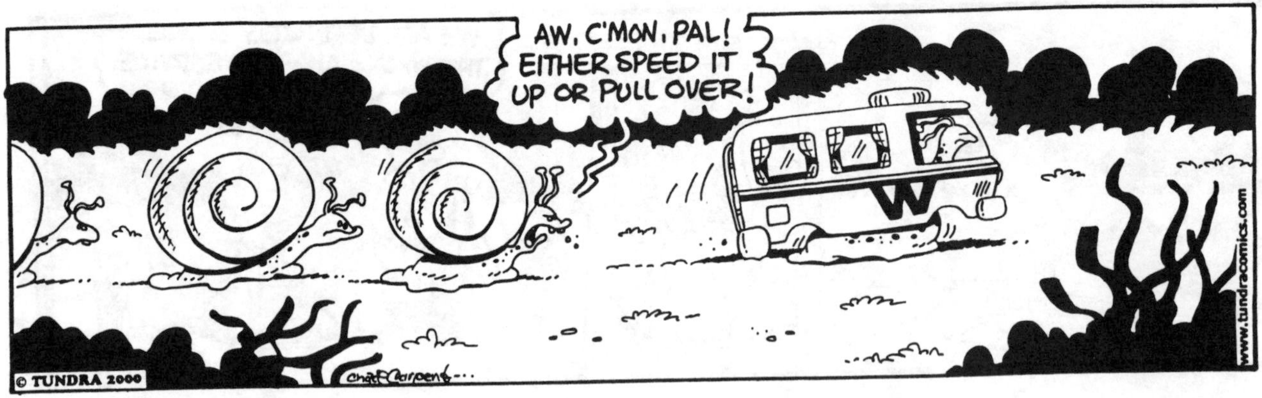
AW, C'MON, PAL! EITHER SPEED IT UP OR PULL OVER!
W
www.tundracomics.com
© TUNDRA 2000

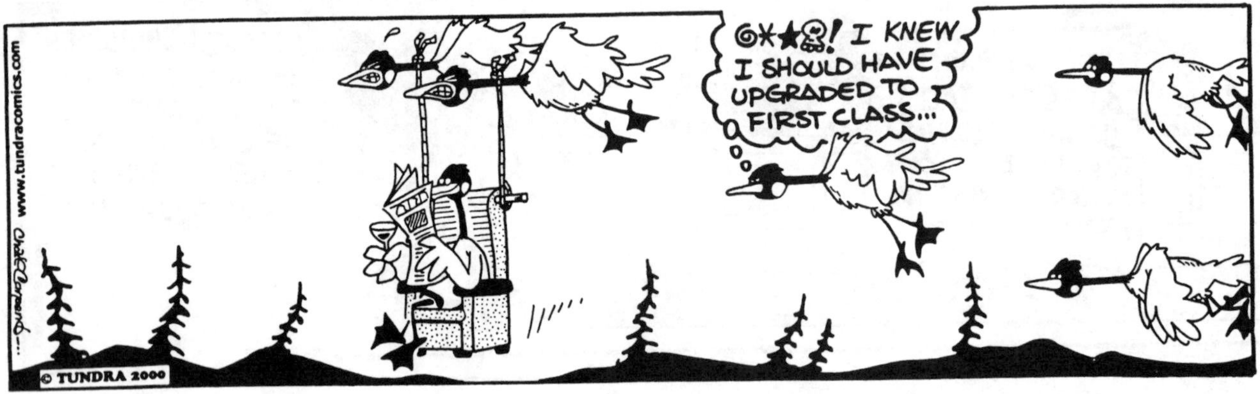
www.tundracomics.com
I KNEW I SHOULD HAVE UPGRADED TO FIRST CLASS...
© TUNDRA 2000

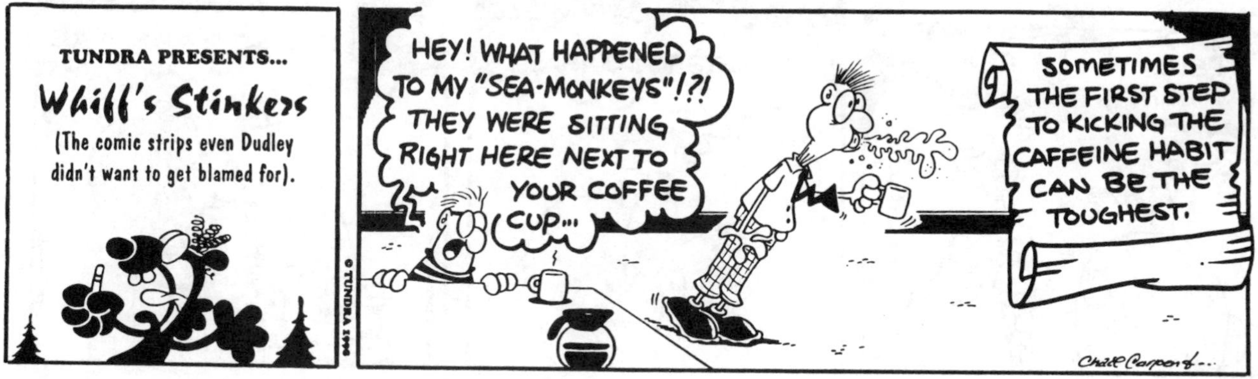
TUNDRA PRESENTS...
Whiff's Stinkers
(The comic strips even Dudley didn't want to get blamed for).
HEY! WHAT HAPPENED TO MY "SEA-MONKEYS"!?! THEY WERE SITTING RIGHT HERE NEXT TO YOUR COFFEE CUP...
SOMETIMES THE FIRST STEP TO KICKING THE CAFFEINE HABIT CAN BE THE TOUGHEST.

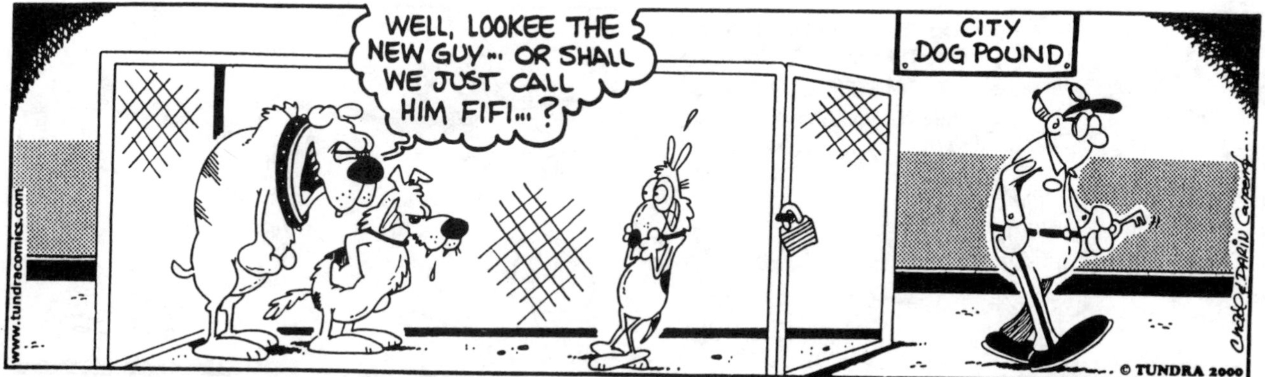
WELL, LOOKEE THE NEW GUY... OR SHALL WE JUST CALL HIM FIFI... ?
CITY DOG POUND
www.tundracomics.com
© TUNDRA 2000

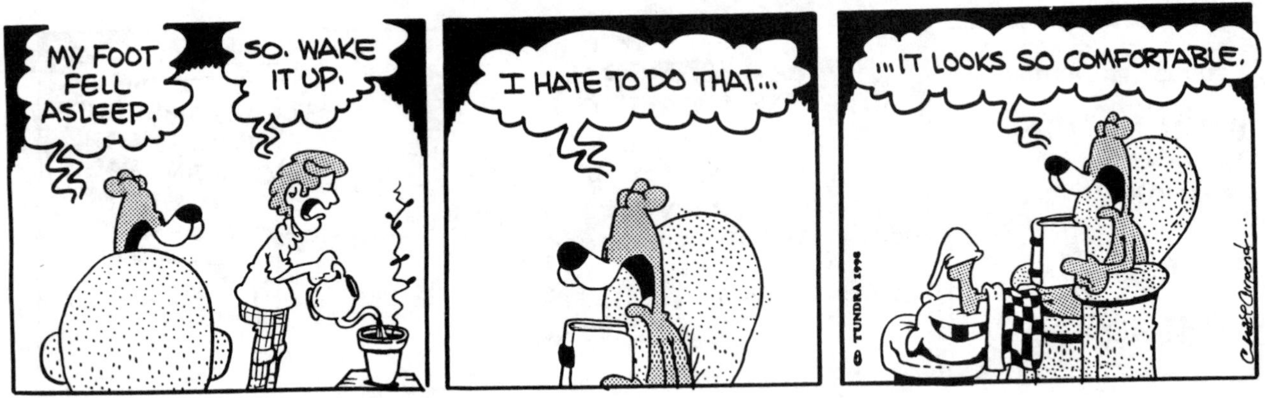
MY FOOT FELL ASLEEP.
SO. WAKE IT UP.
I HATE TO DO THAT...
...IT LOOKS SO COMFORTABLE.
© TUNDRA 1998

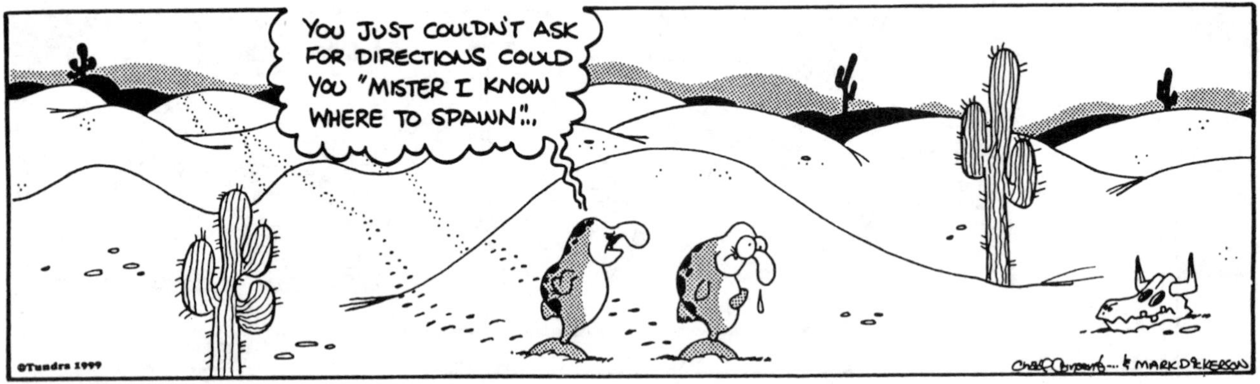
YOU JUST COULDN'T ASK FOR DIRECTIONS COULD YOU "MISTER I KNOW WHERE TO SPAWN"...
©Tundra 1999

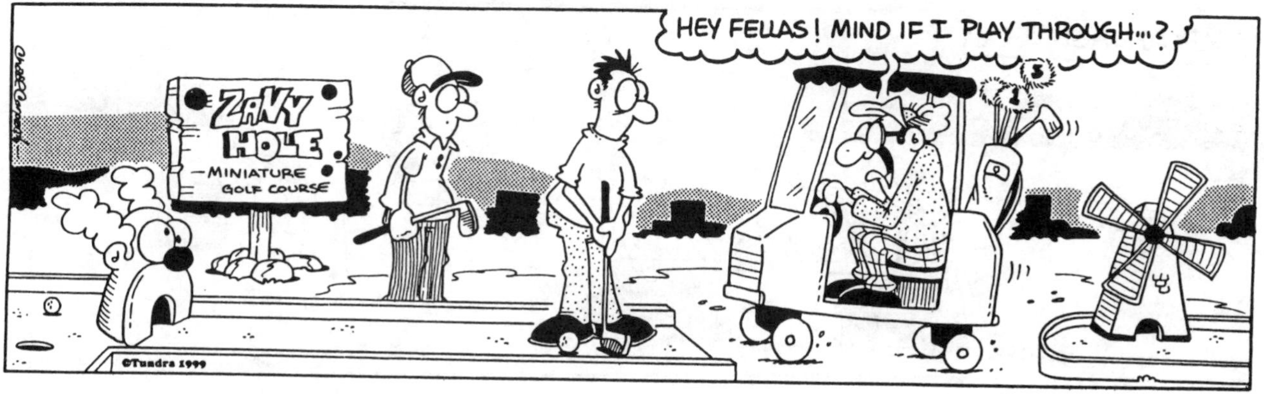
ZANY HOLE
MINIATURE GOLF COURSE
HEY FELLAS! MIND IF I PLAY THROUGH...?
©Tundra 1999

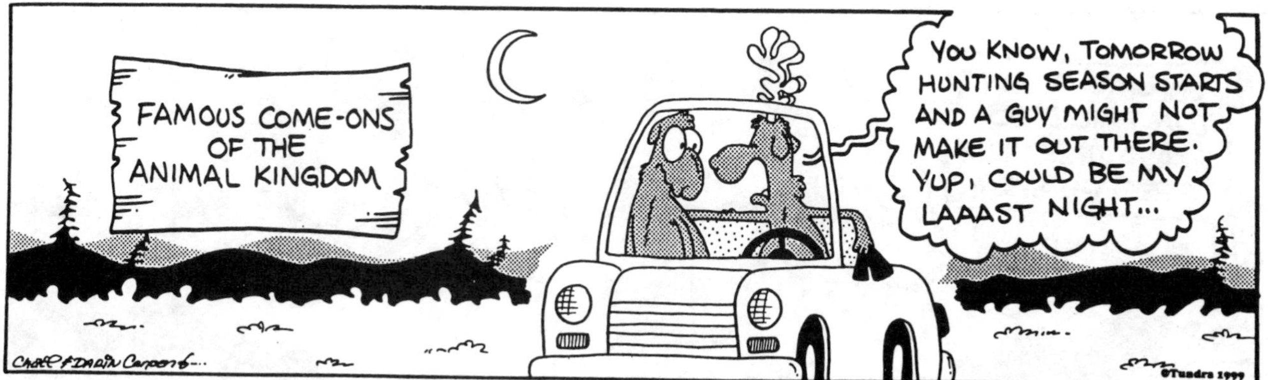
FAMOUS COME-ONS OF THE ANIMAL KINGDOM
YOU KNOW, TOMORROW HUNTING SEASON STARTS AND A GUY MIGHT NOT MAKE IT OUT THERE. YUP, COULD BE MY LAAAST NIGHT...
©Tundra 1999

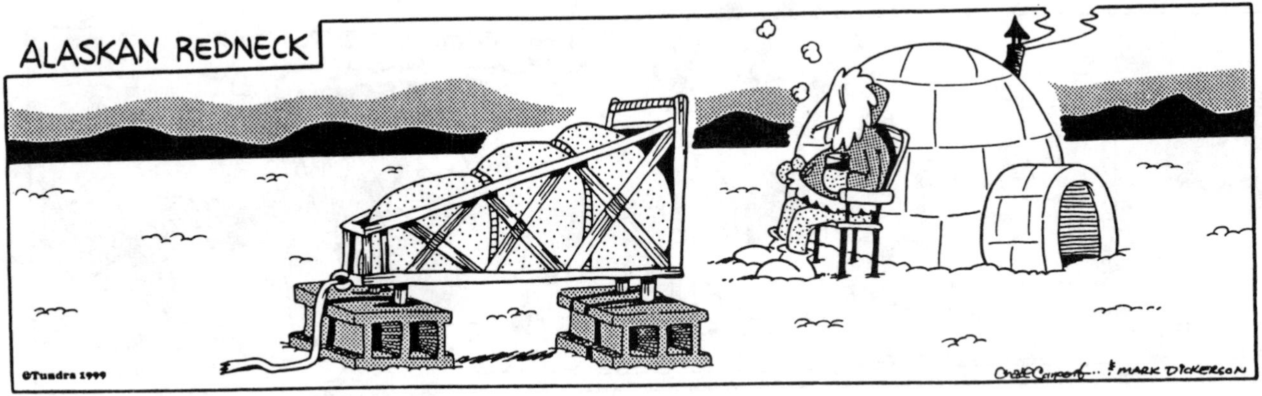
ALASKAN REDNECK
©Tundra 1999
Chad Carpenter... & MARK DICKERSON

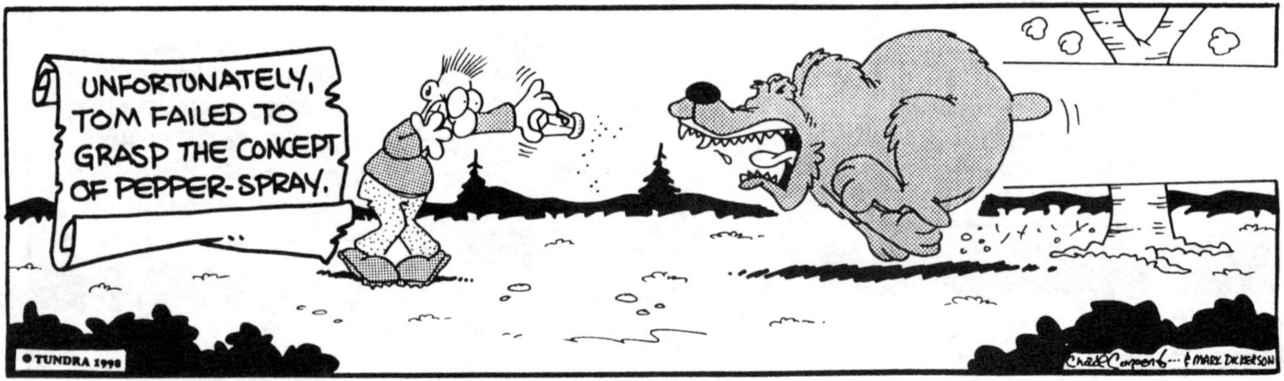
UNFORTUNATELY, TOM FAILED TO GRASP THE CONCEPT OF PEPPER-SPRAY.
© TUNDRA 1998
Chad Carpenter... & MARK DICKERSON

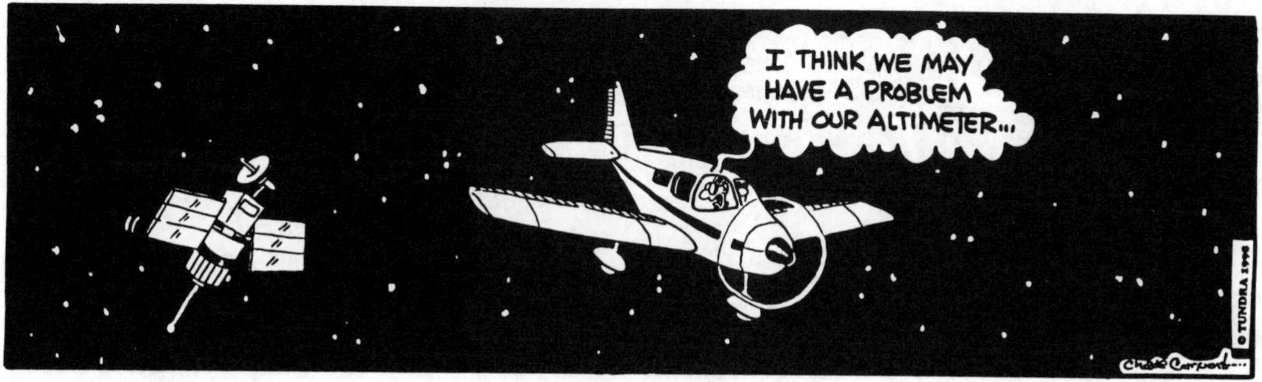
I THINK WE MAY HAVE A PROBLEM WITH OUR ALTIMETER...
© TUNDRA 1998

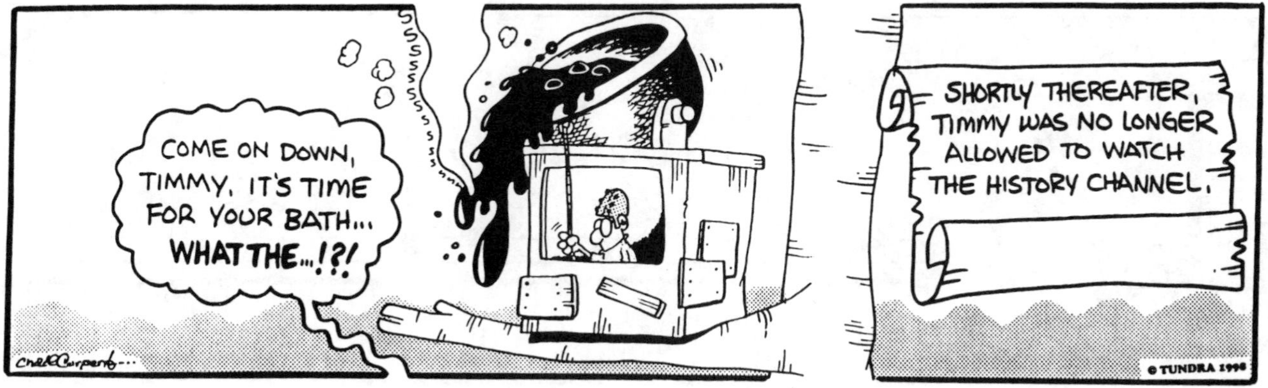
COME ON DOWN, TIMMY. IT'S TIME FOR YOUR BATH... WHAT THE...!?!
SHORTLY THEREAFTER, TIMMY WAS NO LONGER ALLOWED TO WATCH THE HISTORY CHANNEL.
© TUNDRA 1998

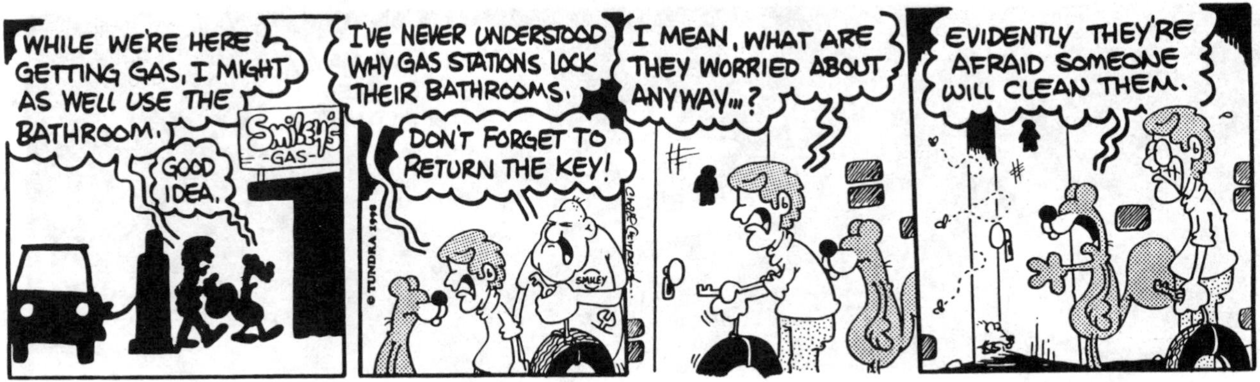
WHILE WE'RE HERE GETTING GAS, I MIGHT AS WELL USE THE BATHROOM.
GOOD IDEA.
Smiley's -GAS-
I'VE NEVER UNDERSTOOD WHY GAS STATIONS LOCK THEIR BATHROOMS.
DON'T FORGET TO RETURN THE KEY!
© TUNDRA 1998
SMILEY
I MEAN, WHAT ARE THEY WORRIED ABOUT ANYWAY...?
EVIDENTLY THEY'RE AFRAID SOMEONE WILL CLEAN THEM.

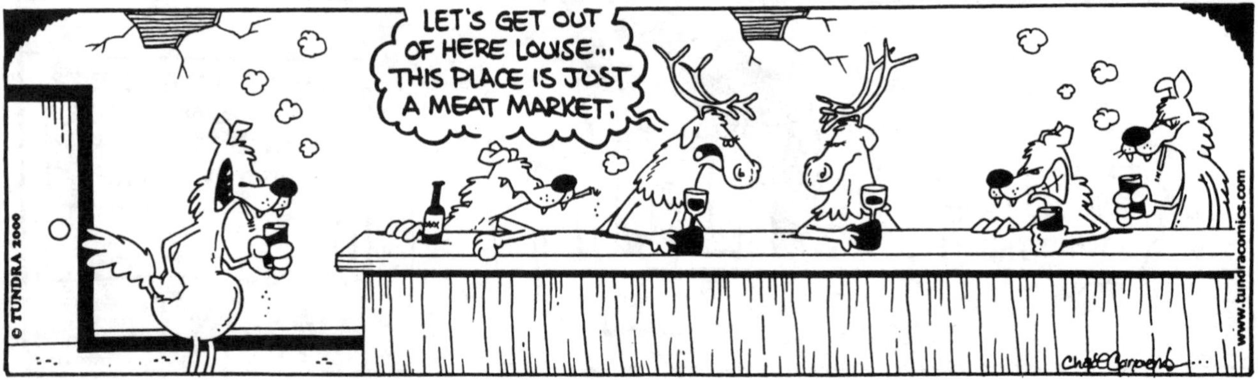
LET'S GET OUT OF HERE LOUISE... THIS PLACE IS JUST A MEAT MARKET.
© TUNDRA 2000
www.tundracomics.com

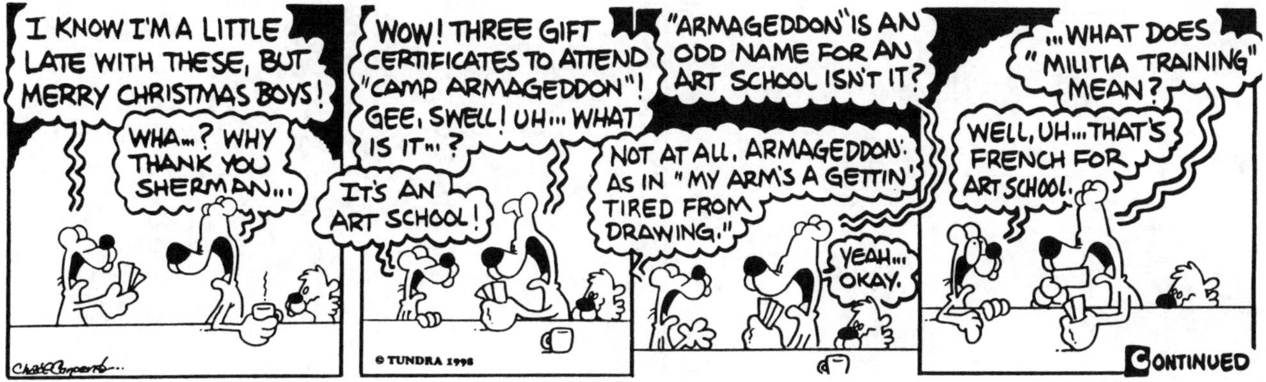
I KNOW I'M A LITTLE LATE WITH THESE, BUT MERRY CHRISTMAS BOYS!
WHA...? WHY THANK YOU SHERMAN...
WOW! THREE GIFT CERTIFICATES TO ATTEND "CAMP ARMAGEDDON"! GEE, SWELL! UH... WHAT IS IT...?
IT'S AN ART SCHOOL!
© TUNDRA 1998
"ARMAGEDDON" IS AN ODD NAME FOR AN ART SCHOOL ISN'T IT?
NOT AT ALL. ARMAGEDDON: AS IN "MY ARM'S A GETTIN' TIRED FROM DRAWING."
YEAH... OKAY.
...WHAT DOES "MILITIA TRAINING" MEAN?
WELL, UH... THAT'S FRENCH FOR ART SCHOOL.
CONTINUED

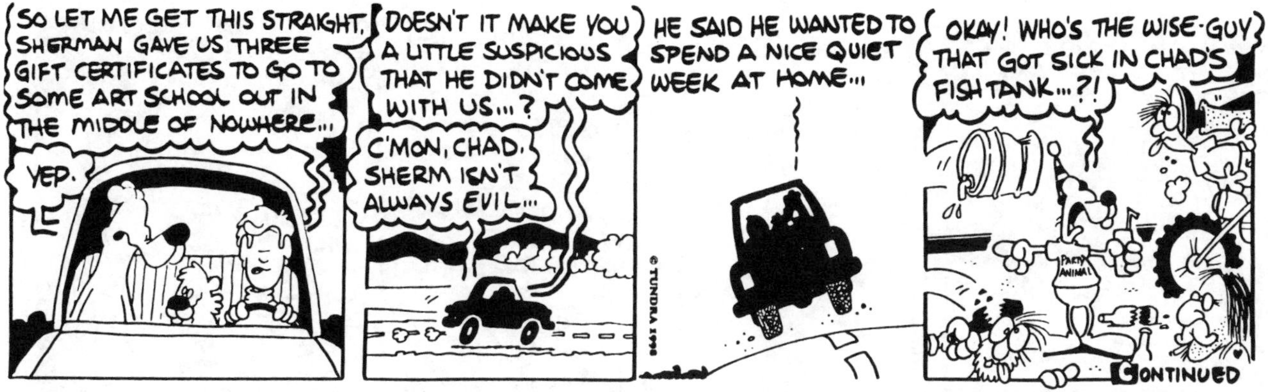
SO LET ME GET THIS STRAIGHT, SHERMAN GAVE US THREE GIFT CERTIFICATES TO GO TO SOME ART SCHOOL OUT IN THE MIDDLE OF NOWHERE...
YEP.
DOESN'T IT MAKE YOU A LITTLE SUSPICIOUS THAT HE DIDN'T COME WITH US...?
C'MON, CHAD. SHERM ISN'T ALWAYS EVIL...
HE SAID HE WANTED TO SPEND A NICE QUIET WEEK AT HOME...
© TUNDRA 1998
OKAY! WHO'S THE WISE-GUY THAT GOT SICK IN CHAD'S FISH TANK...?!
PARTY ANIMAL
CONTINUED

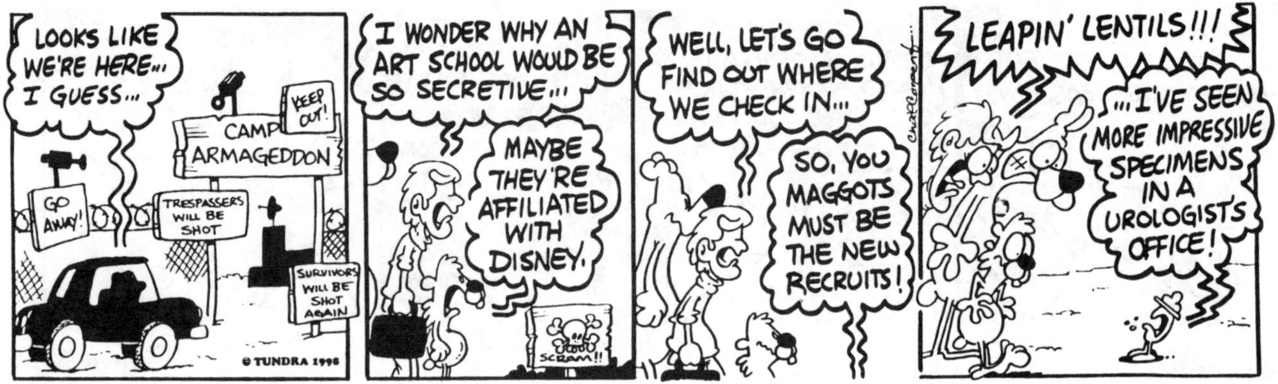
LOOKS LIKE WE'RE HERE... I GUESS...
KEEP OUT!
CAMP ARMAGEDDON
GO AWAY!
TRESPASSERS WILL BE SHOT
SURVIVORS WILL BE SHOT AGAIN
© TUNDRA 1998
I WONDER WHY AN ART SCHOOL WOULD BE SO SECRETIVE...
MAYBE THEY'RE AFFILIATED WITH DISNEY.
SCRAM!!
WELL, LET'S GO FIND OUT WHERE WE CHECK IN...
SO, YOU MAGGOTS MUST BE THE NEW RECRUITS!
LEAPIN' LENTILS!!!
...I'VE SEEN MORE IMPRESSIVE SPECIMENS IN A UROLOGIST'S OFFICE!

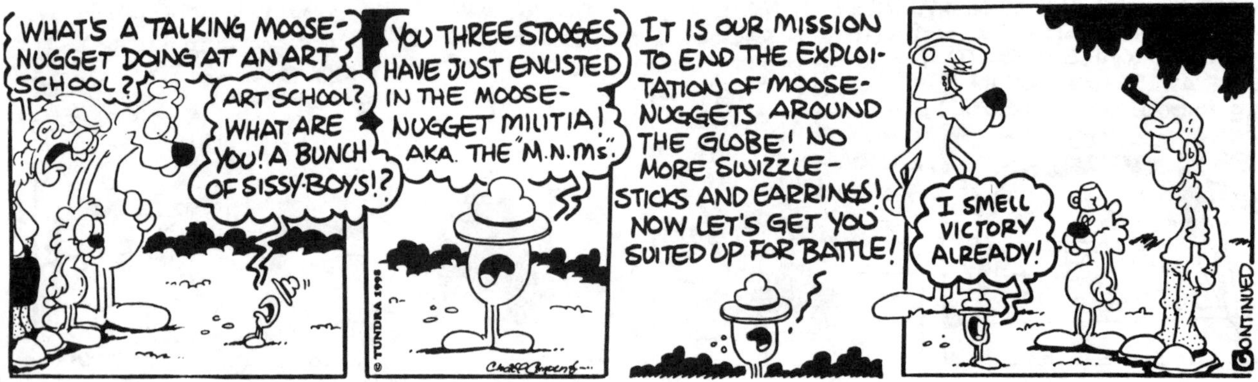
WHAT'S A TALKING MOOSE-NUGGET DOING AT AN ART SCHOOL?
ART SCHOOL? WHAT ARE YOU! A BUNCH OF SISSY-BOYS!?
YOU THREE STOOGES HAVE JUST ENLISTED IN THE MOOSE-NUGGET MILITIA! AKA. THE "M.N.Ms".
© TUNDRA 1998
IT IS OUR MISSION TO END THE EXPLOITATION OF MOOSE-NUGGETS AROUND THE GLOBE! NO MORE SWIZZLE-STICKS AND EARRINGS! NOW LET'S GET YOU SUITED UP FOR BATTLE!
I SMELL VICTORY ALREADY!
CONTINUED

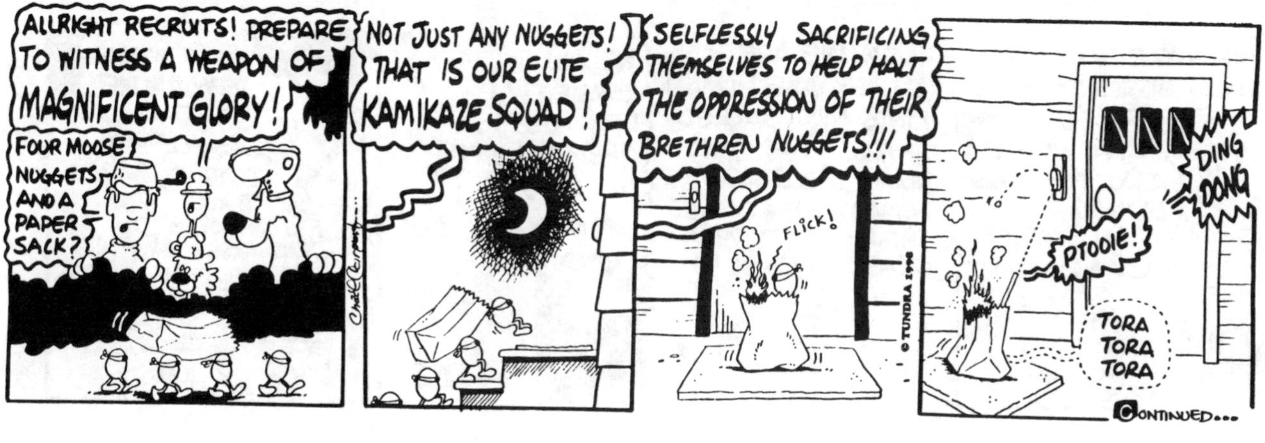
ALLRIGHT RECRUITS! PREPARE TO WITNESS A WEAPON OF MAGNIFICENT GLORY!
FOUR MOOSE NUGGETS AND A PAPER SACK?
NOT JUST ANY NUGGETS! THAT IS OUR ELITE KAMIKAZE SQUAD!
SELFLESSLY SACRIFICING THEMSELVES TO HELP HALT THE OPPRESSION OF THEIR BRETHREN NUGGETS!!!
FLICK!
© TUNDRA 1998
DING DONG
PTOOIE!
TORA TORA TORA
CONTINUED...

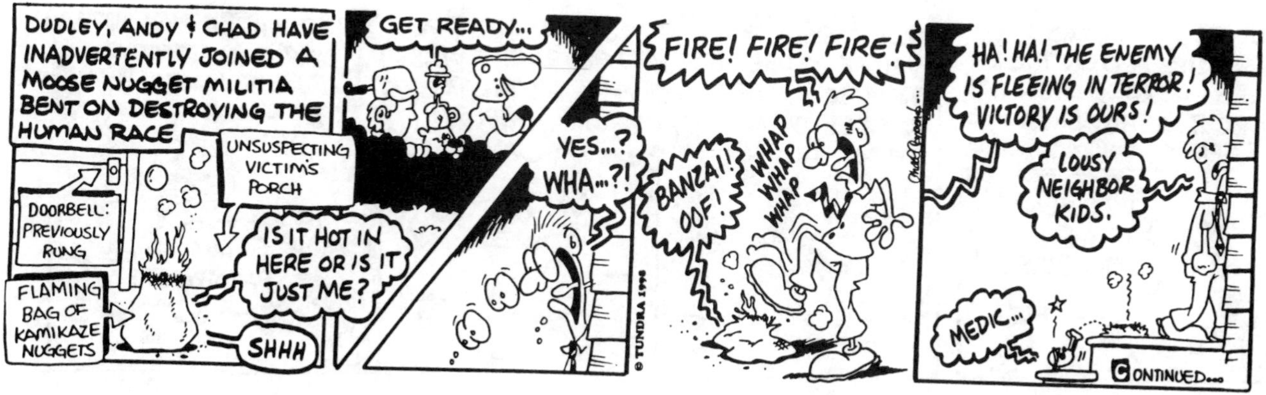
DUDLEY, ANDY & CHAD HAVE INADVERTENTLY JOINED A MOOSE NUGGET MILITIA BENT ON DESTROYING THE HUMAN RACE
UNSUSPECTING VICTIM'S PORCH
DOORBELL: PREVIOUSLY RUNG
FLAMING BAG OF KAMIKAZE NUGGETS
IS IT HOT IN HERE OR IS IT JUST ME?
SHHH
GET READY...
YES...? WHA...?!
© TUNDRA 1998
FIRE! FIRE! FIRE!
BANZAI! OOF!
WHAP WHAP WHAP
HA! HA! THE ENEMY IS FLEEING IN TERROR! VICTORY IS OURS!
LOUSY NEIGHBOR KIDS.
MEDIC...
CONTINUED...

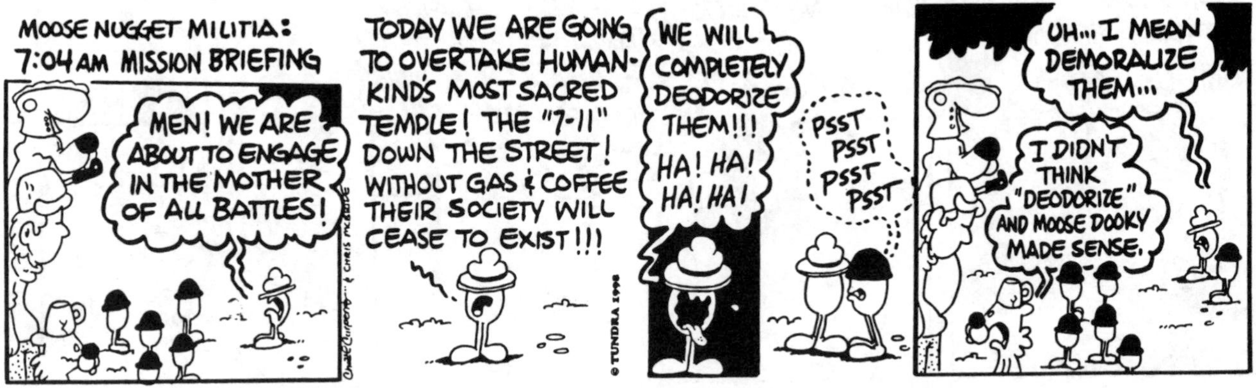
MOOSE NUGGET MILITIA:
7:04 AM MISSION BRIEFING
MEN! WE ARE ABOUT TO ENGAGE IN THE MOTHER OF ALL BATTLES!
TODAY WE ARE GOING TO OVERTAKE HUMAN-KIND'S MOST SACRED TEMPLE! THE "7-11" DOWN THE STREET! WITHOUT GAS & COFFEE THEIR SOCIETY WILL CEASE TO EXIST!!!
WE WILL COMPLETELY DEODORIZE THEM!!!
HA! HA! HA! HA!
PSST PSST PSST PSST
UH... I MEAN DEMORALIZE THEM...
I DIDN'T THINK "DEODORIZE" AND MOOSE DOOKY MADE SENSE.
© TUNDRA 1998

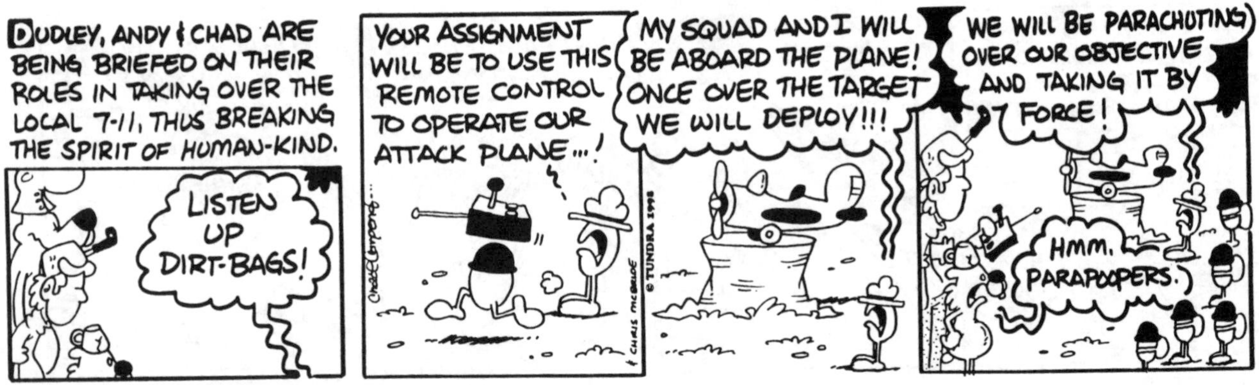
DUDLEY, ANDY & CHAD ARE BEING BRIEFED ON THEIR ROLES IN TAKING OVER THE LOCAL 7-11, THUS BREAKING THE SPIRIT OF HUMAN-KIND.
LISTEN UP DIRT-BAGS!
YOUR ASSIGNMENT WILL BE TO USE THIS REMOTE CONTROL TO OPERATE OUR ATTACK PLANE...!
MY SQUAD AND I WILL BE ABOARD THE PLANE! ONCE OVER THE TARGET WE WILL DEPLOY!!!
WE WILL BE PARACHUTING OVER OUR OBJECTIVE AND TAKING IT BY FORCE!
HMM. PARAPOOPERS.
© TUNDRA 1998

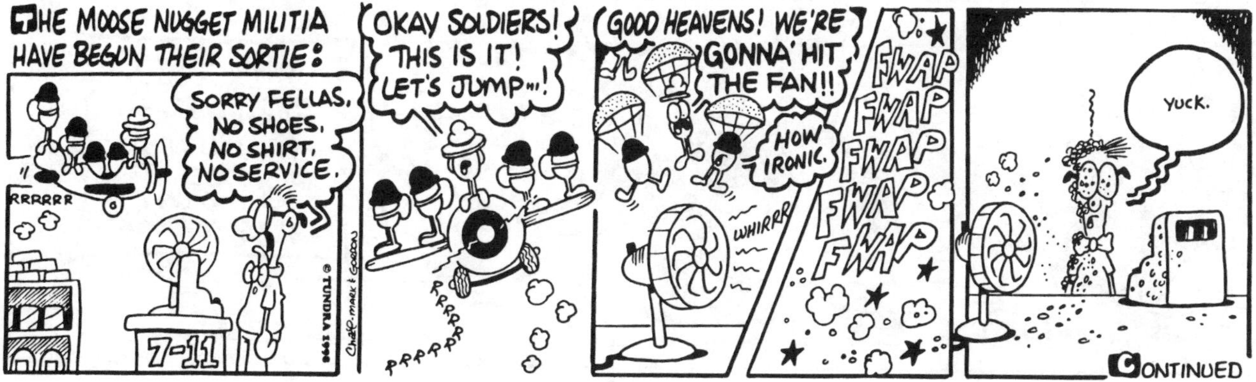
THE MOOSE NUGGET MILITIA HAVE BEGUN THEIR SORTIE:
SORRY FELLAS. NO SHOES. NO SHIRT. NO SERVICE.
RRRRRR
7-11
© TUNDRA 1998
OKAY SOLDIERS! THIS IS IT! LET'S JUMP...!
RRRRRR
RRRRRR
GOOD HEAVENS! WE'RE GONNA' HIT THE FAN!!
HOW IRONIC.
WHIRRR
FWAP FWAP FWAP FWAP FWAP
YUCK.
CONTINUED

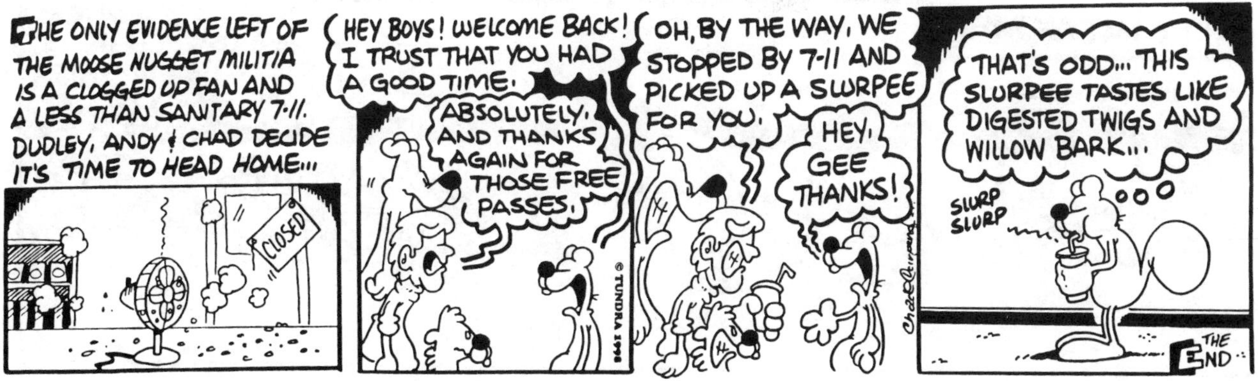
THE ONLY EVIDENCE LEFT OF THE MOOSE NUGGET MILITIA IS A CLOGGED UP FAN AND A LESS THAN SANITARY 7-11. DUDLEY, ANDY & CHAD DECIDE IT'S TIME TO HEAD HOME...
CLOSED
HEY BOYS! WELCOME BACK! I TRUST THAT YOU HAD A GOOD TIME.
ABSOLUTELY. AND THANKS AGAIN FOR THOSE FREE PASSES.
© TUNDRA 1998
OH, BY THE WAY, WE STOPPED BY 7-11 AND PICKED UP A SLURPEE FOR YOU.
HEY, GEE THANKS!
THAT'S ODD... THIS SLURPEE TASTES LIKE DIGESTED TWIGS AND WILLOW BARK...
SLURP SLURP
THE END

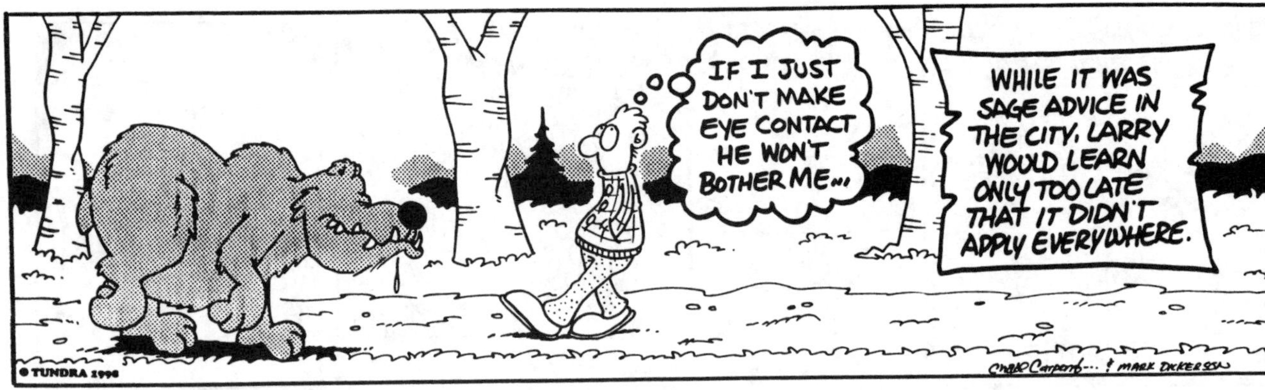
IF I JUST DON'T MAKE EYE CONTACT HE WON'T BOTHER ME...
WHILE IT WAS SAGE ADVICE IN THE CITY, LARRY WOULD LEARN ONLY TOO LATE THAT IT DIDN'T APPLY EVERYWHERE.
© TUNDRA 1998
MARK DICKERSON

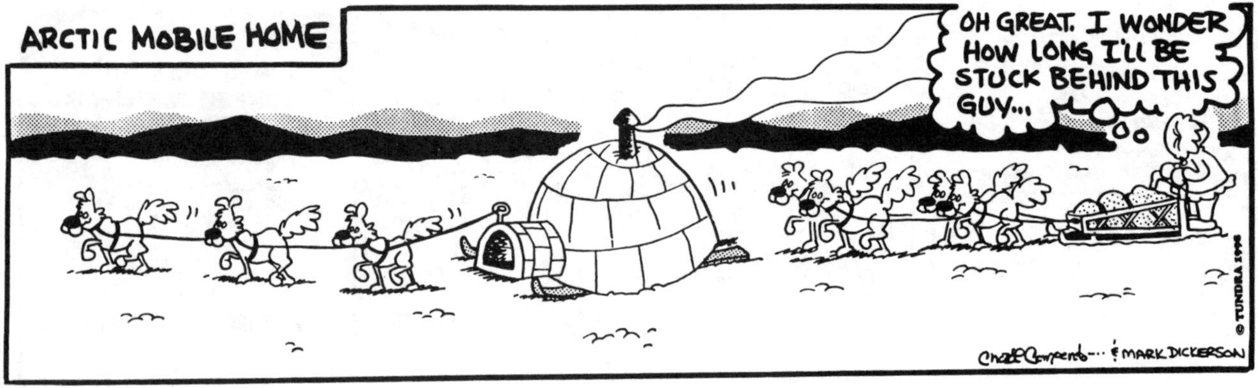
ARCTIC MOBILE HOME
OH GREAT. I WONDER HOW LONG I'LL BE STUCK BEHIND THIS GUY...
© TUNDRA 1998
MARK DICKERSON

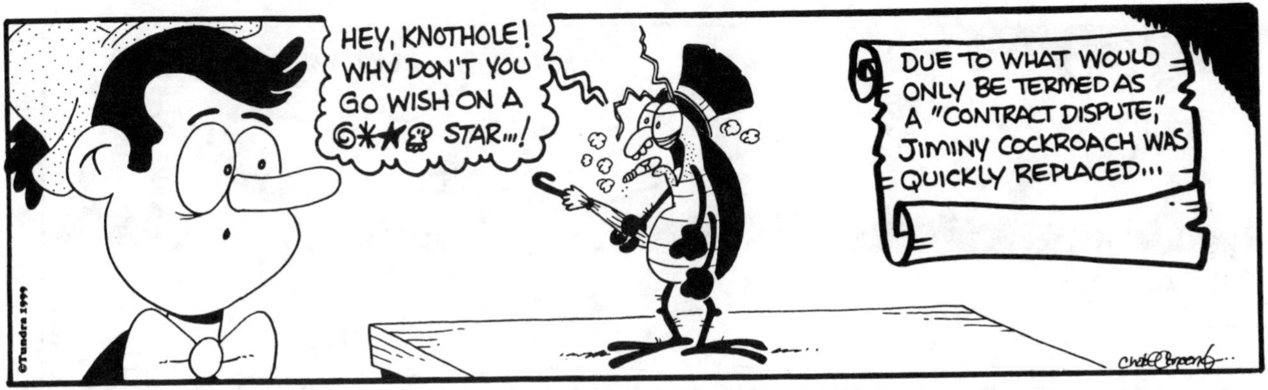
HEY, KNOTHOLE! WHY DON'T YOU GO WISH ON A @*★ STAR...!
DUE TO WHAT WOULD ONLY BE TERMED AS A "CONTRACT DISPUTE," JIMINY COCKROACH WAS QUICKLY REPLACED...
©Tundra 1999

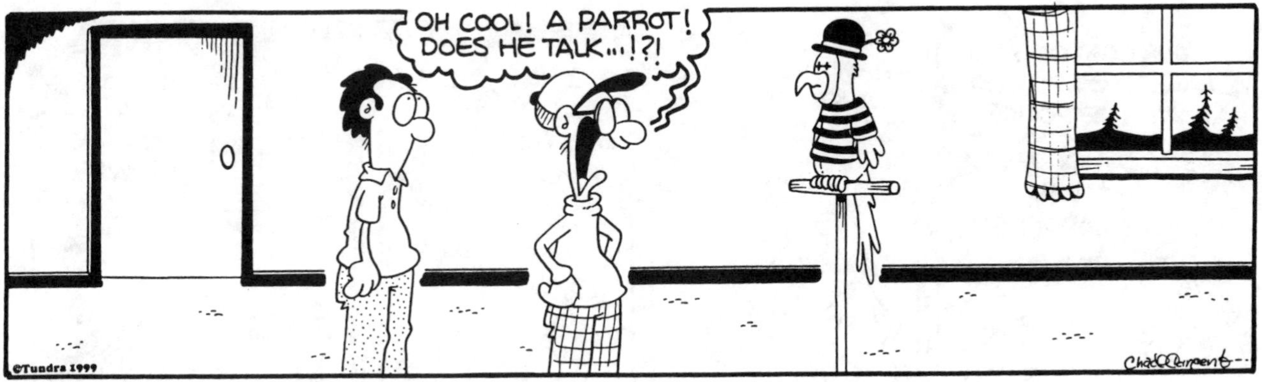
OH COOL! A PARROT! DOES HE TALK...!?!
©Tundra 1999

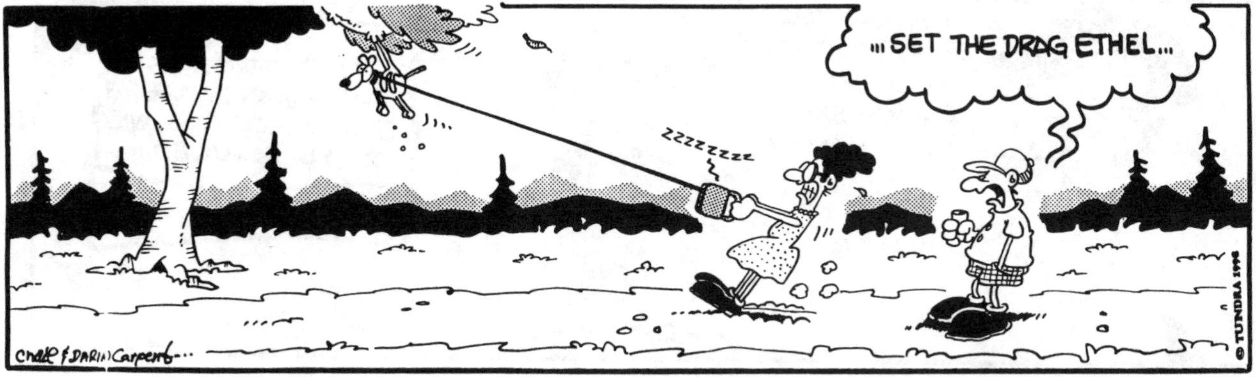
...SET THE DRAG ETHEL...
ZZZZZZZZ
© TUNDRA 1998

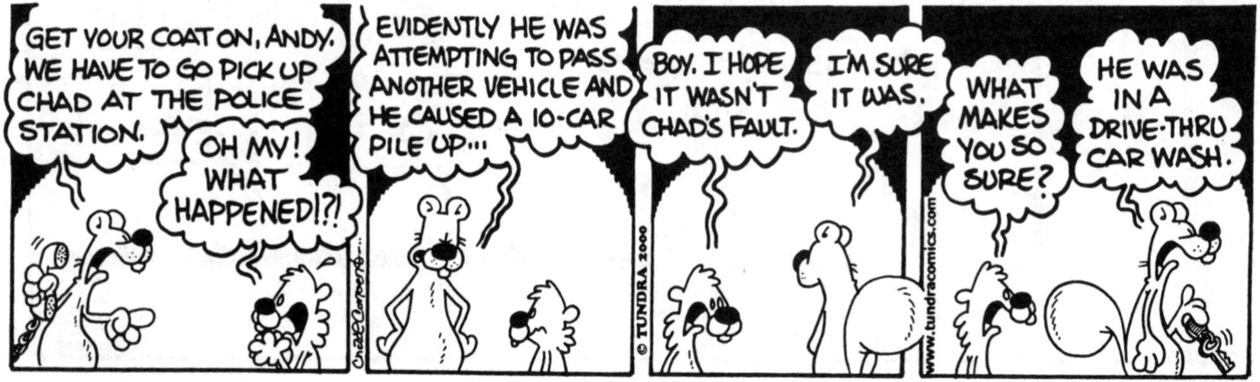
GET YOUR COAT ON, ANDY. WE HAVE TO GO PICK UP CHAD AT THE POLICE STATION.
OH MY! WHAT HAPPENED!?!
EVIDENTLY HE WAS ATTEMPTING TO PASS ANOTHER VEHICLE AND HE CAUSED A 10-CAR PILE UP...
© TUNDRA 2000
BOY. I HOPE IT WASN'T CHAD'S FAULT.
I'M SURE IT WAS.
www.tundracomics.com
WHAT MAKES YOU SO SURE?
HE WAS IN A DRIVE-THRU CAR WASH.

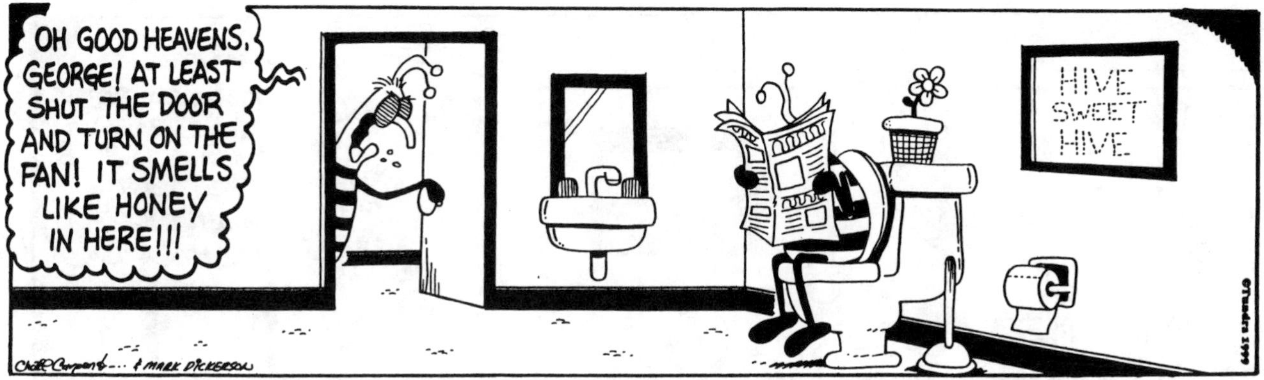
OH GOOD HEAVENS, GEORGE! AT LEAST SHUT THE DOOR AND TURN ON THE FAN! IT SMELLS LIKE HONEY IN HERE!!!
HIVE SWEET HIVE
©Tundra 1999

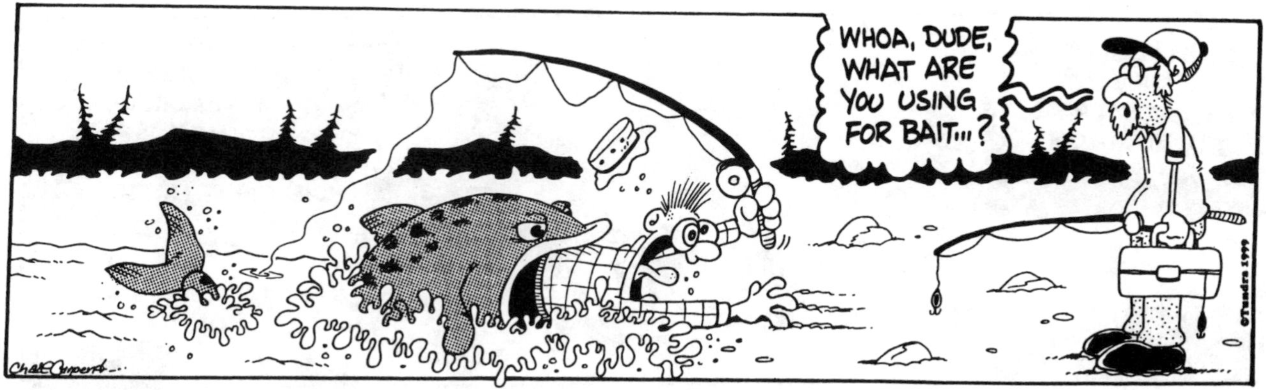
WHOA, DUDE, WHAT ARE YOU USING FOR BAIT...?
©Tundra 1999

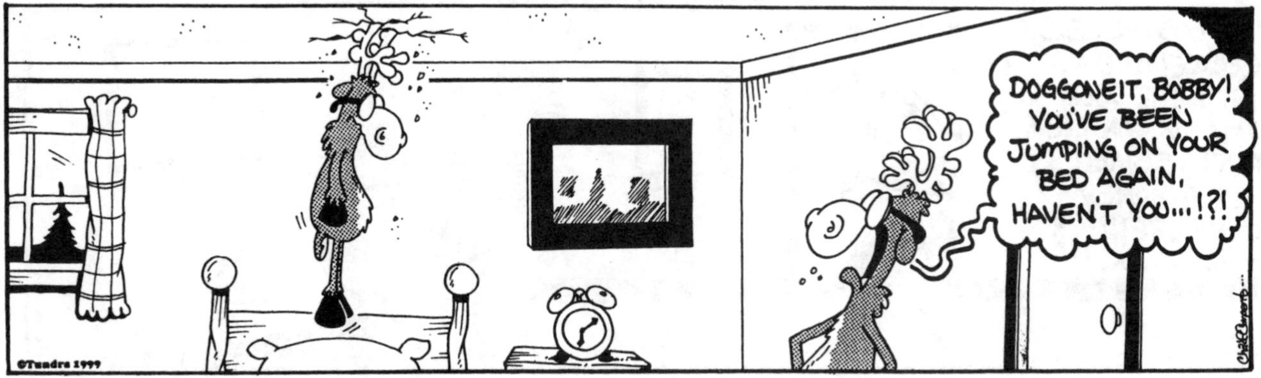
DOGGONEIT, BOBBY! YOU'VE BEEN JUMPING ON YOUR BED AGAIN, HAVEN'T YOU...!?!
©Tundra 1999

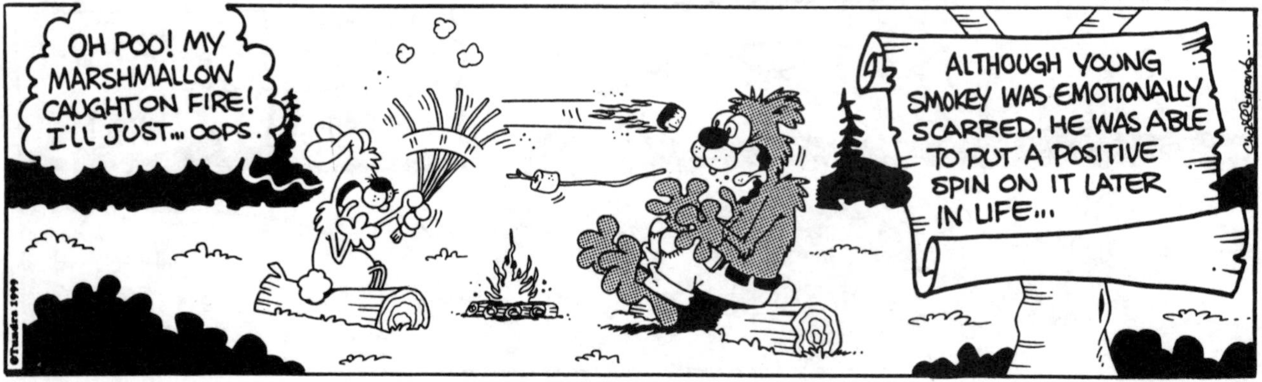
OH POO! MY MARSHMALLOW CAUGHT ON FIRE! I'LL JUST... OOPS.
ALTHOUGH YOUNG SMOKEY WAS EMOTIONALLY SCARRED, HE WAS ABLE TO PUT A POSITIVE SPIN ON IT LATER IN LIFE...
©Tundra 1999

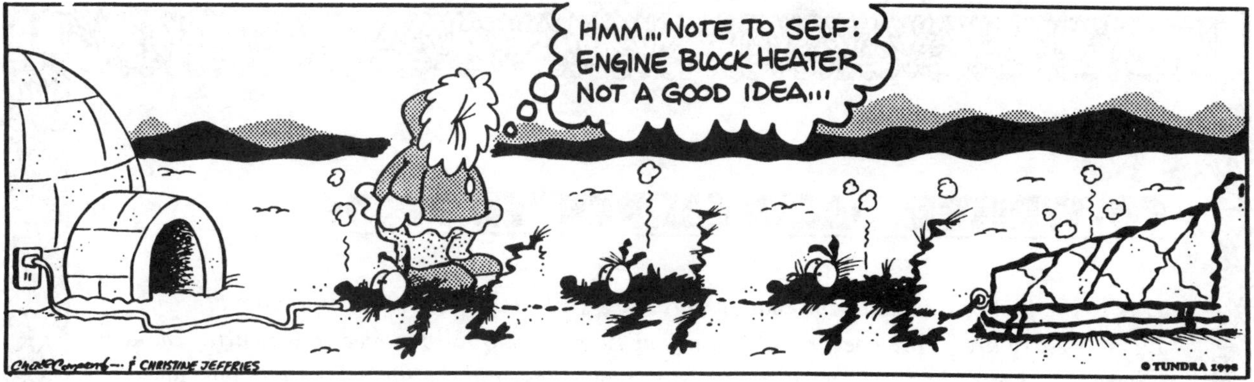
HMM... NOTE TO SELF: ENGINE BLOCK HEATER NOT A GOOD IDEA...
CHRISTINE JEFFRIES
© TUNDRA

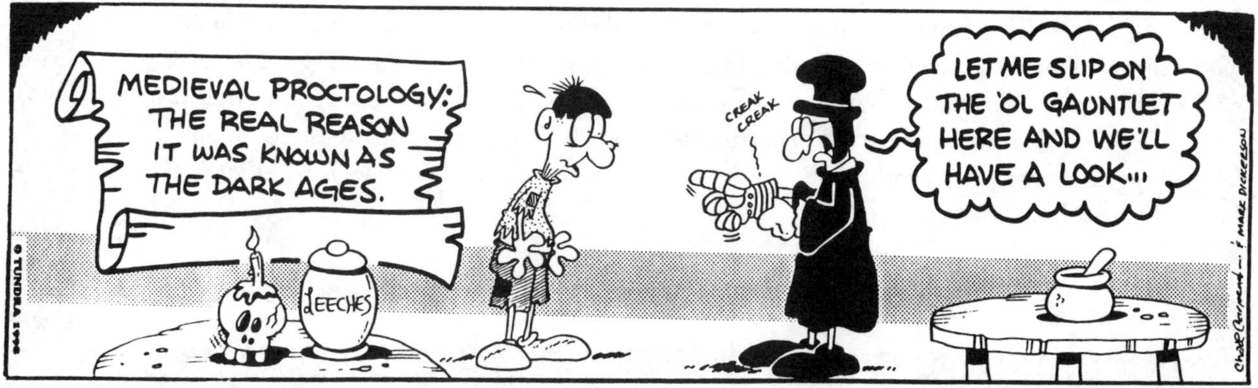
MEDIEVAL PROCTOLOGY: THE REAL REASON IT WAS KNOWN AS THE DARK AGES.
LEECHES
CREAK CREAK
LET ME SLIP ON THE 'OL GAUNTLET HERE AND WE'LL HAVE A LOOK...
MARK DICKERSON
© TUNDRA

CO-WRITER, DARIN CARPENTER'S BIO:

Due to the fact that most of the court records are still sealed, not much is known of Darin's early life. However, it is known that Darin eventually moved to Calcutta, India where he enjoyed the warm weather, the sandy beaches, and the fact that India has no extradition treaty with the United States. While in Calcutta, Darin secured a job as chef at a large Hindu temple. Darin would soon find this career to be short lived when he served a meal that was considered a Hindu culinary faux pas – "Hamburger Helper". It was at this point that Darin was persuaded by dozens of fork-wielding Hindus that it was time to seek other employment opportunities. Darin then moved back to the U.S. and begged his generous brother Chad to let him be a part of the glamorous world that is the Tundra Empire.

CO-WRITER, MARK DICKERSON'S BIO:

Born in the early 1960's to a wandering band of contemporary-dance artists, Mark learned at an early age the pleasures of entertaining as well as keeping limber. During one particularly difficult performance of "Roswell, The Dance of the Abduction," Mark unknowingly wandered into a nearby pasture and soon drifted off to sleep. After a grueling three minutes of searching, the dance troupe finally moved on. Fortunately for Mark, a local family of cows took him in as one of his own. **Unfortunately,** however, due to Mark's lactose intolerance, he almost starved to death. Eventually Mark traveled the countryside until finally settling down with a group of Carhart-backed Brooks Range Mountain gorillas. He lived peacefully with the great apes until one day he was caught in a tofu-baited snare by adventurer/cartoonist Chad Carpenter. Disregarding Mark's poor personal-hygiene habits, Chad quickly recognized his gift for comedy writing as well as picking lice and put him to work.

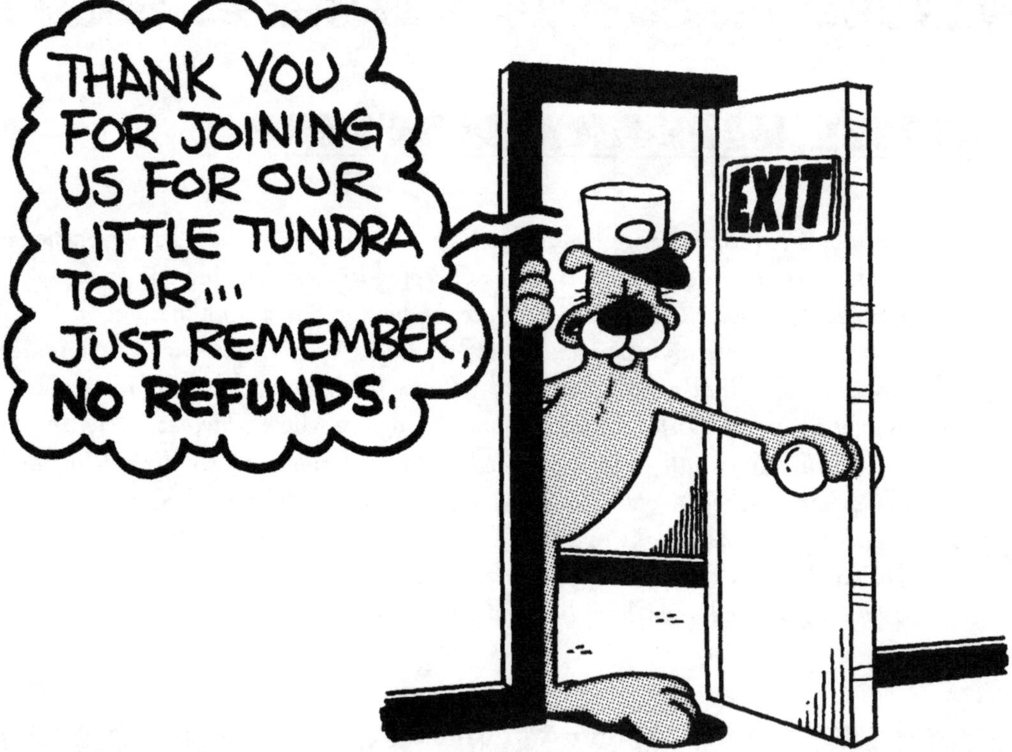
THANK YOU FOR JOINING US FOR OUR LITTLE TUNDRA TOUR... JUST REMEMBER, **NO REFUNDS.**
EXIT